Y0-BDK-151

QUALITY CONTROL
IN DIAGNOSTIC IMAGING

Poor quality (before quality control)   Excellent quality (after quality control)

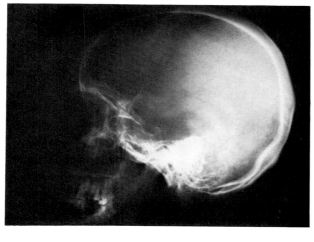 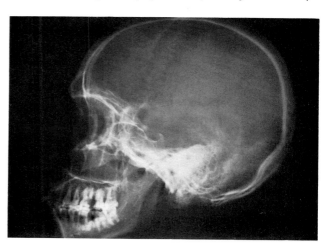

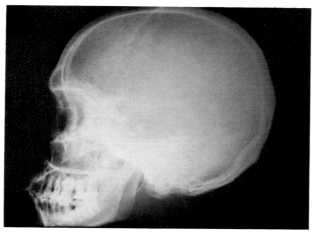 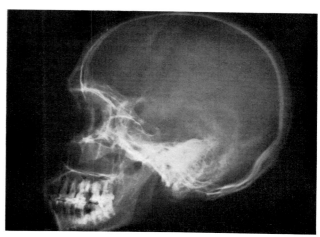

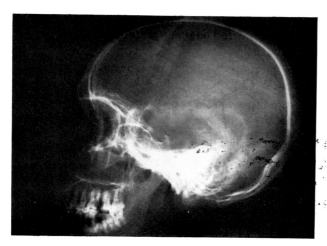 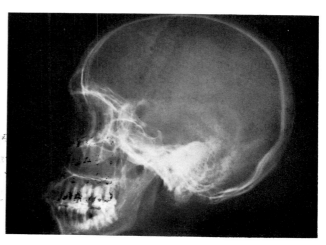

QUALITY CONTROL IN DIAGNOSTIC IMAGING

A Quality Control Cookbook

Joel E. Gray, Ph.D.
Consultant in Radiologic Physics
Department of Diagnostic Radiology
Mayo Clinic and Mayo Foundation

Associate Professor of Radiologic Physics
Mayo Medical School

Assistant Professor of Biophysics
University of Minnesota

Norlin T. Winkler, B.A., R.T.(R), F.A.S.R.T.
Radiologic Technical Analyst
Department of Diagnostic Radiology
Mayo Clinic and Mayo Foundation

Instructor
University of Minnesota

John Stears, R.T.(R)
Quality Control Technologist
Department of Diagnostic Radiology
Mayo Clinic and Mayo Foundation

Eugene D. Frank, R.T.(R)
Quality Control Technologist
Department of Diagnostic Radiology
Mayo Clinic and Mayo Foundation

University Park Press Baltimore

Published by:
UNIVERSITY PARK PRESS
International Publishers in Science, Medicine, and Education
300 North Charles Street
Baltimore, Maryland 21201

Typeset by University Park Press, Typesetting Division

Manufactured in the United States of America by the Maple Press Company

Library of Congress Cataloging in Publication Data
Main entry under title:

Quality control in diagnostic imaging.

   Includes bibliographical references and index.
   1. Radiography, Medical—Quality control.
2. Imaging systems in medicine. I. Gray, Joel E.
RC78.Q34   1982   681 .41   82-13446
ISBN 0-8391-1681-0

CONTENTS

TV Monitors and Videotape and Videodisc Recorders
Fluoroscopic Image Noise
Image Lag
Setting and Maintaining Cine and Photofluorospot (PFS) Film
  Camera Exposures
Fluoroscopic, Photofluorospot Film, and Cine Resolution
Low-Contrast Fluoroscopic Test
Video Waveform Monitoring

10 SPECIAL DIAGNOSTIC IMAGING SYSTEMS / 161

Portable Radiographic and Capacitor Discharge Units
Conventional Tomography
Angiographic Equipment

11 MISCELLANEOUS TESTS AND TECHNIQUES / 175

Video Hard-Copy Cameras
Image Quality Tests for Product Comparisons
Attenuation Measurements

Copy Film
Methods of Lowering the Fluoroscopic Exposure Rate
What to do Before the Service Engineer Leaves
Film Viewboxes

12 EQUIPMENT SPECIFICATION, PURCHASE, AND ACCEPTANCE TESTING / 195

REFERENCES / 199

Appendix

A QUALITY CONTROL FORMS AND CHARTS / 201

Appendix

B EQUIPMENT SPECIFICATION FORMS / 227

INDEX / 245

PREFACE

This book is designed to be used by everyone in diagnostic imaging, each at his or her own level:

For the *radiologist*—We provide basic discussions on what is required for quality assurance and control in diagnostic imaging. We provide information on the type of equipment necessary for quality control (QC), and the training necessary for the QC technologist, as well as an overview of the tests (detailed test instructions are provided separately in the procedures section of each chapter).

For the *physicist*—We provide information concerning the initiation and maintenance of a quality control program. Specific detailed procedures for carrying out tests, including measurement techniques and problems, will help the physicist better guide the direction of the QC program in institutions of various sizes. This book will also provide a basis for other, more specific tests that the physicist may find it necessary to develop.

For the *radiology resident*—We provide a readable introduction to the problems associated with x-ray equipment. The information contained in this book will be of use to the resident entering practice since it will provide insight concerning x-ray equipment he or she will be using and purchasing in the future. This book will also be useful in a residency training program since physics can be taught with a purpose: the quality control and understanding of equipment. The procedures sections of the book can easily be used for laboratory experiences as part of the radiology residency physics program.

For the *radiology administrator*—We provide an introduction to quality control programs, with an overview sufficient for an understanding of the problems associated with administering such a program. The details of the tests, which are not of interest to most administrators, are provided separately in the procedures section of each chapter.

For the *service engineer*—We provide a complete set of noninvasive tests. Although these may not measure exactly what the engineer invasively measures, they can be used to monitor the output of x-ray equipment. These measurements, in conjunction with invasive testing, can be very beneficial in situations such as determining the possible loss of x-ray tube emission. This book will provide the engineer with sufficient insight to better troubleshoot problems reported by quality control technologists who are using these tests on a regular basis. The full complement of image quality tests, including fluoroscopic tests, will be useful to the service engineer. In addition, the tests in this book may be carried out by the less experienced engineer in a training program, providing valuable information as well as experience.

For the *technologist*—Last, but by no means least, we mention the technologist, the person for whom this book is primarily designed since it is this group of professionals who will make the most use of the book and the test procedures that we describe. The staff technologist will benefit from the clearly described test protocols and acceptance limits, as well as the control charts and logs provided. The student technologist will find this book readable and usable. In a student technology program this book can be used as the basic text for a quality control course in conjunction with a physics and imaging text. In fact, physics and imaging can be taught from a new perspective—quality control being taught to make physics and imaging, and the equipment, understandable. This is the opposite approach of many courses, which teach physics and imaging on a theoretical basis and leave it to the student to apply the principles. Now, with this book, the physics and imaging principles can be taught, as needed, to support the practical and necessary work in quality control—at last, a reason for the technologist to study physics!

This book is based upon extensive experience in quality control at our institution. The test procedures have been thoroughly tested in evaluating many rooms of x-ray equipment. The acceptance limits we present have been developed on the basis of our experience, in terms of what we have found is reasonably possible to expect of the equipment and what we have found to be necessary to provide consistent, high-quality radiographic images for diagnostic purposes. The book is based on experience in large and small departments, since our institution supports a cross-section of diagnostic imaging facilities (over 200 x-ray tubes in a large outpatient facility and two hospitals; a small community medicine facility; several outreach facilities ranging in size from a one–x-ray unit facility to a small community hospital).

The contents of this book are unique in that discussions of theory have been eliminated in preference to discussions of practical problems and pitfalls. Material not directly applicable, such as discussions of the components of photographic developer or the difference between Y and delta configuration transformers, is not included in order to make this a succinct, more readable, directly applicable book. Extensive use is made of illustrations and figures both to show the test setup and to demonstrate acceptable and unacceptable results of the tests.

The first chapter ("Introduction") provides an overview of quality control programs. Chapter 2 ("Equipment and Measurement Tips") is a primer on basic quality control equipment and measurement tips for the quality control technologist. (We have studiously avoided the mention of manufacturers' names throughout the book so as not to slight anyone. Most equipment is available from several manufacturers and vendors.)

The use of control charts, the key to a good quality control program, is the subject of Chapter 3 ("Basics of Quality Control"). The establishment of operating levels and control limits as well as room logs is also covered. Chapter 3 should be considered the basis for the quality control program since without adequate records and an easy way to review

the data a quality control program will become a data collection program, with no obvious benefit.

Starting with Chapter 3, each chapter is broken into two sections. First there is a general discussion of the tests and then a detailed procedures section provides a protocol, or cookbook, approach to carrying out the tests and analyzing the data. For each of the procedures we have also included a section called "Problems and Pitfalls," an understanding of which is essential to obtaining reliable data.

Reject-repeat analysis is discussed in Chapter 4, but excessive emphasis is not placed on this aspect of quality control. As we mention, the reject or repeat rate can be reduced to close to zero if the radiologist is willing to read every film that comes out of the processor.

Chapter 5 is devoted to photographic quality control since this is usually one of the major problem areas in diagnostic imaging. Hundreds of thousands of dollars worth of imaging equipment will only produce images as good as that which is produced by the final link in that chain, the processor. The processor can be, and often is, the weakest link in the imaging chain, requiring daily monitoring and constant attention. Also described is a flood replenishment system, which may be the only way to obtain consistent photographic processing quality if fewer than 50 sheets of 14 × 17-inch (35 × 43-cm) film are processed in any processor each day, or in an application where the processor handles an abnormally high percentage of single emulsion films.

Chapters 3 ("Basics of Quality Control"), 5 ("Photographic Quality Control"), and 6 ("Basic Tests") should be considered the backbone and starting point of a quality control program. The basic tests are designed to be carried out with a minimum of test equipment—these tests can be carried out while the department is awaiting the arrival of quality control test tools! However, the fact that these tests are basic does not imply that they should not be part of a more sophisticated QC program. Each one of the basic tests, or a more sophisticated version of each, is an integral part of an ongoing quality control program.

In Chapter 7 ("X-Ray Tubes and Collimators") a significant amount of time is spent discussing rating charts and overload protection, since it has been our experience that the lack of understanding of rating charts probably leads to the majority of x-ray tube failures—tubes that cost from $6,000 to $20,000 each. The purpose of this discussion is to better acquaint the QC technologist with these charts so that he or she can develop technique charts that will allow the optimum usage of the equipment while avoiding tube problems.

Chapters 8 through 11 provide a discussion of the radiographic, fluoroscopic, conventional tomographic, and portable equipment to be evaluated, as well as detailed test procedures. The last chapter ("Equipment Specification, Purchase, and Acceptance Testing") provides some guidelines for specifying and acceptance testing equipment, as well as some comments concerning our experience in working with the vendors.

Quality control forms, control charts, technique charts, maintenance request forms, and equipment specification forms are provided in the appendices. These may be reproduced for use in your institution, but may not be reproduced for sale without permission of the authors and publisher.

This book describes the basis for the quality control program at our institution, of which we are, naturally, quite proud. We feel that we produce some of the best diagnostic films in the world while main-taining the exposure to our patients and staff at a minimum level. In addition, since our retake rates have been minimized through the use of quality assurance (including QC, staff training, and in-house service) we have minimized the cost of operating our department. In other words, we feel we are doing our best in the three areas of importance in diagnostic imaging—

Diagnosis—best diagnostic image quality
Dose—minimized exposure to patients and staff
Dollars—reducing the cost of health care

We hope this book and your quality control program will benefit your department as they have benefitted ours.

Joel E. Gray, Ph.D.
Norlin T. Winkler, B.A., R.T.(R), F.A.S.R.T.
John Stears, R.T.(R)
Eugene D. Frank, R.T.(R)

1 INTRODUCTION

Quality assurance and quality control are rapidly becoming familiar words in diagnostic imaging. The federal government has published recommendations for quality assurance programs in diagnostic imaging facilities (Bureau of Radiological Health, 1980). The Joint Commission on the Accreditation of Hospitals (JCAH) states that one of the responsibilities of the director of radiology services is the "maintenance of a quality control program to minimize the unnecessary duplication of radiographic studies and to maximize the quality of diagnostic information available" (Joint Commission on the Accreditation of Hospitals, 1980). In addition, most of the professional societies are endorsing quality control and are publishing guidelines for quality assurance and quality control programs.

Before continuing, let's examine the differences between quality control and quality assurance. First of all, quality assurance is defined as:

> A system of activities whose purpose is to provide assurance that the overall quality control job is in fact being done effectively. The system involves a continuing evaluation of the adequacy and effectiveness of the overall quality control program with a view to having corrective measures initiated where necessary (Thomas, 1973).

Quality assurance includes many facets of activities such as quality control, preventive maintenance, equipment calibration, in-service education of the technologists and darkroom personnel, specification and acceptance testing of new equipment, and evaluation of new products.

Quality control is defined as:

> The overall system of activities whose purpose is to provide a quality of product or service that meets the needs of the users; also, the use of such a system. The aim of quality control is to provide quality that is satisfactory, adequate, dependable and economic (Thomas, 1973).

In other words, the quality assurance program is the overall management program, whereas the quality control program is that segment of the quality assurance program that is responsible for the measurement of the image quality and the integrity of the equipment.

It is interesting to note that these definitions are provided in a publication issued by a photographic science and engineering society. Quality assurance and quality control have been integral parts of the photographic industry and many other industries for decades for both the manufacturer and the user (e.g., the motion picture industry and the field of aerial reconnaissance and mapping). Up until the early 1970s most radiology departments were not familiar with the concept of quality control, to say nothing of having active quality control programs.

We concern ourselves primarily with quality control (QC) throughout this book, although some of the aspects of quality assurance (QA) are discussed briefly. We look at the justifications for QC, discuss the number of people needed for an effective program, and most importantly, provide a step-by-step approach for QC, along with suggestions concerning the extent and frequency of tests for various types of equipment.

WHY QUALITY ASSURANCE?

Quality assurance is becoming similar to motherhood, apple pie, and the American flag—everyone must believe in it, enjoy it, and respect it. But why are we really interested in quality assurance? The real justification for QA and QC efforts rests with the results we hope to obtain, which we refer to as the three Ds:

Dose
Diagnosis
Dollars

First of all, we hope to minimize the "Dose" to the patient so that as much as possible the potential benefit of the examination outweighs the risk. (While we are reducing the dose to the patient, we are also reducing the exposure to the staff.) If we accomplish the reduction in dose while maintaining and improving the quality of the image or diagnostic information, then we can be sure we are optimizing the "Diagnosis" or, more specifically, the diagnostic information upon which the diagnosis will be based. Last, and perhaps least, if we reduce the number of retakes, we will be improving the utilization of our resources and reducing the amount of film and chemicals we consume, and ultimately reducing the cost of the examination and saving "Dollars."

We place the cost savings lowest in our priorities since it is difficult, at best, to justify the cost of a quality assurance program on the basis of financial savings alone. One could always argue that the best way to reduce the number of retakes and the cost of supplies is to have the radiologists accept and read every film that comes out of the processor.

In many institutions, it is difficult to identify actual cost savings because of the many other variables one must take into consideration in carrying out such a study. However, there are several studies available in the literature indicating savings that at least cover the cost of the quality assurance program (Blackham, 1977; Goldman et al., 1977; Hall, 1977; Nelson et al., 1977; Linton et al., 1979; Fields et al., 1980; Noyes, 1980). In addition to savings in direct costs due to savings in film and chemicals, one may realize indirect savings in terms of a reduced workload for the technologist. This in turn may lead to increased patient flow and better utilization of the equipment and facilities.

In terms of direct costs, Nelson et al. (1977) found that their annual savings in film and chemicals alone was about $27,000 after the initiation of a quality control program. Blackham (1977) noted a 20% de-

crease in film costs after initiating a QC program even though there was a 3% increase in the number of studies carried out. Hall (1977) found that an institution spending $150,000 annually for film and chemicals could save $10,000 with a QC program. Goldman et al. (1977) estimated savings for just a photographic QC program would amount to $6300 per year for a facility producing 100,000 radiographs. Noyes (1980) estimated annual savings ranging from $33,000 to $51,000 for a department with 12 examining rooms.

Another area of potential savings is in the reduction of downtime of the equipment. However, it has been our experience that this is even more difficult to quantitate than the cost savings since breakdowns still occur (usually in the middle of a very busy morning with many patients waiting) and it is difficult to identify impending equipment failures before they occur. In fact, failures can occur immediately after QC checks have been carried out, thereby casting doubt on the efficacy of quality control in the mind of the more cynical administrator. Also, it must be remembered that QC checks require the use of the x-ray equipment and may reduce the patient flow. If you are concerned about downtime, the best answer to this problem is to establish, if feasible, an in-house service program to go along with the quality control program.

QUALITY CONTROL AND THE PROFESSION

Even though there are real savings with quality control programs in terms of the cost of expendables and potential savings through the better utilization of facilities, an even more important reason to initiate and maintain a QC program is related to the professionalism and pride the technologist should take in doing the best job possible. You, as a technologist, are an important contributor to the care of the patients at your clinic or hospital. The radiologists rely on the competency of the technologists to produce the best films possible, a trust and reliance that is rather unique in the medical field. As technologists you should do everything that you can to assure that your professional relationship with the radiologists is maintained and nurtured. A QC program will be a real asset to you, to your department, to your patients, and to your radiologists.

WHO IS RESPONSIBLE FOR QUALITY CONTROL?

The ultimate responsibility for quality control in a radiology department rests with the radiologist responsible for that facility (Bureau of Radiological Health, 1980; Joint Commission on the Accreditation of Hospitals, 1980). However, in most instances this responsibility will be delegated to the radiologic physicist, the chief technologist, or a QC technologist. In actuality, quality control is everyone's responsibility.

You must decide how best to initiate and maintain a quality control program in your facility. For example, one approach is for each technologist to be supplied with simple test tools to evaluate the particular room of equipment that he or she uses. In other words, every technologist is responsible for assuring that his or her equipment is working properly at all times. Another approach designates one or two technologists to carry out all of the necessary checks on a part-time basis, usually in the afternoon when the work load is lighter. Still another approach assigns a technologist to carrying out the QC tasks full time, although this is usually only feasible in larger institutions. In very few facilities does the chief technologist carry out the QC checks, since the chief technologist is usually already overburdened with other responsibilities and administrative tasks.

There are distinct advantages and disadvantages to each of these approaches. If every technologist is responsible for his or her individual room, then each technologist must be trained in the use of the test tools. This usually limits the complexity of the tests that can be carried out and increases the amount of test equipment that must be available. In addition, unless the technologists are highly motivated individuals who are interested in quality control, the QC tests become secondary and most frequently are neglected after a few months.

If one or two technologists are designated on a part-time basis to carry out the QC checks, especially in the afternoons when work loads are lighter, a strong commitment must be made by the department to assure that time is made available to them to do these tests. Frequently the workload requires that these technologists be utilized to fill in for someone else and the QC tests are neglected as a result.

In both of the above approaches several technologists must be trained in QC techniques. This dilution results in everyone involved being less experienced, in addition to making the training of several individuals costly in terms of dollars and time.

It would seem that a full-time technologist with sole responsibilities for quality control would be the ideal solution, but this is only feasible in larger institutions with a strong commitment to quality control. The individual with such responsibilities may obtain specialized training in quality control. In addition, this provides another possible pathway for advancement of technologists in the department and perhaps a stepping stone to higher positions.

A QUALITY ASSURANCE COMMITTEE?

Although committees in hospital facilities are known to be the largest consumers of man-hours, a quality assurance committee may prove quite useful. The committee should consist of at least one radiologist (additional radiologists representing subspecialties should be included in larger departments), a diagnostic radiologic physicist, the chief technologist, the QC technologist(s), and a representative from the in-house x-ray service or engineering group. This group should meet regularly and should provide direction to the program, determine the frequency of checks, assure that proper documentation is maintained (i.e., that which is necessary to meet JCAH requirements), and review the effectiveness of the program.

TECHNOLOGIST, PHYSICIST, ENGINEER?

Who should do what? This will depend on the relationships between the technologist, the physicist, and the engineer and on the individual expertise of each. We believe that the technologist, with proper training, should be able to carry out all of the QC tests that we describe. The physicist should be available to assist during the period when the technologist is learning to carry out and interpret the tests, but should not be required to get involved in most of the day-to-day operations of the QC program. The physicist should then be available to the technologist on a consulting basis.

Since all of the tests that we describe are noninvasive, the technologist should be able to carry them out without the assistance of an engineer. The engineer, however, should be available on a consulting basis to discuss design functions of the components and problems found by the QC technologist, and to provide the necessary expertise in calibrating and repairing the equipment. The QC technologist and engineer should work together closely in attempting to locate the cause of problems in x-ray systems. Finally, the technologist must verify the integrity of the equipment after the service engineer has completed his work, since the technologist must assure that quality diagnostic images are produced at a minimum dose to the patient after equipment service. If the technologists and engineers coordinate their work, they will find that both of their jobs are much easier.

In summary, the physicist oversees the program, develops tests as required, and monitors the measurements of radiation levels and image quality. The QC technologist carries out the day-to-day measurements in the program and maintains the QC logs. The service engineer carries out all repairs, preventive maintenance, and calibration on the diagnostic imaging equipment.

HOW MANY PEOPLE AND HOW MUCH TIME?

The number of people needed for a quality assurance program will depend on the size of the facility. A large proportion of the QC work should be done by the staff technologists in a small facility (with 5 or fewer rooms), but they should rely on a larger facility for some of the more complex measurements requiring sophisticated testing equipment. A small facility should have the services of a consulting physicist who visits the facility at least one day a month. The small facility should have a service engineer available for emergency repair calls and should establish regular preventive maintenance checks with the engineer.

A medium-sized facility (with 5 to 15 rooms) should have a part-time QC technologist and a full-time service engineer. A facility of this size should have a consulting physicist available in the facility at least one day a week and available at all times by telephone for consultation with the QC technologists and other department personnel.

A large facility (with 15 to 20 rooms) should have a full-time QC technologist and two or more full-time service engineers. A facility of this size should have a physicist working at least half-time and available in the facility 20 hours per week on a fixed schedule. In addition, the physicist should be available for consultation by telephone at all other times.

An extra-large facility (25 to 30 or more rooms) should have at least one QC technologist for each 25 rooms of equipment and one full-time engineer for each $3 million worth of equipment (this is based on replacement cost, not purchase value, of the equipment). There should be a full-time physicist available in the facility at all times.

Remember, small facilities need quality control as much as large facilities. A small facility may want to consider "time-sharing" the services of the QC technologist, the physicist, and the engineer with other facilities, or a larger facility may wish to consider providing such services to smaller facilities on an "outreach" basis. However, some quality control must be carried out by in-house technologists, including daily processor QC checks and some basic "go/no-go" tests. Consequently, each small facility must make a minimum investment in equipment, as described in the next chapter.

The QC technologist must be allotted adequate time to carry out the required tests. He or she *must* be released from clinical duties to carry out the QC tasks at specified times. For example, the QC technologist must be released from clinical responsibilities at 12:00 noon each day, *without fail,* or must be free of clinical duties on Tuesdays, Wednesdays, and Thursdays.

The amount of time needed to carry out room checks will depend on the sophistication of the tests. To check out a general radiographic room (without fluoroscopic or tomographic capabilities) will take from 1 to 2 hours. A radiographic and fluoroscopic room will take from 2 to 4 hours, and a tomographic room will take about 1½ to 3 hours. In addition, the QC technologist must have time to carry out daily processor quality control, or to supervise a designated individual who will process and read the densities of the control strips. The QC technologist must have sufficient time to troubleshoot other problems as they occur. Normally after a quality control program is initiated and the other technologists accept the program, the QC technologist will be called upon more and more to troubleshoot problems. This may mean that the technologists who are responsible for patient care are passing some of their responsibilities off to the QC technologist, but, at the same time, this is usually a more efficient use of resources since the QC technologist has the experience and equipment to quickly isolate the problems.

In addition to actual QC tasks, the QC technologists must have sufficient time allocated to update their skills, which will mean travel to other institutions and professional meetings. The QC technologist should participate in all QA committee meetings and departmental conferences as well as assist in the preparation of equipment purchase specifications. He or she will also need time to maintain adequate records of all work (this is required by JCAH), and to consult with the physicist and engineers on equipment and QC problems.

HOW FREQUENTLY SHOULD EQUIPMENT BE CHECKED?

The major goal of a quality control program is to detect changes in the equipment and have corrections made *before* these changes become significant enough to affect the quality of the radiographs produced. Consequently, the frequency of tests will depend on many variables, such as the complexity of the equipment, the age of the equipment, the criticality of the equipment usage (special procedure labs versus general radiography), and the volume of work.

One must also consider the amount of variation that is inherent in the individual equipment being monitored. For example, photographic processors are about the most variable pieces of equipment in any department and consequently should be monitored on a daily basis. Special procedure labs, especially ones doing more than two or three cases per day, receive a lot of hard use and a failure in any component is quite critical. Consequently, special procedures rooms should be checked at least monthly and preferably before every case, by imaging a patient ID device along with an image quality indicator. General radiographic rooms are much less complex than radiographic and fluoroscopic (R and F) rooms and will probably require checking about every 6 months, whereas R and F rooms will probably require quarterly checks. The simpler the generator, the less there is to go wrong, and the less QC effort is required. For example, a single-phase, nonfluoroscopic generator without phototiming will normally require much less attention from the quality control and preventive maintenance programs than a three-phase, falling load, fluoroscopic generator with phototiming.

You must decide from your experience how frequently you should check the rooms and how often preventive maintenance and calibration will be required. Every x-ray generator and imaging system should be calibrated and thoroughly checked at least once a year (Joint Commission on the Accreditation of Hospitals, 1980). QC checks should be carried out immediately following annual calibration and preventive maintenance as well as at 6-month intervals between annual invasive servicing. In addition, QC checks should be made immediately after any servicing that may affect the quality of images or the radiation output of the equipment. These checks need not be as extensive as those carried out in between the invasive calibration and preventive maintenance tests (for example, if a collimator has been removed then the half-value layer and collimator alignment should be checked).

WHAT SHOULD BE EVALUATED?

Simply stated, everything that affects the quality of the radiograph, the dose to the patient or staff, the safety of the patient and staff, and the comfort of the patient should be checked as part of the quality control program. However, you should determine the parameters to be tested or checked on the basis of the usage of the particular room.

Only those functions required for a particular room need to be checked on a regular basis. For example, if an x-ray generator is only used between 65 and 100 kVp and at 200 and 400 mA there is no need to check the entire range of kVp values, which may be from 30 to 150 kVp, nor to check all of the mA stations, which may range from 25 to 1000 mA. (If this is indeed the case, you should ask why a 150-kVp, 1000-mA generator was purchased in the first place since a less expensive unit would have been sufficient.) This makes the job of the QC technologist easier, as well as that of the service engineer, while providing an additional benefit—the possibility that you will get better generator calibration over the more limited range, allowing for the matching of x-ray outputs from room to room with all of the inherent advantages. As in the above example, you should also evaluate the stations on either side of the useful range, e.g., from 60 to 120 kVp and from 100 to 600 mA.

IN-HOUSE EQUIPMENT SERVICE?

For the best possible quality assurance program, and for a significant savings in service costs, every department with 5 to 15 or more rooms of x-ray equipment should consider establishing their own in-house service program. Smaller facilities should consider time-sharing the services of an x-ray engineer.

In terms of cost, in-house service is a real bargain. Most manufacturers are charging between $50 and $60 per hour (door-to-door) for service plus parts. This means that a service call that takes the vendor's engineer approximately 1 hour will cost you $55 plus the cost of travel time, say ½ hour each way, for a total cost of $110. In addition, most firms charge mileage at 20¢ to 30¢ per mile plus a 50% premium for work on weekends or after normal working hours. Most firms charge approximately 7% of the *replacement* cost of the equipment for a service contract, although this may include some parts. However, a service contract does not include overtime, for which the customer is billed the 50% premium, nor does it include special modifications.

Obviously in-house service has a significant cost advantage over vendor-supplied service. However, there is another major advantage that is often overlooked. If you have your own in-house engineer, he or she will become intimately familiar with all of your equipment and learn the quirks of each individual piece. In addition, the engineer will be available to assist in other projects when not busy repairing equipment. More importantly, he or she will be available at all times on short notice for equipment breakdowns and to repair minor nuisance items for which you would not want to call in a vendor's service engineer.

Another advantage of in-house service, which has become apparent in our facility, is the reduction in staff required to maintain the quality control program after a period of time. We are able to maintain the quality and service of our 173 rooms of equipment with three full-time quality control technologists, 25% of the effort of a physicist, and 7 service engineers. This is partly due to the fact that all of the calibration of all of the equipment is maintained within very tight tolerances from the day it is installed. Consequently, we carry out QC checks on our general radiographic equipment every 9 months, while carrying out preventive maintenance every 18 months, unless intermediate checks indicate otherwise. In some instances, certain types of equipment will require additional calibration, preventive maintenance, and QC checks. This is why it is necessary to start out a QC program with more frequent checks than may be necessary after all of the problems are corrected and the program is functioning smoothly.

Find out how much your department paid for x-ray equipment service last year and consider the possibility of an in-house service program. You will surely realize a cost savings while benefiting from minimum downtime, better equipment calibration, and better maintenance.

2 EQUIPMENT AND MEASUREMENT TIPS

WHAT EQUIPMENT IS NEEDED?

Actual equipment needs will depend on the size of the facility, the expertise of the individuals carrying out the tests, and the extent of the testing program (see Tables 2.1, 2.2, and 2.3). Note that the equipment needs should *not* be constrained by fiscal considerations. Although a complete collection of equipment as described in Table 2.3 may cost between $15,000 and $20,000, you should consider this in terms of the total investment of equipment in the diagnostic imaging department and the value of the services that can be provided with such equipment.

Most of the test equipment that we describe as part of our test procedures is available commercially. We do not mention manufacturers' names specifically since many firms make or market similar equipment, and it would be difficult to include all vendors. The Bureau of Radiological Health has published quality control catalogs (Burkhart, 1977, 1978) that list a large number of test items and vendors.

We have found it necessary, for one reason or another, to develop a few pieces of test equipment at

Table 2.1. QC tools for a small facility

Sensitometer
Densitometer
Thermometer
Collimator alignment template
Phantom or step wedge
Simple instructions on how to use phantom to check linearity, compare rooms, and evaluate fluoroscopic images
Screen-film contact mesh

Table 2.2. QC tools for a medium-sized facility

Sensitometer
Densitometer
Thermometer
kVp measurement device
Collimator and beam alignment test tools
Dosimeter (direct readout preferable)
HVL aluminum
Star focal spot test target
Tomographic phantom
Synchronous or electronic timer test tool
Phantom (patient equivalent and mammographic)
Mesh resolution pattern
Low-contrast test tool
High-contrast lead resolution pattern
Screen-film contact mesh

our institution. This equipment is described in detail in the Procedures sections so that the reader can reproduce it. One of these pieces is our patient equivalent phantom (PEP).

The patient equivalent phantom is based on a design for a phantom by the American National Standards Institute (ANSI) for the testing of photosensitive radiographic materials and photographic processing (American National Standards Institute, 1980). Its construction is based on transmission measurements at various kVp values, and has been modified so that the absolute transmission as well as the spectral transmission best simulates that from an actual patient, using readily available and inexpensive materials.

Table 2.3. QC tools for a large or extra-large facility

Sensitometer

Densitometer

Dosimeter (some have time duration option)

Full range of dosimeter chambers

Collimator and beam alignment tools

kVp test device

HLV aluminum

1.5° and 2° star focal spot patterns

Pinhole camera

Tomographic phantoms

Phantoms (full range of body part phantoms, uniform density phantoms, and resolution and contrast evaluation phantoms)

Step wedges

Full range of lead resolution targets

Mesh resolution patterns

Low-contrast test tools

Screen-film contact mesh

Oscilloscope

Scope camera

Output detector

Video waveform monitor

Video signal generator

Photometer

General purpose tools

Chart recording thermometer

Digital thermometer

The PEP, its specific dimensions, and materials are shown schematically in Figure 2.1a. It consists of six slabs of plastic (polymethyl methacrylate, also known as Plexiglas or Lucite) each 1 inch (2.5 cm) thick by 12 inches (30.0 cm) square. The six slabs are arranged in pairs so that the PEP actually is three phantoms in one:

1. Skull, abdomen, and pelvis phantom—consists of the chest phantom with an additional 2 inches (5.0 cm) of plastic added in the air space of the chest phantom (Figure 2.1b).
2. Chest phantom—consists of a 1-mm thick sheet of aluminum sandwiched between two slabs of plastic together with a second sandwich similar to the first but with a 2-mm sheet of aluminum (Figure 2.2a). [**Note:** Type 1100 aluminum should be used.] When this is arranged with a 2-inch (5.0-cm) air gap between the two sandwiches, as shown in Figure 2.2a, a typical chest is simulated for testing purposes.
3. Extremity phantom—consists of a 2-mm sheet of aluminum sandwiched between two slabs of plastic (Figure 2.2b).

As mentioned before, the PEP was chosen since it provided spectral and absolute transmissions that closely simulate patients. We have found, for example, that the pelvis phantom simulates a 21-cm patient abdomen. In addition, its simple construction and relatively low cost make it available to most institutions. We should note that it is necessary to obtain a phantom of these dimensions, especially the 12 × 12 inch (30.0 × 30.0 cm) dimensions, to properly simulate the patient and the scatter generated by the patient.

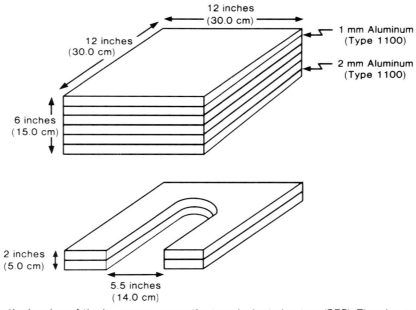

Figure 2.1a. Schematic drawing of the homogeneous patient equivalent phantom (PEP). The phantom and base, made of acrylic and aluminum, are used extensively in a quality control program.

Figure 2.1b. Basic PEP, which is used to simulate the abdomen, skull, and pelvis.

Figure 2.1c. Base for the PEP, which is used when dosimeter readings are to be made under the phantom.

Figure 2.2a.   PEP for chests and extremities. The basic PEP can be modified to provide a phantom that simulates the chest and extremities. The chest phantom is similar to the basic phantom, but two slabs of acrylic [2 inches (5 cm)] are removed from the center. A 2–inch (5–cm) air gap is left between the remaining layers.

Figure 2.2b.   The extremity phantom consists of a 2–mm sheet of type 1100 aluminum sandwiched between two 1–inch (2.5–cm) sheets of acrylic.

In addition to the PEP, we have developed a similar phantom containing several test objects that allows us to provide quantitative measurements of an imaging system as well as provide the clinical radiologist with objects to which he can relate (Figure 2.3). As can be seen in Figure 2.3a, it contains bone, catheters, simulated low-contrast "stones" in contrast media, steel wool, resolution targets, and a step wedge in a circular configuration. These are placed at various levels, as shown in Figure 2.3b. Of particular importance is the construction, type, and placement of the resolution targets. These contain frequency patterns to 5 cycles/mm since the large majority of imaging systems are limited to this level in the clinical situation, especially with the scatter produced by the phantom. Two of these, 0.10 mm and 0.01 mm thick, are placed on the bottom side of the phantom and allow determination of the high and low contrast resolution of the image recording system. The third, 0.10 mm thick, is placed on the top of the phantom and allows determination of the amount of unsharpness introduced by the focal spot and screen-film system in combination.

When we refer to the PEP, we will be referring strictly to the skull, abdomen, and pelvis phantom without any objects included, unless specifically noted.

DOSIMETERS

A dosimeter, properly understood and used, is an important tool in a quality control program. It is needed to determine the half-value layer (HVL), to determine how well a generator is calibrated (in terms of the mR/mAs measurements), and to measure the maximum and standard fluoroscopic exposure rates. A dosimeter can also be used to measure the attenuation of grids, tabletops, or any other item in the x-ray path, and it is beneficial in evaluating new products such as screens and films.

There are many factors that must be considered in the use of a dosimeter. There are basically three types of radiation measurement instruments (Figure 2.4). The survey meter is designed for measuring low levels of radiation such as those in an isotope lab or in evaluating x-ray exposure room shielding. This device is not suitable for quality control purposes. Pen dosimeters are sometimes recommended for quality control purposes, but we feel that they have many shortcomings that render them all but useless for an effective QC program. General purpose dosimeters with ionization chambers are the most expensive type of radiation measurement devices and the best for quality control purposes.

Dosimeters can be used with ionization chambers designed for specific purposes (Figure 2.5). Small volume chambers (less than 20 cc) are designed for high exposure rate measurements, e.g., high kVp, high mA, and short exposure time with measurements being made in air. These chambers must also be used with most dosimeters for the measurement of exposure times if that feature is available on the dosimeter. Large volume chambers (greater than 50 cc) are designed for lower exposure rate measurements such as low mA, low kVp, or heavily attenuated x-ray beams, e.g., for measuring the exit beam exposure behind a phantom, or the exposure in the Bucky tray where the exposure to the screen-film combination is on the order of 1 mR. These chambers are usually unsuitable for the measurement of exposure times because of their capacitive characteristics. Another type of ionization chamber is designed for use in mammography and has an extremely thin entrance window. This thin window is necessary to avoid the attenuation of the soft radiation used in mammographic applications. Finally, there are special chambers designed for CT applications. These are small, pencil-shaped chambers designed for insertion into CT phantoms.

All chambers have two limitations of which the user must be aware—energy and rate dependence. The use of the chambers for x-ray energies or rates other than those for which they were designed will provide confusing, meaningless results. The energy dependence is specified in terms of the keV range over which the calibration is within a certain percentage of the true value (usually ± 5%). For example, most dosimeters for diagnostic purposes are within ± 5% calibration over the range of 30 to 120 keV. (The effective keV of the beam is ½ of the kVp, so if you want to use a chamber that is calibrated from 30 to 120 keV, your measurements should be limited from 60 to 240 kVp.) The rate dependence of chambers is quite important since most diagnostic x-ray exposures will exceed the rates allowed for many chambers. The rate dependence results in readings lower than you should obtain since recombination of the ionized air and electrons occurs in the chamber (the dosimeter measures the amount of ionization), resulting in a low, false reading.

The entire volume of the ionization chamber must be irradiated to obtain proper readings, with the exception of the CT chamber. In the latter case, a correction factor is supplied with the chamber to assure proper readings.

Dosimeters are delicate, sensitive, electronic instruments and must be treated with tender loving care. Ask your physicist to go over the operation of

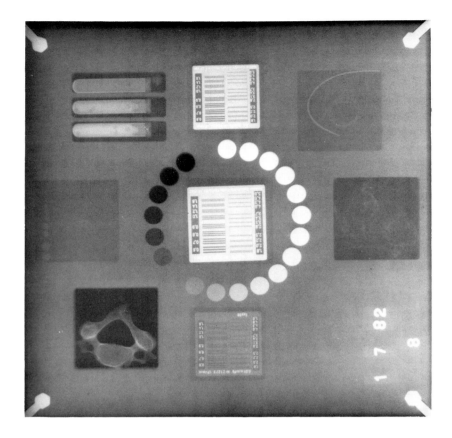

Figure 2.3a. Patient equivalent phantom containing special test objects. A radiograph of the phantom containing test objects shows that both quantitative and qualitative judgments can be made about image quality.

the dosimeter with you and explain all of the precautions of which you must be aware. Like any sensitive electronic instrument, dosimeters and their associated ionization chambers require recalibration on a regular basis. Most manufacturers offer recalibration, repair, and preventive maintenance services for a reasonable fee. We recommend that every dosimeter and chamber be serviced and recalibrated on an annual basis.

QUALITY CONTROL
FORMS AND CONTROL CHARTS

As we discuss in Chapter 3, all of the data collected in a QC program should be maintained in a way that allows you to review each measurement over the history of the equipment. We have provided all of the forms and control charts that we have developed for our QC program in Appendix A. (These may be copied for individual use without the permission of the authors or publisher, but they may not be copied for resale.) Keeping these forms and control charts up to date will provide you with the appropriate information

for troubleshooting and also for determining the reliability of each piece of equipment, a real asset for a radiology department.

SERVICE REQUEST FORM

Also in Appendix A is a copy of a service request form that we use to request in-house service. This is a four-part form that is initially filled out by the individual detecting the problem—the staff technologist, x-ray supervisor, or QC technologist. The first copy is retained by the x-ray supervisor as an indication that service is required and the three remaining copies are given to the service engineer. Upon completion of the service work, the engineer gives one copy to the x-ray supervisor indicating that the work is complete. Another copy is placed in the QC room log by the service engineer to alert the QC technologist that service has been performed, and the final copy is maintained by engineering in their room file to indicate what service has been carried out in a particular room.

Prior to a room QC check, or any other time the QC technologist goes into an x-ray room, the service

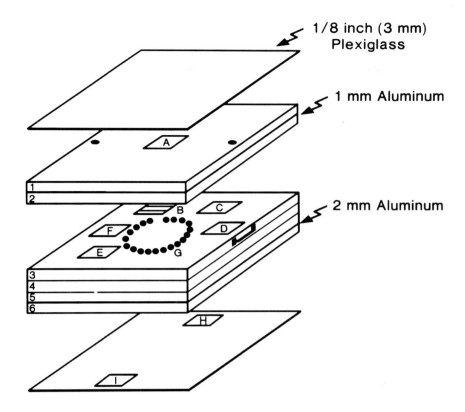

1/8 inch (3 mm) Plexiglass

1 mm Aluminum

2 mm Aluminum

Figure 2.3b.   The placement of the objects is important. Objects are placed in specific layers as follows:

Layer 1: A 0.10–mm lead resolution target *(Item A)* provides information concerning the focal spot characteristics since this is closest to the x-ray source. This layer also contains markers indicating the anode and cathode ends of the image.

Layer 3: This layer contains: dilute contrast media in small plastic vials with several plastic beads in the contrast media *(Item B)* to simulate a gallbladder with stones; a cutout with short pieces of catheter material *(Item C)*; a cutout containing steel wool *(Item D)*; a deeper cutout containing a portion of a vertebral body *(Item E)*; a cutout containing various sizes of plastic beads *(Item F)*; and a step wedge *(Item G)* made by inserting aluminum rods of various lengths to obtain film densities lighter than the surrounding material and by drilling holes into the acrylic to obtain film densities darker than the surrounding material.

Layer 6: On the underside of layer 6 there are two lead resolution targets *(Items H and I)*; one is 0.01 mm thick, providing a low-contrast image to assist in determining the effects of quantum mottle, and the other is 0.10 mm thick, providing a measure of the resolution of the screen-film system.

request copies in the QC log are reviewed and summarized in the maintenance log (a permanent part of the QC room log). These copies are then discarded. This procedure ensures that the QC technologist is aware of what service has been performed. However, if the service engineer has performed any work in the room that may affect image quality or the x-ray output of the system, he immediately notifies the QC technologist upon completion of the service work. The QC technologist then carries out the necessary tests to assure that integrity of the equipment and image quality and patient exposure are optimal.

QC EQUIPMENT CART

The amount of QC test equipment needed, especially for medium- or larger-sized facilities, can present

some difficulty in transporting it to the room to be evaluated. To simplify the movement of this equipment around the department, and to assure that all of the equipment is available in the room when needed, we have developed an equipment cart that contains all of the necessary test equipment and tools (Figure 2.6).

Since several of the pieces of test equipment require electrical power, and since most x-ray rooms usually have a minimum of electrical outlets, we have mounted a multiple outlet box with an integral circuit breaker on the cart (Figure 2.7). This means that only one electrical connection must be made when the QC technologist enters the room, with all of the equipment being powered from the multiple outlet box.

Since film, cassettes with film, and Polaroid film are carried on the cart, and it is in the room during

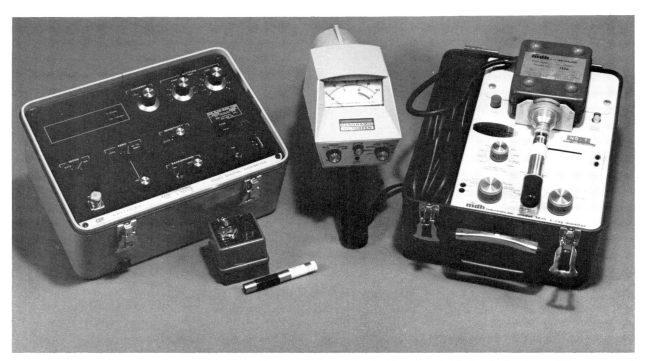

Figure 2.4. Radiation measurement equipment. The survey meter *(center)* is not suitable for dosimetry or QC purposes. A pen dosimeter, shown in the lower left with its charger-reader, can be used for limited purposes, but because of its inherent limitations we do not feel it is accurate enough for QC purposes. Direct readout dosimeters *(on the left and right),* although somewhat costly, are essential for reliable and accurate dosimetry and for a good QC program.

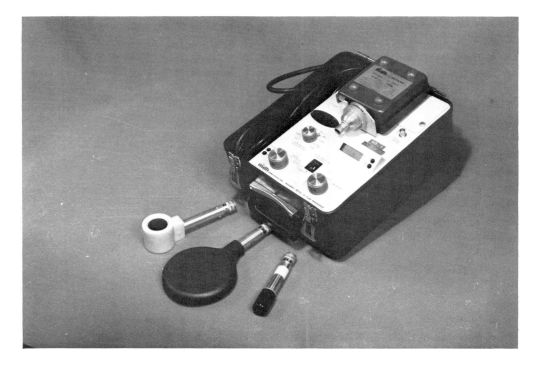

Figure 2.5a. For QC purposes we recommend a direct readout digital dosimeter that digitizes the signal at the ionization chamber. Three chambers are necessary for specific purposes: a thin-windowed chamber for mammography *(left);* a large volume chamber for use under phantoms and in making measurements at low radiation levels *(center);* and a small volume chamber for making measurements at high radiation flux levels as well as monitoring the x-ray waveform *(right).*

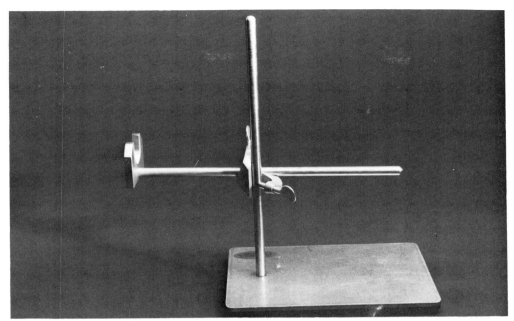

Figure 2.5b.   Although not essential, a stand can be constructed with a lead-weighted base to hold the dosimeter at the appropriate level for measurements.

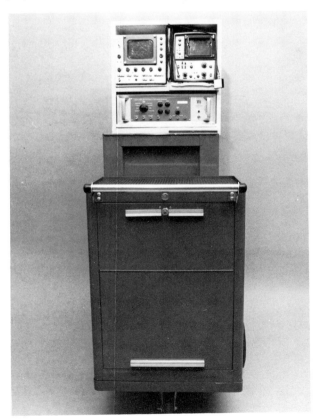

Figure 2.6a.   Quality control equipment cart. It is convenient to have all of your equipment on one cart so that it is available when you are working in a room. The locked section contains tools (screwdrivers, pliers, etc.) and the readout section of the dosimeter. The rack on top was added to the cart to hold electronic test gear.

Figure 2.6b.   All QC test tools are contained in the locked drawers and lower storage area (including the PEP). One small drawer is lead-lined so that film can be stored in the cart without risking film fog. The flat area to the left provides a writing area. Various ionization chambers are stored in one drawer, which has been lined with foam containing cutouts to fit each chamber.

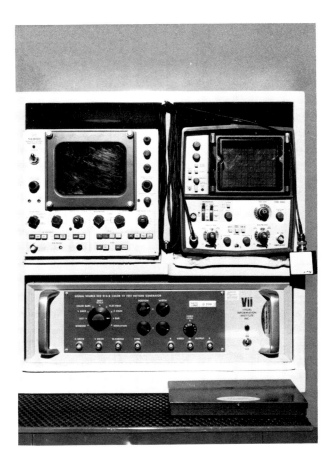

Figure 2.6c. Electronic test equipment includes a video waveform monitor *(upper left)*, a storage oscilloscope with a solid-state detector connected to it *(upper right)*, and a video signal generator *(bottom)*, all sitting on foam (for shock absorption) in a specially designed cabinet. Note also the lead letter and number identification kit on the lower right.

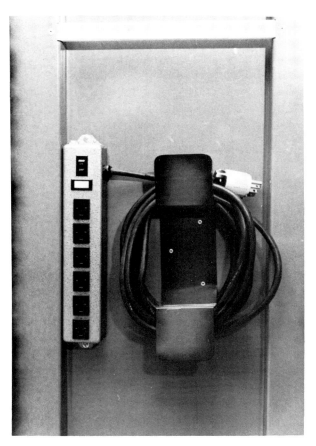

Figure 2.7. Multiple outlet box. Since most radiographic rooms do not have sufficient outlets to support all of the test gear, and to make set-up easier and quicker, a multiple outlet box with a switch and circuit breaker is mounted on the right side of the cart (relative to Figure 2.6b). In addition, an extra-long electrical cord is provided so that the cart can be positioned anywhere in the x-ray room.

x-ray exposures, one drawer of the cart is lead-lined to prevent film fog.

A writing surface is also provided on the cart, allowing the cart to be placed just inside the control booth door. This allows the technologist to have the dosimeter and oscilloscope available near the control panel and reduces the number of steps required in checking out the x-ray system.

HEEL EFFECT

Heel effect is the term given to the change in intensity of the x-ray beam along the anode-cathode axis of the x-ray tube. It varies with the anode angle (being greater for shallow angle tubes) and with the distance from the x-ray source. The intensity of the x-ray beam will be lowest on the anode side of the x-ray beam, in-creasing to its highest value somewhere past the central ray and dropping off again toward the cathode side of the beam (Figure 2.8). With a greater source-to-image distance (SID), the effect is less significant since you are only using the central portion of the beam. For example, at a 40-inch (100-cm) SID, the intensity of the beam will decrease to 55% at the anode end of a 17-inch (43-cm) field and to 98% at the cathode end of the same field. At a 72-inch (180-cm) SID, the intensity of the beam will decrease to 78% at the anode end of a 17-inch (43-cm) field and increase to 107% at the cathode end of the same field. (All measurements are normalized to 100% under the central ray.)

Whenever possible, radiation measurements should be made with the ionization chamber under the central ray. If measurements cannot be made in

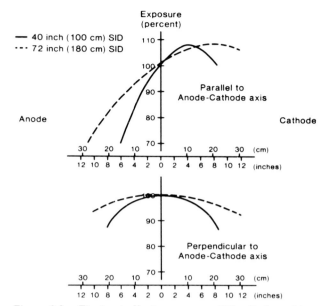

Figure 2.8. The heel effect can cause difficulty in making radiation measurements. Considerable variability will be noted as the ionization chamber is moved parallel to the anode-cathode axis, expecially with a 40–inch (100–cm) SID. Variation is not nearly as significant perpendicular to the anode-cathode axis, but it is still present.

this manner, always make each of them with the ionization chamber positioned on the same side of the beam (e.g., on the cathode side), and with the chamber the same distance from the central ray.

Whenever you are making measurements from film, such as in the use of the kVp cassette, the dimension of interest should be placed perpendicular to the anode-cathode axis. Step wedges should be placed in this orientation also since the change in intensity is much less than along the anode-cathode axis (Figure 2.8).

In clinical practice, the heel effect can be used advantageously. For example, in a radiographic room used mainly for abdominal procedures, the x-ray tube should be mounted so that the cathode side is toward the patient's head, placing the highest intensity point of the beam over the thicker portion of the abdomen. On dedicated chest systems, the x-ray tube should be mounted with the cathode end of the beam toward the patient's feet. Consideration should be given to the position of the x-ray tube whenever a new system is installed or a tube is replaced so that the heel effect is used to the best advantage.

3 ■ BASICS OF QUALITY CONTROL

OBJECTIVES OF A QUALITY CONTROL PROGRAM

The major objective of the quality control program is to detect changes in image quality that may affect diagnosis or cause changes in the radiation exposure to the patient before they become significant and, most importantly, to request service or calibration of the imaging systems before the radiologist comments on the loss of image quality. In other words, we want "...to provide quality that is satisfactory, adequate, dependable and economic" (Thomas, 1973).

Let's examine those four words in detail and see what they really mean.

Satisfactory—we want to assure that the quality of the images fulfills the needs of the radiologist, i.e., that the clinical images are satisfactory.

Adequate—the quality of the images should be sufficient for a specific requirement, i.e., the quality is adequate. Note that we very specifically indicate here that the quality is sufficient for a *specific* requirement. This is important in that less expensive systems may be utilized where appropriate. For example, the image intensifier for GI examinations need not be of as high a quality as one used for cardiac catheterization (in the former case, the system is limited by the TV chain and in the latter case, if you are recording the images on cine film, the intensifier limits the quality of the images).

Dependable—the quality should be consistent, the density and contrast should be the same on any day the exam is carried out, and the radiologist should be able to compare films from one day to the next or from year to year without having to "read through" differences in the images due to changes in the equipment, image quality, etc.

Economic—In addition to all of the above we would like to keep the costs of operating a radiology department as low as possible. Along these same lines, we want to select the equipment or materials that will give us the best examination for the specific situation. Why purchase a $75,000 three-phase, falling load, phototimed generator for a limited-purpose situation such as an operating room when a $15,000 single-phase generator will do the same job? In addition to the equipment and materials being economic, you must remember that the quality assurance and control programs should be as economic as possible, but this doesn't mean cutting corners when it comes to purchasing QC equipment. Good QC equipment will save considerable time in a quality control program and is well worth the investment.

In summary, the major objective of the QC program is to maintain the quality of clinical images at an optimum level, at a reasonable cost, and to request service or calibration of the equipment *before* the clinical quality of the images deteriorates. Consequently, the measurements you make must be accurate, reproducible, and sensitive enough to detect changes less than those that would be objectionable to the radiologist.

MEASUREMENTS AND CONTROL CHARTS

In a QC program we want to deal with data that are objective and that can be easily quantitated. In other words, we don't want to deal with one individual's opinion of whether the contrast is sufficient; we prefer to measure the contrast and then determine from past experiences whether the contrast (the numerical value) is optimum. This may create some difficulty since personal preferences of radiologists vary, but the best solution to this problem is to work to the requirements of the most critical radiologist. If you satisfy the most critical individual, you will satisfy all of the radiologists.

All measurements you make will contain two types of errors—systematic and random. Since we want to use these measurements to detect slight changes in the parameters we are measuring (changes that are less than those that are visually apparent), you must exercise extreme caution to assure that the measurements are made properly and made *in the same manner each time.* If the radiation output is to be measured at 100 cm, this means that the center of the ionization chamber is to be 100 cm from the x-ray focal spot and not 99 or 101 cm. Errors of this type, errors introduced by the QC technologist making the measurements, are systematic measurement errors and must be avoided at all costs. Also in the category of systematic errors would be differences in measurements made by two different QC technologists, even though the measurements made by each may be consistent. (For example, one technologist measures the exposure with the center of the ionization chamber 100 cm from the focal spot and the other measures the exposure with the top of the chamber 100 cm from the focal spot.) We will try to point out the major sources of systematic error in each of the tests we describe, but we can't stress too strongly that you must do everything possible to eliminate all sources of systematic error.

Random errors are errors in your measurements over which you have no control. For example, you set up the dosimeter properly to measure x-ray exposure and make six exposures without changing any of the generator settings or moving any of the equipment and you get the following series of readings:

105 mR, 98 mR, 103 mR, 100 mR, 101 mR, 97 mR

Which of the readings is the true reading? They are all correct in their own way but there is an inherent, random variation in these six readings. The average value ($\overline{X}$) here is 100.7 mR.

One word of caution is appropriate here concerning the accuracy of measurements. The actual average value of these six readings is 100.666666666... mR. However, we will work with the rule of thumb that you carry only one additional digit along after the calculation beyond the significant digits displayed by

the instrument. In the case of these six readings the dosimeter provided, at most, three significant digits so we will report the result in terms of four digits.

Now if we make six additional measurements and determine their average, we will find that the average values also vary because of random variation. How can we cope with this variation so we know that the results we get are real and that changes we are seeing are due to changes in the equipment and not to random variations in the measurements? In order to help us sort out these problems, we will use control charts for logging all of our data.

Control charts are the key and backbone of a quality control program. A control chart is a graphical means of recording data that allows for the easy inspection of those data from the present measurement back over the history of the control chart (Figure 3.1). Each measurement is recorded along the horizontal axis of the control chart as a function of time. For example, if we are making measurements on a daily basis, the increments on the horizontal axis are in terms of days. The vertical axis represents the numerical value of the measurement we are making. In

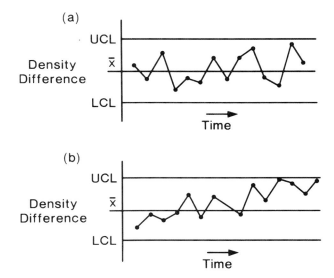

Figure 3.1. Basic control charts. Control charts are plots of numerical values with time. The data will contain inherent variation **(a)** and should oscillate around the operating level *($\overline{X}$)* and remain within the upper and lower control limits *(UCL and LCL).* Any time a single data point reaches or exceeds the control limits corrective action *must* be taken, although the test should be rerun to verify that the process is indeed out of control. Also, any time that a control chart shows trends (an increase or decrease in data over at least three data points) corrective action should be taken. The control chart in part **b** shows an out-of-control process since there is a steady increase evident over a long period of time—in fact, corrective action should have been taken after the fourth or fifth data point.

the example in Figure 3.1a, we are looking at the density differences from a daily photographic processor quality control program. Consequently, the values along the vertical axis represent the density differences we are measuring. There are three important numbers on this axis: the average value, the upper control limit (UCL), and the lower control limit (LCL). The average value, $\overline{X}$, is the value at which we would hope to find the density difference every day when we make the measurement. However, because of random variation, we really find that the measurement of the density difference seldom falls on the average value line, but oscillates around that value. How do we determine if the magnitude of these variations is acceptable and is indeed due to random error?

This is where the upper and lower control limits come into play. The control limits indicate the maximum and minimum values of the measurement that we will accept as normal random variation. If the measured value reaches or exceeds the control limits, then we must assume that a significant change has occurred in the operating level of the process. If a change has occurred, we then must *immediately* make a correction or take what is referred to as corrective action. In many instances, this will mean that we must call in a service man, change the chemistry, and so forth. Consequently, since corrective action may involve a considerable effort, it is always prudent to *make a second measurement* to verify the fact that your data have really reached or exceeded the control limits, and that the process is out of control. If after repeating the measurement the process is still out of control, then corrective action must be taken immediately. We cannot stress enough that **when the control limits are reached or exceeded, corrective action must be taken *immediately*.** Why make measurements and determine that something is not functioning properly if you are not going to do anything to correct the situation?

Another condition that you will encounter in the use of control charts is one in which all of the data points remain within the control limits but steadily increase or decrease (Figure 3.1b). This also indicates an out-of-control condition for which corrective action must be taken *immediately* since the control limits will be reached if the process is allowed to continue operating. This slow change in the process is known as "drift" and it is most frequently encountered in photographic processing.

Caution must be taken in determining if drift is occurring in the process. Normally, you must see at least three data points moving in the same direction, either upward or downward, before it is possible to determine if the process is really drifting. In other

words, if you can draw a line through three data points as shown in Figure 3.1b and that line is moving upward or downward then the process is probably shifting and the problem should be investigated to determine its cause. Note that we stated that the problem should be investigated—in this case corrective action should be taken only after you determine the cause of the problem. If the cause cannot be ascertained, then the process should be monitored closely to determine if the drift was in fact real.

ESTABLISHING OPERATING LEVELS AND CONTROL LIMITS

The operating level of the control chart is the central line about which we expect our day-to-day measurements to fluctuate. In order to establish this level, we must know something about the measurements, about the process, and about the history of the process.

Let's take, for example, the operating level of an x-ray generator in terms of the kVp. This is quite simple since we know that when we set 80 kVp on the generator we want the measurements we make using the test cassette to indicate that we are indeed getting 80 kVp. We then must know something about the measurements so we know what each line above and below the operating level represents. Do we want the divisions to be in terms of ½ kVp? Since we know that we cannot measure the kVp more accurately than 1 or 2 kVp, then looking at ½ kVp changes would be meaningless. In this case, we will make each division equal to 1 kVp.

If we want to set up a control chart for a photographic processor, this becomes more difficult since there are no standards defining what density we should get on our film for a specific exposure. Consequently, we must know something about the measurements, about the process and about the history of the process (we already do—we know there are no standards!). We know in advance that the measurements cannot be made more repeatably than ± 0.01, the inherent limitation of the densitometer. We also know that measurements cannot be made more accurately than ± 0.02, a limitation associated with the instrumentation as well as the measurement process in general. Consequently, we will make each division equal to 0.02.

What about the operating level? To establish this, we must know something about the history of the process. In this case, we must put fresh chemistry and starter in the processor, allow the chemistry to equilibrate, and process a sufficient number of films [one hundred 14 × 17-inch (35 × 43-cm) films or the equivalent of assorted sizes] to assure that the chemistry is stable before we can determine the correct operating level. This methodology is described in detail on pages 44–45.

Once the operating level and the divisions on the control chart are determined, these should be placed on the control chart (Figure 3.2). In addition, the upper control limit and the lower control limit values should be determined and recorded on the control chart, and indicated by a red line. The operating levels and control limits that we provide in this text are ones that are based on statistical analyses of QC measurements and that, through experience, we have found to provide the sensitivity to detect significant changes in the measurements we are making while not indicating changes in the process when they do not exist. You may wish to consult with your physicist and service engineer to determine if these operating levels and control limits are reasonable for your facility or if other levels may be more appropriate. However, it is important to remember that these levels and limits should be such that you can detect changes *before* they are visually apparent to the radiologist reading the radiographs. At the same time, you do not want the operating level set at an artificial level that is difficult or impossible to maintain, nor do you want the control limits set so close to the operating level that you are calling for corrective action unnecessarily. [**Note:** The control limits can be determined on a statistical basis and your physicist may want to refer to a standard statistical textbook for information on how this is done (Crow et al., 1960; Rickmers and Todd, 1967)].

ROOM LOGS FOR QUALITY CONTROL

Next to control charts, room logs are the most vital part of a quality control program. The room log, kept in a single three-ring binder, consists of all of the control charts associated with a particular room, room inventories, maintenance logs, sample images, and so forth—all of the data needed for reference during a quality control check of a room (see Appendix A). (It may be useful to keep a duplicate set of logs in the quality control office for quick reference and to minimize the problems created as a result of a lost QC room log, although this means that both sets of logs

must be updated during the QC check.) The items that should be maintained in the room log are listed in Table 3.1. Most items are self-explanatory, but special attention should be paid to those items noted below.

The "Quality Control Procedure" section of the room log may contain detailed instructions for carrying out the QC tests, but this is usually not necessary since all tests should be carried out in the same manner from room to room to assure that results are meaningful. However, detailed procedures for all tests should be maintained with the test equipment. It is necessary to note any deviations from normal procedures in this section and to indicate which kVp and mA stations, for example, are used for evaluation (normally only those stations that are used in a particular room, and adjacent stations, need to be checked on a regular basis). If deviations from the normal procedures are noted in this section, then this fact should be clearly indicated on the appropriate control charts so that anyone doing the tests or analyzing the data is aware that differences may exist.

The "Visual and Manual Quality Control Checks" are necessary checks of items in the room that may affect image quality or patient safety and comfort. These checks should be done by the QC technologists since they are not in the room every day and will be more alert to missing items and problems. This list may be modified to meet the individual needs of a department, but our experience has indicated that the same list should be used in almost every room in the department.

The "Maintenance Logs" are a very important part of the room log. Each time service of any type is performed on the equipment, an indication of this service should be noted in this log. You may wish to have the engineers leave a copy of the service form in the room log so the QC technologist can review the service forms and summarize them in the Maintenance Log, or you may have the engineers directly enter the information in the Maintenance Log. In either case, it is essential for the QC technologist to review the forms before carrying out the QC tests so he or she is aware of potential changes resulting from the recent service requests. The Maintenance Logs also provide a quick way to determine the amount of service that has been required on a specific piece of equipment in

Figure 3.2. Sample photographic processor control chart. Several important points are apparent on this control chart. The upper and lower control limits are emphasized with short dashed lines (normally, red lines for the control limits would be added to working control charts). Information concerning replenishment rates and chemicals temperature is recorded. Each time any single data point reaches or exceeds the control limits all of that test's points are plotted and then circled. The data points resulting from retesting after corrective action was taken are then plotted and connected to the previous day's data points. Also, the specific corrective action is noted in the "Remarks" section of the chart for future reference and assistance.

X-RAY PROCESSING CONTROL CHART

Department of Radiology

Processor: **# 2 Angio**   Month: **July 1982**

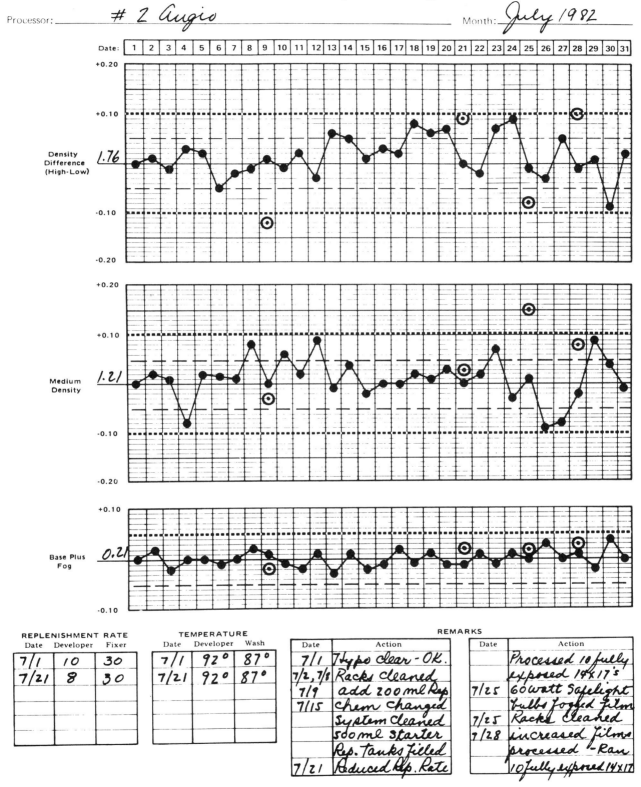

REPLENISHMENT RATE		
Date	Developer	Fixer
7/1	10	30
7/21	8	30

TEMPERATURE		
Date	Developer	Wash
7/1	92°	87°
7/21	92°	87°

REMARKS

Date	Action
7/1	Hypo clear - OK.
7/2, 7/8	Racks cleaned
7/9	add 200 ml Rep
7/15	chem changed
	System cleaned
	500 ml starter
	Rep. Tanks filled
7/21	Reduced Rep. Rate

Date	Action
	Processed 10 fully
	exposed 14x17's
7/25	60 watt Safelight
	bulbs fogged film
7/25	Racks cleaned
7/28	increased films
	processed - Ran
	10 fully exposed 14x17

Table 3.1. Contents of QC room logs

Room equipment survey (including overload protection factors for x-ray tubes)

Quality control procedures

Visual and manual quality control checks

Control charts for:
  mR/mAs
  Linearity
  Repeatability
  kVp
  Timer accuracy
  Half-value layer
  Focal spot size
  Collimator
  Standard fluoroscopic exposure rate
  Maximum fluoroscopic exposure rate
  Phototiming
  Phantom film entrance exposure and film density
  Tomography

Maintenance logs

Miscellaneous
  Polaroid photos of standard x-ray output waveforms
  Star and/or pinhole focal spot images
  Collimator test images

the department when you are considering the potential for new equipment. (It may also be worthwhile to indicate total downtime for the equipment since this may be considerable in cases where a service company may have difficulty in providing rapid response to your calls or may have difficulty in obtaining repair parts—the specific facts and times should be noted for future reference.)

The items listed under the "Miscellaneous" category provide important information. All of the standard images—x-ray output waveform, focal spot, tomographic phantom, and collimator test—are needed for reference in the future to determine if changes have occurred. However, don't become a collector and end up with piles of these images—the only ones that are valuable are the initial ones made on the equipment (which ideally should have been made when the equipment was installed) and the most recent images. These two sets of images should always be compared critically with the images from the present QC checks to assure that no significant changes have occurred. You may want to consider keeping copies of "interesting cases" in your office file for teaching purposes or to show to your colleagues when they ask what types of problems you are finding.

Like control charts, room logs are only as good as the data in them. Be sure to keep them up to date and assure that all necessary information is present. Most importantly, assure that anyone could go to the log, if necessary, and determine how the tests were carried out and equate the results.

PROCEDURES

3.1. CONTROL CHARTS

Purpose

To provide a graphical means of recording data for easy analysis and interpretation.

Equipment Needed

1. Graph paper or specialized control charts
2. Pencil and ruler

Procedure

1. All data collected *must* be plotted on control charts, including the actual data points, the date the data were collected, and the corrective action taken, if any.
2. The operating levels and control limits (both upper and lower control limits) must be determined and indicated on the control chart (see the sample control chart in Figure 3.2). If you are plotting the measured kVp, then the operating level becomes that level at which the control panel is set, e.g., 80 kVp.
3. The control limits are those levels that, if exceeded, require that corrective action be taken (e.g., a service engineer is called to calibrate the equipment). For example, we may wish to maintain our generators within ± 3 kVp, so the upper control limit becomes 83 kVp and the lower control limit is set at 77 kVp.
4. Sometimes it is not as easy to establish the operating level and control limits. For example, with photographic processors there are no absolute values you can use. These will have to be established in a manner similar to the operating levels and control limits described on pages 44–45.
5. As soon as you have plotted the data points you should immediately determine if any of the points lay outside of the control limits.
6. To assure that you did not make some mistake or that your data are not incorrect because of experimental error, it is wise, and probably time saving, to repeat any test that indicates that the process is out of control, especially if a data point lies on or just outside of the control limits.
7. If corrective action is required, repeat the test after the correction has been made. [**Note:** This is especially important to do if you rely on service engineers who are not affiliated with your institution. Remember, as a QC technologist, you were delegated the duties by your radiologist and are responsible for the safety of your patient and for assuring that the radiographs you produce are of the best quality possible.]
8. Circle the data points for out-of-control results and then plot the in-control data points (obtained from postcorrection testing), connecting the latter points to the in-control data points from the previous QC test with straight lines.
9. Record the corrective action taken on the bottom of the control chart or on the maintenance record log, which should be part of your QC room log.
10. You may encounter a condition in which the data points are all within the control limits but in which the process is considered to be out of control. This occurs when a process exhibits trends or drift. A trend, or drift, is indicated when *at least three* data points move in either the upward or downward direction. This means that the process is not in control. If allowed to continue to operate in this manner, the data points will soon be outside of the control limits. Be sure to scrutinize your control charts for trends whenever you plot the data.
11. In addition to the possibility of control limits and trends becoming apparent, your control charts will exhibit normal random variation (see Figures 3.1 and 3.2). This type of variation is to be expected since it is due to the normal variation in the process and the experimental error in your measurements.

Problems and Pitfalls

1. The major problem associated with control charts is failing to keep them up to date with the pertinent measurement data, the date of the measurements, and the corrective action and corrected data points. A control chart only provides the history of your equipment or processes if you keep the history up to date.

2. An important pitfall is that many people do not recognize random variation in the data, which is inherent, and they expect the data to fall along the operating level at all times. The data will vary randomly around the operating level but should remain within the control limits, not exhibiting any trends.

3. There is a tendency to record data on various bits and pieces of paper or to develop a survey sheet for a room of x-ray equipment that contains all of the information about the room on a single date. The purpose of a control chart is to provide a working sheet that can be filled in while you are making the measurements. A control chart should be a single graph exhibiting all the measurements of a single parameter made at different times so you can visually scrutinize the changes that may be taking place in that single variable, rather than a single sheet containing all of the various measurements made on one day.

4. The major pitfall in using control charts is the reticence of the user to call for corrective action when the control chart so indicates, i.e., when the control limits are exceeded or trends are apparent. When the control limit is reached or exceeded, the test should be repeated. If the second set of data still indicates that the control limits have been met or exceeded, *corrective action is required immediately.* If trends are apparent over three or more data points, *corrective action is required immediately.* The purpose of control charts and a quality control program is to *control quality,* not to monitor quality or the lack of quality.

3.2. QUALITY CONTROL ROOM LOGS

Purpose

To provide a source of information concerning the operating conditions of equipment, equipment failures, preventive maintenance, or any other activity that may influence the quality of the end product.

Equipment Needed

1. Three-ring notebooks
2. Notebook dividers
3. Control charts, maintenance logs, etc. (see Appendix A)
4. Pencil and ruler

Procedure

1. Establish a complete QC room log for each room of x-ray equipment. This should include all of your control charts for that room, a set of instructions on how the measurements are made in that particular room (including kVp, mA, and exposure time settings), the source-to-image distance, and any settings peculiar to the room, plus a maintenance log. A complete survey of the equipment, including serial numbers and dates purchased, should be an integral part of the log.

2. It is the QC technologists' responsibility to see that the QC room logs are established and maintained. It is also their responsibility to enter the data on the control charts as the measurements are being made.

3. It is the responsibility of the service engineer to enter the appropriate information in the maintenance log, which is part of the QC room log, so that the technologist will know what adjustments or changes have been made to the equipment. This is particularly important if maintenance work is carried out during off hours.

4. The QC technologist should review the entire QC log every time he or she evaluates the room and every time any changes are made in the equipment. The QC technologist must make evaluations of any parameters that may be affected by changes carried out by the service engineers and enter the appropriate data in the control charts. In addition, all data that are not fully understood or are confusing must be reviewed with the radiologic physicist as soon as possible.

Problems and Pitfalls

1. The most prevalent problem is not entering *all* data in the QC room log as soon as it is collected. If it is first recorded on bits and pieces of paper, it will become confused and ultimately lost, thereby negating the efforts of the quality control technologist.

2. Not only must new data be entered but previous data must be reviewed to see if the new measurements are meaningful.

4
REJECT-REPEAT ANALYSIS PROGRAM

One of the main goals of a quality control program is to reduce the number of films that are rejected and repeated. By rejects we mean all scrap film including green film, black film, clean-up films, and patient films. We limit repeat films to those radiographs of patients that were not accepted and required an additional exposure of the patient. This accomplishes two things—1) it reduces the amount of film and chemistry that will be needlessly wasted; and 2) it reduces the number of times patients will have to be exposed two or more times without providing additional diagnostic information. Consequently, we should consider the analysis of rejected and repeated films a key to how a radiology department is functioning. Although a Reject-Repeat Analysis Program (RAP) could be considered a measure of the effectiveness of a QC program, it should be used with caution in this vein since many other factors should be considered in determining the efficacy of such a program. The reject-repeat rate can be reduced to zero if the radiologist reads every film that comes out of the processor, but these films may not contain the necessary diagnostic information.

The steps necessary to carry out a Reject-Repeat Analysis Program are outlined in the Procedures section of this chapter, and also discussed in the literature (Goldman, 1979). However, we should look at what we can and cannot learn from such a program. First of all, we can determine what the reject rate is for a specific department and compare this to the average reject rates from around the country, as shown in Table 4.1. However, anytime you compare data from a single institution with that of others, it is important to be certain that the data were collected in

the same manner and that the facilities are similar. For example, does one institution include all "green" film in the count of rejected films whereas another does not? Does one institution rely on an estimate of the number of films consumed whereas another relies on a counter attached to the entrance roller of the processor to determine the number of films processed? [This also provides an inaccurate count since small films—e.g., 8 × 10 inch (20 × 25 cm)—should be processed two at a time.] Does one institution notify the technologists that a RAP is being carried out whereas another does not? In terms of facilities, one must consider many variables—does the institution have student technologists; is the patient mix at the institution similar (e.g., all inpatients, all outpatients, mostly trauma patients); are the number of cases per technologist similar at both institutions; what is the attitude of the radiologists toward quality films (i.e., will they read anything that comes out of the processor)? All of these variables, and many more, will affect the results of a RAP, so comparison of data between two or more institutions is difficult to say the least.

The attitude of the staff technologists is very important in a RAP. If QC and the RAP are seen as policing measures, every effort will be made, intentionally or unintentionally, to thwart the RAP. Even unconsciously a technologist may pass films that he or she might normally repeat on to the radiologist to read, if a RAP is in progress, just to reduce the overall repeat rate. In some institutions, technologists have been known to take their repeat films home with them for disposal while a RAP was going on.

There are several key guidelines to carrying out a RAP. Everyone in the department should be aware

Table 4.1. Reject-repeat rates

	Reject rate (%)		Repeat rate (%)	
	Before QC	After QC	Before QC	After QC
DuPont (Hall, 1977)	13[a]	7	9	
University of Connecticut		14.3	8.4	
PHS Hospital (Goldman et al., 1977)			8	6.2[b]
Donelson Hospital			9–10	3–5
Hammond Clinic (ACR, 1981)	6.5–8	2.75–3.75		
Medical College of Virginia (ACR, 1981)			8	3
Morton F Plant Hospital (ACR, 1981)	12.6	6.2		
McLaren Hospital (ACR, 1981)			10	7.4
Mercy Hospital, Baltimore (ACR, 1981)	24	13.6	14	8.6
Fountain Valley Community Hospital (ACR, 1981)			15	7.7
Mercy Hospital, Davenport (ACR, 1981)			14	7.5

[a]Hall indicated a range of reject rates before QC from 2% to 46% over 150 facilities.

[b]After photographic processor QC only.

that such a program will be going on sometime in the future and they should be made aware of the results in a constructive manner. Individual technologists should never be identified as being at fault for the results of the RAP. Consequently, technologists' identification should be removed from the rejected films if any of them are to be used as teaching cases for in-service education.

You will find a considerable diversity of opinion in trying to determine why films were rejected. A radiologist who is involved in the analysis may find that many rejected films would have been acceptable for readings. Consequently, there should be a category on the analysis sheet for "good" films. The fact that these films were acceptable should be communicated to all of the technologists. The same people should analyze the films each time since different individuals will have different criteria for judging a good film, whether a film is too light or too dark, whether the radiograph was retaken due to motion or position, and so on.

The results of the RAP should never be used competitively between areas of a hospital, different hospitals, or different groups of technologists since such competition is not fair and the results of the RAP, under such conditions, will be less than reliable. The results of the RAP should be communicated to all of the technologists in terms of the overall reject rate at their institution, and perhaps relative to the national averages where appropriate. Such results can be used to demonstrate the effective efforts of *all* personnel in the department in reducing the number of

rejected or repeated films but should never be used to demonstrate the effectiveness of the QC program to the staff technologists or radiologists since *everyone* in the department is responsible for the rejected and repeated films. The results of a RAP indicate the effectiveness of the QA program, which represents the overall quality assurance efforts of everyone.

Before a RAP can be carried out, strict guidelines must be established concerning the methods of film collection and analysis. The following guidelines are an example of the necessary "ground rules" to assure that the study is carried out in the same manner each time:

1. No copy or subtraction films should be included in the reject count or total film count.
2. "Positioning" includes any errors generally attributed to the technologist; for example, no labels on the film, snaps from patient gowns, or dual exposures.
3. Scout films, although normally rejected, will be included in the count as "Scouts."
4. Films from special procedure areas (cardiovascular and neurological) will not be included in the reject count or the total number of films used.
5. The "miscellaneous" category should be used for films that cannot be fit into the other categories. Notation should be made concerning the cause of the rejects in miscellaneous categories.
6. Examples of "good films" should be saved.
7. You should look at three separate categories: (A) total waste films—all films that are in the

scrap bin; (B) total rejects—all films except clear films and quality control films; and (C) total repeats—only those films for which you are fairly certain that an additional film was made of the patient.

The results of a *reject* analysis, based on the above guidelines, are shown in Figure 4.1, Table 4.2, and Table 4.3. There are several notable points in Table 4.2., especially the fact that the type and mixture of patients will significantly affect the results. For example, an outpatient clinic would expect to have a lower overall reject rate than a hospital general radiology department. Likewise, a hospital emergency room would be expected to have a higher reject rate than a hospital general radiology department.

Location _St. Mary's General_
From _12/1/81_ To _12/29/81_

Cause	Number of Films	Percentage of Rejects	Percentage of Repeats
1. Positioning	46	30	37
2. Patient Motion	5	3	4
3. Light Films	21	14	17
4. Dark Films	14	9	11
5. Clear Film	20	✕	✕
6. Black Film	17	11	13
7. Tomo Scouts	12	8	✕
8. Static	—	—	—
9. Fog—Darkroom	2	1	2
10. Fog—Cassettes	6	4	5
11. Mechanical	6	4	5
12. Q.C.	10	✕	✕
13. Miscellaneous (?)	15	10	✕
14. Good Films	9	4	7
Total Waste (1–14) 7.8 %	183	✕	✕
Total Rejects (All except 5 and 12)	153	(6.5)	✕
Total Repeats (1–4, 6, 8–11, 14)	126	✕	5.4
Total Film Used 2354			

Figure 4.1. Worksheet for reject and repeat analysis.

Table 4.2. Mayo Clinic reject rates

Section	Rate (%)
Clinic (outpatients)	3.1(weighted average)
Heads	6.6
General	2.8
Mammography	1.8
Pediatrics	8.6
Community Medicine	5.8
Methodist Hospital	6.4
St. Mary's Hospital—General	6.5
St. Mary's Hospital—ER	7.7
Weighted average	5.2

Table 4.3. Percentage of rejects by category, St. Mary's Hospital—general radiology

	Rejects (%)
Positioning	30
Patient motion	3
Light films	14
Dark films	9
Black films	11
Tomo scouts	8
Static	—
Fog—darkroom	1
cassette	4
Mechanical	4
Good films	6
Miscellaneous	10

Even within one type of facility there will be a diversity of reject rates depending on the type of examinations. For example, in an outpatient facility the highest reject rate is found in pediatrics, not surprising since one would expect problems with patient motion. (The reject rates shown in the breakdown of the outpatient clinic exams are statistically significant since they are based on the analysis of over 8,000 *processed* films.)

The next aspect to consider in a RAP is that of the percentage of rejects by category (Table 4.3). In this analysis, you take all of the *rejected* films and determine what percentage of the total number of rejects fall into each of the categories. The results of this analysis can be used to guide the efforts of the quality control program.

When a QC program is first initiated, it will usually be found that a large percentage of the rejected films falls into the categories of light films and dark films. After a good QC program has been in effect, you will find that the percentage of films in these categories *decreases* but that the percentage in other categories such as positioning and patient motion *increases*. This is to be expected since the total number of rejected films is decreasing and the number in the light and dark film categories is decreasing. Consequently, if the *number* of films in the positioning and motion categories stays the same the *percentage* of these films relative to the total number of rejected films must increase.

There is a wealth of useful information in the results of a RAP. However, the data must be collected with extreme care and the results must be analyzed with great caution to assure that the conclusions drawn from the study are correct and meaningful.

PROCEDURES

4.1. REJECT-REPEAT ANALYSIS PROGRAM (RAP)

Purpose

To provide a method for the analysis of the rejected radiographs in a radiology department. The results of such an analysis will provide information concerning those aspects of radiologic imaging that need the most attention. If you plan to initiate a quality control program then you should carry out an analysis of your rejects before starting the QC program so you will have some idea of the impact of your quality control efforts.

Equipment Needed

1. Rejected radiographs and a count of the total number of films consumed during the survey period
2. A QC technologist and, preferably, a radiologist

Procedure

1. Clean out all rejected film bins throughout your departments.
2. Establish a method to accurately determine the amount of raw film consumed starting on the day that you cleaned out the reject bins.
3. After at least 1 week, or the period of time that it takes to produce about 1,000 radiographs, collect all rejected radiographs and determine the actual number of radiographs exposed (i.e., the number of sheets of raw films consumed) during this period.
4. Analyze, with a radiologist if possible, all of the rejected films and determine the reason that they were probably rejected.
5. Record these numbers on a tally sheet (see the examples in Figure 4.1 and Appendix A) as you are reviewing the films. (Don't be surprised if there are many radiographs for which you can't determine the cause of rejection.)
   [*Note:* It will be difficult to determine if a light or dark radiograph was rejected because of poor technique or improper processing. Consequently, these must be classed simply as ''light'' or ''dark.'']
6. Determine the overall reject rate. For example, if there were 153 rejected films and a total of 1225 films produced, then the overall rate is

$$\frac{153}{1225} \times 100\% = 12.5\%$$

7. Now determine the percentage of rejects from each of the categories. For example, let's say that 49 films fell into the category labelled ''too dark.'' The percentage of rejected films falling into this category is then

$$\frac{49}{153} \times 100\% = 32\%$$

Problems and Pitfalls

1. Many technologists regard a reject analysis program as a means of ''checking up on them.'' Consequently, you should not use the reject analysis program to determine which technologist is producing the most rejected radiographs.
2. If possible, it would be better not to let your technologists know when you are collecting the rejected films. If they know you are collecting rejects, they will often pass more radiographs through to the radiologists or throw rejected films in the trash can rather than the reject box. In fact, in one institution, the technologists actually carried rejected films home with them to avoid having their supervisors find out how many films were not acceptable.
3. Once you have completed the reject analysis, share the results of your study with the radiologists and technologists, explaining to them what these results mean and how you plan on reducing the number of rejects. Remember to point out to them that reducing the number of rejects will reduce the technologists' work load and frustrations and will save the department money in terms of reduced film and chemical consump-

tion, while higher patient throughput may be realized. Also, the radiation exposure to the patients and staff will be reduced.

4. One problem in this type of analysis is the "acceptance level" of the radiologist. We all know which radiologist in our department will "accept anything." Consequently, if the department has become accustomed to poor and variable quality radiographs and the radiologists accept them, the overall reject rate may be quite low. However, this does not mean that a quality control program is not needed. It does mean that the technologists are not exhibiting pride in their work, and the radiologists are not providing the best medical care possible to their patients. This, of course, means a QC program is needed to improve image quality and consistency. Once the radiologists start reading good quality, consistent films they will appreciate the need for QC and the efforts of their technologists while having more confidence in the diagnostic information content of the images.

5. In general, special procedures should not be included in the overall departmental reject analysis but should be analyzed separately.

Acceptance Limits

1. The overall reject rate should be less than 10%. Ideally, you should attempt to get the overall reject rate down to about 5%. This depends not only on a good QC program but on a good rapport between the radiologists and technologists, as well as an understanding between them as to what constitutes a good radiograph and what should be rejected.

2. Compare your percentage of rejects (from Procedures Step 7) to those from other institutions (Tables 4.1, 4.2, and 4.3; Hall, 1977). Those categories that contain the highest percentage of rejects should receive the most attention. For example, Hall (1977) showed that before the initiation of a QC program the combination of light and dark films accounted for 73% of all rejects. After the QC program had been in operation, this percentage dropped to 32%.

Corrective Action

1. If your overall reject rate is in excess of 10%, you are desperately in need of a good quality control program.
2. If your reject rate is between 5% and 10%, then you may be in one of two situations:
   a. The quality of your radiographs is good. If you don't presently have a QC program, you should initiate one to assure that you maintain the present quality of your radiographs.
   b. Your radiologists are accustomed to accepting poor quality radiographs since they can "read through" the poor quality films (Goldman et al., 1977). In this case you should work closely with your radiologists to establish a QC program and demonstrate to them the difference quality can make.
3. Remember, as your QC program becomes effective the overall reject rate should decline. Likewise, you should see a decrease in percentage of rejected films that are due to faulty equipment, processing, and so on—such as films that are too light or too dark. However, as the percentage of rejects due to a specific cause decreases, this means that the *percentage* due to the other causes will increase, but you should not see an increase in the total *number* of rejected films due to the other causes. The percentage of rejects should be used only as a guide to direct your efforts to those areas needing the most attention. The effectiveness of your quality control program should only be judged from the overall repeat rate.

5 PHOTOGRAPHIC QUALITY CONTROL

Of all of the areas requiring quality control in medical imaging photographic processing equipment is probably the one that demands the most attention, most frequently, and with the most care, since the photographic film is quite sensitive to changes in the processing system. All of the efforts expended in QC in other areas can be quickly negated if the processor is not well controlled.

There have been several studies made throughout the nation indicating the difficulties with photographic processing, but the study by Suleiman et al. (in press), conducted in New Jersey, is the most recent and provides excellent documentation of these problems. They evaluated 479 film-chemistry-processor systems in medical x-ray facilities. The results indicated that variations in relative speed of the same radiographic film processed in the various processors ranged from 35 to 210 (with 100 being the "normal" speed). This is a sixfold variation in film speed from processing alone! More significantly, the 245 processors producing speeds from 35 to 100 required an increased exposure to the patient to produce a radiograph—that's more than half of the processors.

The base-plus-fog levels on the films (the density of the unexposed portion of the film after processing) from all of the processors ranged from 0.09 to 0.53 with a range of about 0.15 to 0.20 being considered optimum. This is particularly important since increased fog decreases contrast and reduces diagnostic information content.

Fog can also be caused by the improper use of safelights in the darkroom or by light that is "unsafe," i.e., light that can fog the film, such as white light. Of the darkrooms studied, only 48% did *not* significantly fog the film in 1 minute (Suleiman, personal communication).

Obviously, a large portion of the darkrooms in the country are producing less than optimal results in terms of speed variations due to processing (contrast is also affected by improper processing) and in terms of light fog on the films. Consequently, we recommend that the first efforts of a quality control program should be directed at the photographic processing and darkroom aspects of the medical imaging department.

We have adopted the term "mechanized processors" as opposed to "automatic processors" in this book for a specific purpose. We would like to dispell the idea that processors are "automatic." In fact, processors are merely a mechanized method for processing film. They need a considerable amount of attention to assure that they function in the way the manufacturer intended and to maintain the activity of the chemistry at the intended levels.

A caveat is required at this point. You should not cut corners when purchasing a processor since it is the last element in the imaging chain, and perhaps the most important one. Many cardiac catheterization labs purchase an inexpensive processor with no recirculation, no chemical filtration, and no replenishment system to save a few dollars, after spending in excess of $500,000 to $700,000 for the x-ray equipment in the lab. [It is recommended that at least 2–3% of the cost of a cardiac catheterization lab be spent for a cine film processor (Inter-Society Commission for Heart Disease, 1976).] Likewise, many inexpensive conventional film processors do not come with the necessary controls to produce consistent, high-quality radiographs.

It might be argued that for small offices or radiology departments a large "expensive" processor cannot be justified. However, a mechanized processor will *not* operate properly unless at least 25 to 50 14 × 17-inch (35 × 43-cm) films, or the equivalent number of square inches of smaller sizes, are processed daily. Unless this quantity of film is processed, replenishment will be insufficient, the developer will quickly oxidize, and the processed films will become degraded, producing lower contrast. This requires the technologist to modify the techniques, with a resulting increased exposure to the patient and a decrease in diagnostic information content. It might sound like a step backward but, in most situations where low-volume processing is necessary, hand processing will provide better overall quality at a lower cost as long as the technologist processes all films at the proper temperature and for the correct time. If it is essential to use mechanized processors with low volumes, then a flood replenishment system which we describe in this chapter must be installed.

IS YOUR DARKROOM IN A FOG?

As we noted before, 52% of darkrooms fog film. The basic reasons are quite simple (Gray, 1975):

1. Either faded or improper safelight filters are being used (in some cases the filters must be placed in the safelight filter holder so that the lettering can be read from the outside).
2. The light bulb in the safelight is of too high a wattage for the conditions being used.
3. "Unsafe" light is reaching the film.

Safelights fade and age with time. If the safelights are left on 24 hours a day, the filters should be replaced every year. If they are on 12 hours a day, the maximum life should be 2 years. The date of the last filter change should be indicated on the safelight. In addition, if a higher wattage bulb has been used with a safelight then the chances are that the filter is already faded and should be replaced. Be sure to check with the manufacturer of your film to determine what filters you should be using with the films you use in your darkroom and remember that not all films can be handled under the same safelights.

In an effort to increase the brightness of darkrooms many people install higher wattage bulbs. No more than a 15-watt bulb should be used in the small "beehive" safelights, and no more than a 25-watt bulb in the large square safelights used for *indirect* lighting. Darkrooms can still be well illuminated and easy to work in with a few considerations. First of all,

no surfaces in the darkroom need to be black. The walls can be painted white or a light pastel color, and countertops can be white or light colored. Just changing to light-colored surfaces in the darkroom will make a major difference and you will be able to see much better. Next, a sufficient number of safelights should be used. One or more of the large rectangular safelights should be aimed at the ceiling to provide overall illumination. Each work surface should have about two of the small circular safelights (at least 4 feet above the surface), and there should be a safelight directly over the processor feed tray that turns off automatically when film is feeding into the processor (this safelight also provides a visible indication of when additional film can be fed into the processor).

"Unsafe" light can cause a major problem in darkrooms. Darkrooms with maze entrances, i.e., without a double or revolving door system, are not acceptable in any medical imaging darkroom. Neither can one accept anything other than dual door pass boxes with an interlock so that both sets of doors cannot be opened at the same time.

Other sources of "unsafe" light include white light leaks and "unsafe" indicator lights and luminous panels. To look for white light leaks, go into the darkroom and, with all of the lights turned off, allow your eyes to dark adapt for at least 5 to 15 minutes and then start looking for light leaks. Any white light leaks that you can see will fog film. Be particularly observant around door frames, where the processor abuts to the darkroom, around pass boxes and anywhere there is a break in the wall (around light switches, for example). Also, look very closely at the ceiling. Many suspended acoustical tile ceilings will allow light to leak into the darkroom from adjacent areas—the ceiling looks like a starry night sky.

Indicator lights, although they appear red, may actually be emitting light that can fog your film. Also, luminous panels or clock dials will fog film since they emit light in the region of the spectrum where the film is sensitive. One other potential problem area is in room lighting. Fluorescent lights should never be installed in a darkroom since some of these produce an afterglow when they are turned off. Some of the afterglow may be in the ultraviolet region, which will fog your film but is not visible to the human eye.

The methods of testing your darkroom for fog are described in the Procedures section of this chapter. Every darkroom should be checked for fog using this technique every 6 months or at any time you suspect there might be an increase in darkroom fog.

The technique for testing for darkroom fog requires that you preexpose the test film and then test for fog. This is extremely important since unexposed film is much less sensitive to fog light. This applies in both ways: if the film is fogged before exposure the film is more sensitive to the regular exposure it receives; and if the film is fogged after exposure the film is more sensitive to the fog light.

This difference in sensitivity is due to the non-linear nature of the photographic film. Each grain of the silver halide in the film must be "hit" with several light photons before it becomes developable. If a few hits occur during a fog exposure then it will take fewer hits to make the grain developable and, hence, the film is more sensitive.

Figure 5.1 is an excellent example of the effect of the increased sensitivity of exposed film as com-

Figure 5.1. Effect of fog on radiographic film. One half of the step wedge image (screen-film exposure) was exposed to safelights for 4 minutes. It is apparent that the fog is not perceptible in the unexposed portion of the image nor is it apparent in the dense portions of the film. Fog tests carried out with unexposed film will not indicate the true effect of fog in the mid-densities, the region of primary importance in radiology. Also, in visually judging if the fog is excessive it is necessary to cover the line between the fogged and un-fogged areas with a pencil. Eliminating the sharp border significantly changes your perception of the density difference between the two sides.

pared to unexposed film. A radiograph was made of an aluminum step wedge using a conventional x-ray system and a screen-film system. Half of the film was then covered with opaque paper in the darkroom and remained on the counter for 4 minutes so that one half of the area of the step wedge was fogged. It is easy to see that there is no apparent fog in either the radiographically unexposed area of the step wedge or the dark portion of the step wedge, but in the intermediate densities the effect of the fog is quite apparent.

There is a problem in judging the amount of fog that is acceptable unless a densitometer is used. A density difference of 0.05, as measured with a densitometer, between the exposed and unexposed portion is the most fog that is acceptable, and this amount of fog should not be apparent for safelight exposure times of 2 minutes or less. If the films must be judged visually, you must obscure the border between the fogged and unfogged portion of the film with a thin opaque object, since over edges that are not obscured, the eye can discriminate density differences on the order of 0.005 to 0.01. With the boundary between the two areas obscured, a visible density difference is about 0.05, or the level at which one must judge the safelighting unacceptable. (To demonstrate this to yourself, cover the boundary between the exposed and fogged and unfogged portions of Figure 5.1.)

What "fog time" is acceptable? We feel that, unless the darkroom can pass the fog test (a density increase of 0.05 or less) for a safelight exposure time of 2 minutes, it is unacceptable. Film is exposed to safelight and other light in the darkroom for considerable periods of time if one considers that each time the film bin is opened all of the film in the bin is exposed. The film is exposed as it is transported into the processor and it is exposed while it is lying on the counter while unloading and loading cassettes.

We have one final precaution concerning the measurement of fog. First of all you should test every type of film you use in the darkroom. Second, all film tested must be preexposed to light (e.g., from an intensifying screen) as it would be in use. If you are testing x-ray film expose it in a cassette with screens to a density of approximately 1.0. Direct x-ray exposed film does not have the same sensitivity as film exposed with light from screens.

ESTABLISHING A DAILY PHOTOGRAPHIC PROCESSOR QUALITY CONTROL PROGRAM

The major problem we face in establishing a photographic processor QC program is that there are no preset standards that tell us what our operating levels should be. You should follow the manufacturers' recommendations concerning the proper chemistry to be used with a specific film, the appropriate temperature for the chemistry and wash water, the proper processing time, and the correct temperature for drying the film. However, this does not tell you what density to expect for a specific step on the step wedge.

When we discuss step wedges in regard to a photographic processor QC program, we are referring to a step wedge exposed with a sensitometer (Figures 5.2 and 5.3). Processor QC *cannot* be carried out with a step wedge exposed with an x-ray machine. In order to control the quality of photographic processing we would like to eliminate as many other variables as possible, and if the wedge is exposed with an x-ray generator we will not know whether the generator or the processor is causing the changes in the density of the film.

Likewise, when we discuss sensi-strips we are referring to sensitometric exposures made with your sensitometer on the film normally processed in the machine you are evaluating and processed not less than ½ nor more than 4 hours after exposure. By waiting ½ hour, some of the inherent variability you would see from strip to strip is reduced. However, if you wait more than 4 hours, the effects of latent image decay may become apparent. Furthermore, it has been demonstrated that sensi-strips that were aged more than a few hours are less sensitive to changes in chemistry in terms of chemical activity or variations in temperature (Poznansky and Smith, 1968; Gray, 1976, 1977). In addition, it has been demonstrated that films exposed directly to x-rays, as opposed to x-ray exposure with screens, are extremely insensitive to changes in the chemicals of the photographic processor.

Since we would like the processor to be working under optimum conditions before starting our photo-

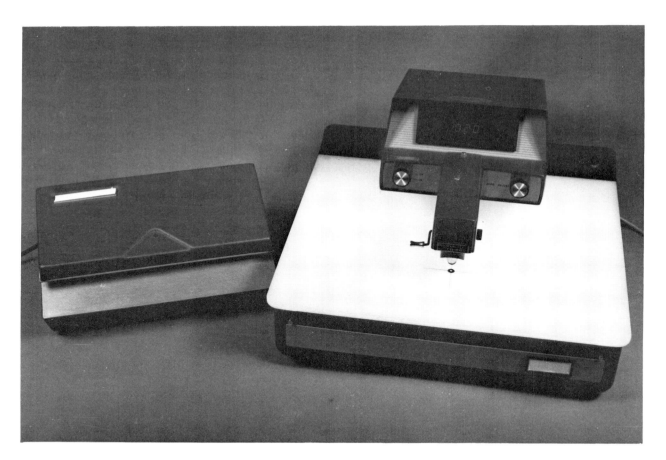

Figure 5.2.   A sensitometer *(left)* and densitometer *(right)* are essential for a photographic quality control program. Densitometers with a built-in light source are preferred. The color of the light used for quality control purposes in either the sensitometer or densitometer does not matter. However, sensitometers should *never* be used to compare different radiographic films since such comparisons are only meaningful if the film is exposed with the *exact* type of light with which it is used clinically, i.e., screen light emitted from the appropriate intensifying screens.

Figure 5.3. Sensitometrically exposed step wedge. The sensitometer provides a known, stepped exposure to film. The step wedge on the sensitometer has been marked to indicate which steps produce densities close to 0.25, 1.0, and 2.0 above the base-plus-fog level of the film so that the appropriate steps are read each time a strip is processed for QC purposes.

graphic processor QC program, it should be cleaned and any necessary repairs made before further work is done on the QC program. **Do not use systems cleaner at this time!** Systems cleaner is a strong acidic solution and if even minute traces of it remain in the processor it will contaminate the chemistry and invalidate your setup procedures. In addition, extreme care should be taken to ensure that not even a few drops of fixer are allowed to contaminate the developer since it takes only a few milliliters of fixer to cause significant changes in the developer (Figure 5.4) (Stears et al., 1979).

Follow the procedure described in the Procedures section of this chapter very carefully. Be sure to set the developer and fixer replenishment at those levels recommended by the manufacturer and verify

that you are actually getting the amount of solution indicated by the metering devices.

In photographic QC, as in all QC, one must be extremely cautious to carry out all tests in the same manner each time. It is absolutely essential to run the sensi-strips for both the initial setup procedure and the daily photographic QC with the thin (low-density) end of the strip leading and at the same location on the processor feed tray each time.

The by-products of the development process, primarily bromide ions, diffuse out of the film and can retard development. If processor agitation is less than ideal the by-products will flow over the film and retard the development on trailing portions of the film. The thin end of the strip is fed into the processor first to minimize this effect. (It will be necessary to notch or punch a hole in the sensi-strip at the time of exposure to indicate the thin end of the strip.)

Many processors exhibit differences in agitation and/or temperature from one side of the development tank to the other. Consequently, films processed at

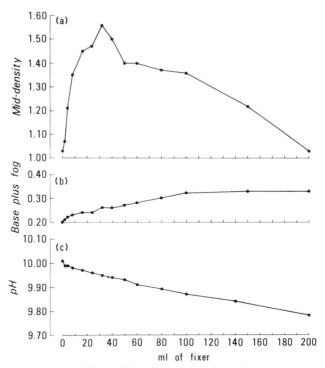

Figure 5.4. Effect of fixer contamination of developer activity and pH. Very small amounts of fixer can cause severe contamination of the developer (only a few milliliters of fixer in a 2.5-gallon developer tank caused the mid-density to exceed control limits). Other measures suggested in the literature, such as the fog level and pH, are not sensitive enough to provide an advance warning of such contamination. (Reproduced with permission from: Stears, J. G., Gray, J. E., and Winkler, N. T., 1979. Evaluation of pH monitoring as a method of processor control. *Radiologic Technology* 50:657–663.)

one location on the feed tray one time and then at another location the next time will produce different sensitometric results. A good rule of thumb is to always process the film at the extreme right of the feed tray each time—and with the thin end of the strip leading.

After determining the proper operating levels, record these values on the control charts and indicate the upper and lower control limits as shown in Figure 3.2. Now you can adjust all of the processors in your department to operate at the same levels (adjusting the temperature or replenishment rates as a last resort), assuming that you are using the same film in all of the processors.

DAILY PHOTOGRAPHIC QUALITY CONTROL OF MECHANIZED FILM PROCESSORS

Now that you have established the operating levels and control limits, you must maintain your checks on your processor on a regular basis. First of all, it is not necessary to monitor any parameters other than the densities of the sensi-strips on a regular basis unless problems arise. You should have already recorded the replenishment rates and temperatures on the control chart for reference. These can quickly be checked on a regular basis using the replenishment flowmeters and the thermometer built into the processor. It is not necessary to check the chemistry and water temperatures every day, nor to record these on a control chart, since any changes in the developer temperature will be immediately evident on the density of the sensi-strips and fluctuations in the fixer and wash water will not normally cause significant problems (in fact, some processors today operate with a "cold water" system, i.e., they use cold tap water so it is not necessary to monitor the temperatures).

It is not necessary to plot an entire characteristic curve each day since this provides no significant information that cannot be obtained by monitoring several density points and the density difference. In fact, it may be possible to monitor only the medium-density level, but the density difference and the base-plus-fog levels do provide useful additional information with little additional effort.

Daily photographic quality control should, as the name implies, be carried out on a daily basis. It is usually not necessary to make processing QC checks more often than this if the processor is stable and it is not being run for long periods of time without films being processed (such as overnight). (You should consider attaching a standby kit to every processor because this reduces the water and electrical consumption while helping to conserve chemistry, since the processor operates normally only when film is being processed. At other times the drive is turned off and water flow is reduced, but the recirculation pumps and dryer fan are operating enough to maintain the machine in a "ready" status.)

In some situations it may be possible to monitor the processor on a less frequent basis, but this is quite risky unless several other controls are initiated. In this situation it would be necessary to pretest the freshly mixed chemicals (perform a dip test) to assure that their activity meets the standards set by the quality control program (Winkler, 1975). In addition, only machines that are known to be stable and are in a high-volume area where a consistent mix of films is processed should be considered for less frequent monitoring. For the small amount of time it takes to expose, process, and read sensi-strips the risk of reducing the frequency of testing far outweighs any benefits.

One problem in photographic quality control is due to the fact that photographic films vary slightly in characteristics (speed, contrast, etc.) from emulsion batch to batch. Consequently, one should maintain a quantity of film sufficient for quality control for a 6-month period in a cool, dry place away from sources of radiation (refrigeration is ideal for such storage) and away from any sources of chemicals that may produce vapors. Before the last box of this emulsion batch is used you should perform a cross-over as described on page 46 and adjust the operating levels and control limits on the control charts if the new emulsion characteristics are different from the previous batch. (The range of the control limits, e.g., ±0.10, should not change.)

In some areas of the country (the south and southwest) water as cold as that required for the processor may not be available during the summer months. Most processors require that the wash water temperature be 5–10°F below the developer temperature since this cooler water acts as part of the temperature control system. In many of the warmer climates the tap water temperature can approach 90–95°F, resulting in a loss of control of the processor. If you attempt to use chilled or refrigerated water to bring the normal 120–140°F hospital hot water down to the required 85°F a considerable amount of refrigeration will be required. Only a relatively small amount of chilled water will be required to drop the tap water (at 95°F) to 85°F. Figure 5.5 shows a plumbing arrangement that allows for adding refrigerated water to tap water in the summertime while still using the conventional temperature control valve (Gray, 1977). You should be sure, at any rate, that the water chiller used has sufficient capac-

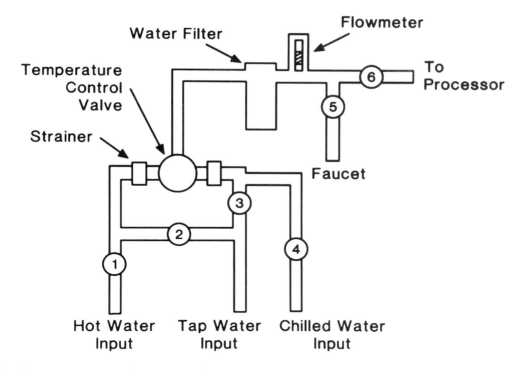

Figure 5.5. Temperature control, filtration, and flow monitoring system. A water filter should be installed before the point where the wash water enters the processor, along with a flowmeter, not a pressure gauge. In areas where the tap water temperature may approach the temperature required for the wash water, it is difficult to control and maintain the appropriate temperature without using refrigerated water. If refrigerated water is mixed with hot tap water [usually around 120–140 °F (49–60 °C)] a large quantity will be needed, requiring a large refrigeration plant. With the plumbing arrangement shown here it is possible to cool the normal cold tap water [around 90 °F (32 °C)] with refrigerated water, but only a small quantity of refrigerated water is needed. For normal operation valves 1 and 3 are open with valves 2 and 4 being closed. If the cold tap water approaches the desired wash water temperature then valves 1 and 3 are closed and valves 2 and 4 are opened.

ity to handle the volume requirements of the photographic processors (some require as much as 2.5 to 3 gallons of water per minute).

PROCESSOR CLEANING AND MAINTENANCE

Processor cleaning and maintenance is a major part of the photographic quality control program. Unless the processor is maintained in a clean and mechanically sound condition you cannot expect the best photographic processing results. You should follow the manufacturer's cleaning and maintenance schedule very closely.

With a good QC program, including cleaning and maintenance of the processor, it will not be necessary to change chemistry except as recommended by the manufacturer of the processor or when your control charts indicate that a change is required. In many instances the chemistry only need to be changed every 3 or 6 months. A good QC processor cleaning and maintenance program will actually reduce your workload while providing optimum processing.

A processor maintenance log is essential so that the QC technologist knows when maintenance has been performed on the processor, chemistry has been changed, or more replenisher added to the replenishment tanks—all changes that could affect the quality of the films produced.

Systems cleaner is a rather caustic (pun intended) topic. Although it is necessary at times to utilize systems cleaner, if it is not used properly it can cause havoc with your quality control efforts. Follow the instructions on pages 47–48 carefully and be sure to season the tanks and racks after using systems cleaner. Seasoning consists of placing developer and fixer in the appropriate tanks and then, with the racks in place, operating the processor for 10 to 15 minutes without processing film. These chemicals should then be discarded and fresh chemicals added, starting the processor operation in a normal manner at this time. The seasoning with the developer and fixer allows for the neutralization of the chemicals in the systems cleaner, which would normally leach into the chemistry during processor operation and change

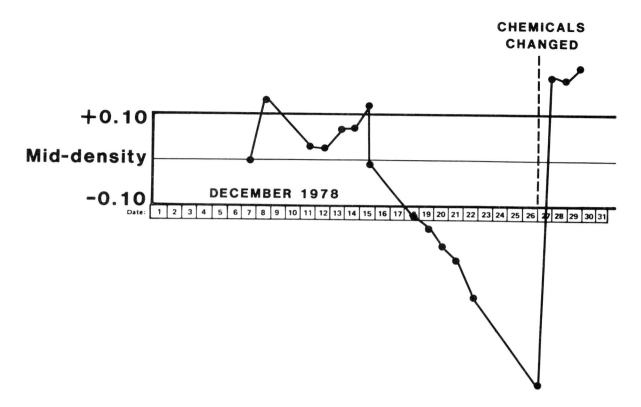

Figure 5.6a. Effect of flood replenishment on photographic processors. Rapid deterioration of developer activity is apparent in this control chart from a low-volume processor. (Reprinted with permission from: Frank, E. D., Gray, J. E., and Wilken, D. A. 1980. Flood replenishment: A new method of processor control. *Radiologic Technology* 52:271–275.)

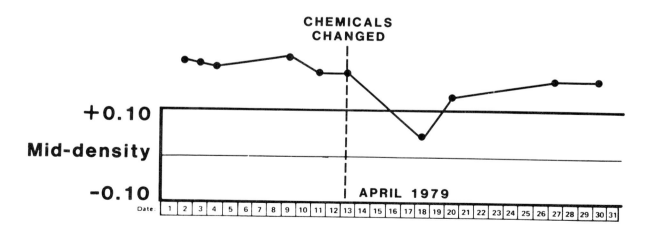

Figure 5.6b. After initiating a program to adjust replenishment rates and temperatures, along with changing the chemicals every month, the processor was a bit more stable but operated at levels outside the control limits and required constant attention (pampering).

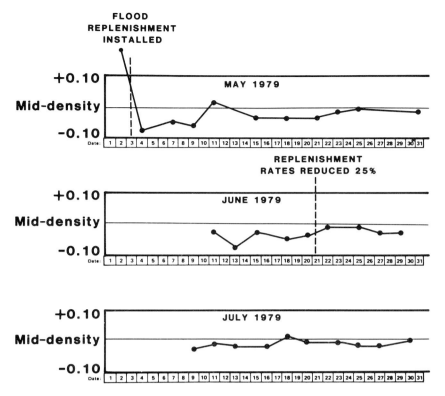

Figure 5.6c. After installation of a flood replenishment system it is apparent that the excessive variability of this processor has been eliminated and, in fact, it has become one of the most stable processors in our institution.

change their activity, causing the processor to go out of control.

FLOOD REPLENISHMENT

In many situations, it is necessary to operate a mechanized processor even though the daily workload is less than the minimum 25 to 50 14 × 17-inch (35 × 43-cm) films per day or the equivalent area of film in smaller sizes. Normally the developer is rapidly oxidized, resulting in a continual decline of chemical activity with subsequent drops in the mid-density levels, as well as changes in contrast (Figure 5.6). It is easy to increase the technique to compensate for this decline, but this results in less than satisfactory films and an increased patient exposure.

Flood replenishment was first introduced for both industrial and medical x-ray film processors by Titus (1979a, 1979b, 1979c). A discussion of the technique is available in the papers by Titus, and a thorough discussion of clinical applications along with control charts before and after flood replenishment can be found in a paper by Frank et al. (1980).

The basic idea of flood replenishment is quite simple. Since sufficient replenishment is not being

introduced into the processor by the films being processed, and other chemical components are also being introduced at less than an ideal rate (e.g., bromide, a by-product of the development process), it is necessary to artificially add these to the processor at a rate that will assure constant chemical activity. This is done by disconnecting the replenishment pumps from the automatic replenishment control system and connecting them to a timer that adds a predetermined amount of developer replenisher (with starter) and fixer replenisher at set intervals. The amount of solution added through the flood replenishment should replace the entire volume of the solution tanks in the processor every 16 working hours. This usually results in an increase in the consumption of chemistry but produces a stable processing environment. It also helps to prevent excessive chemical buildup on the rollers and, in general, keeps the processor much cleaner.

A word of caution is necessary concerning flood replenishment: **starter solution must be added to the developer replenisher in the replenisher tank each time fresh replenisher is mixed.** The amount of starter should be that specified by the manufacturer of your developer for mixing fresh developer solutions.

PROCEDURES

5.1. DARKROOM FOG CHECK

Purpose

To assure that the safelights and other potential sources of "unsafe" light will not fog the film being handled in the darkroom.

Equipment Needed

1. Unopened box of x-ray film (must be the type normally processed in the darkroom to be tested)
2. Screen-film cassette
3. Two pieces of black, opaque paper each as long as the film to be used and one-half of the film width
4. Densitometer
5. Clock with second hand or stopwatch

Procedure

1. Turn off all of the safelights and other lights in the darkroom.
2. After your eyes have had time to adapt to the darkness (about 5–15 minutes) look for any source of light you can find. Pay particular attention to the seals around processors, passboxes, darkroom doors, etc., and to ceilings (suspended ceilings can leak light from surrounding rooms). If you can see any light in the darkroom these sources should be eliminated.
3. After you have made sure there are no apparent light leaks, turn off all safelights, cover indicator or pilot lights on equipment with opaque material, and remove any luminous dial clocks from the darkroom.
4. Open a new box of film. [**Note:** This box of film must be the same type that is normally used in the darkroom. If more than one type of film is used the following tests should be carried out with each type of film.]
5. Load the film into the cassette in total darkness.
6. Expose the film.
   a. To evaluate x-ray film, make a uniform radiographic exposure with the film in a cassette (with intensifying screens) so that the density on the film is approximately 1.0.
   b. To evaluate other types of film, make a uniform exposure with the imaging device normally used so that the density is approximately 1.0.
7. Place the film on the counter in the darkroom with all of the lights off.
8. Cover the left half of the film with the one opaque sheet of paper. Keep this half covered throughout the next two steps.
9. Turn on the safelights and indicator lights.
10. Cover all but the upper quarter of the remaining portion of the film with the second piece of opaque paper and expose that portion for 2 minutes. Shift the opaque paper so that one-half of the film is uncovered and expose for 1 minute. Shift the paper again so that three-quarters of the film is uncovered and expose for another minute. (This film now has a total exposure of 4, 2, and 1 minutes in the three exposed areas and should look similar to Figure 5.7.)
11. Determine the density difference between the exposed areas and the *corresponding* unexposed area and record these values. If a densitometer is not available, cover the border between the adjacent areas with a thin strip [about 1/8 inch (3 mm)] of opaque material and compare the visual appearance of the areas.

Problems and Pitfalls

1. It is essential to use the same film as is handled in the darkroom.
2. The densities of the films must be read on adjacent areas to avoid processor and exposure variations.

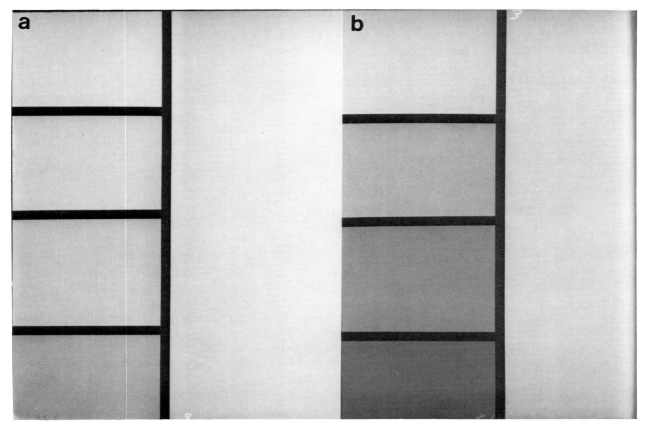

Figure 5.7. Darkroom fog check results. Any comparison of fog tests should be made with a densitometer. However, visual comparisons can be made if the borders between the various areas on each film are covered with a pencil or strip of opaque material. (**a.**) Virtually no density difference is visually apparent between the 1- and 2-minute fog times (center two areas on left) and the large, unfogged area, but a visual difference is apparent between the 4-minute fog time and unfogged area. This result would indicate an acceptable amount of fog in the darkroom. (**b.**) Even at 1 minute a visual difference is apparent when compared to the unfogged portion of the film. The safe lighting in this darkroom is in need of improvement.

Acceptance Limits

The density difference between the fogged and unfogged portions of the film should not exceed 0.05 for the 2-minute exposure area and *must not* exceed 0.05 for the 1-minute exposure area. For visual comparison, you should see no density difference between fogged and unfogged sides of the film for the 2-minute exposure area and must not see a difference in density for the 1-minute exposure area.

Corrective Action

If the density difference exceeds the limits noted above:

1. Check to assure that the proper safelight filter is in the safelight.
2. Check the safelight filter for signs of fading, aging, or cracking and replace it if indicated.
3. Assure that the proper wattage bulb is being used in the safelight. (Check the film manufacturer's recommendations for the recommended type of safelight, wattage of the bulb, and distance of the safelight from the working surface.)
4. If after these checks fog still exists, cover all indicator lights and repeat the tests with just the darkroom safelights on. [**Note:** It would be ideal to carry out this test in every darkroom every 6 months or whenever you suspect that fog may be creating problems.] A darkroom can be quite bright and not fog film if it is properly designed and lighted. There is no need for black walls or countertops—walls can be white and countertops either white or stainless steel. If the safelights are really safe and there is no source of "unsafe" light in the darkroom you will be better able to see and work in a darkroom with light-colored surroundings.

5.2. ESTABLISHING A DAILY PHOTOGRAPHIC PROCESSOR QUALITY CONTROL PROGRAM

Purpose

To determine the operating levels for all photographic processors in the department. (The operating levels should be the same for all processors processing the same type of film.)

Equipment Needed

1. Sensitometer
2. Densitometer
3. Digital thermometer or metal-stemmed dial thermometer
4. Stopwatch
5. Control emulsion
6. Fresh chemicals

Procedure

1. Drain the developer and fixer tanks in the processor and flush the tanks and racks with fresh water. [**Note:** **Do not** use systems cleaner at this time.]
2. Replace the developer recirculation filter with a new filter and assure that the processor is functioning normally.
3. Drain and flush the replenisher tanks and hoses with fresh water.
4. *Carefully* mix fresh developer-replenisher and fixer.
5. Refill the replenisher tanks, operating the replenisher pumps temporarily to assure that all fresh water is flushed out of the replenisher lines and to assure that the replenisher pumps are functioning properly.
6. Flush the processor fixer tank again with fresh water.
7. Fill the fixer tank in the processor with fresh fixer and replace the fixer rack.
8. Again flush the developer tank.
9. Fill the developer tank with fresh developer-replenisher and add the correct amount of starter as noted in the manufacturer's instructions.
10. Carefully replace the developer rack, crossover racks, etc.
11. Allow the processor to operate for 30 minutes.
12. Check the developer temperature, fixer temperature, and wash water temperature. The chemistry temperatures should be within 0.5° of those recommended.
13. Check the replenishment rates and the time it takes a film to pass through the processor (the time it takes from when the leading edge enters the processor until the leading edge exits the dryer).
14. Allow the processor to be used until 50 14 × 17-inch (35 × 43-cm) films, or the equivalent, *per gallon of developer* have been processed.
15. Expose six sensi-strips. If you are using a double emulsion film and a sensitometer that exposes only one side you should expose strips on both sides of the film, i.e., three sheets of film with two exposures each.
16. Wait at least 30 minutes before processing the strips.
17. Process the sensi-strips—**thin end leading, same side of the feed tray.**
18. Zero and calibrate the densitometer.
19. Read the densities on the six strips. Be sure to read the densities in the center of each strip, not near the edges. (Check the zero and calibration of the densitometer after reading each strip.)
20. Determine the average of the densities of the six strips for each step.
21. Select and mark the steps producing the densities nearest to 0.25, 1.0, and 2.0 above the base-plus-fog level of the film (Figure 5.3).
22. Determine the appropriate values and record these values and the control limits on the control chart (Figure 3.2). Three values should be recorded:

    DD (Density Difference) = high − low (± 0.10)
    MD (Medium Density) = mid (± 0.10)
    B + F (Base-Plus-Fog) = B + F (± 0.05)

23. Adjust *all* processors using the same film and chemistry to produce the same values.

Problems and Pitfalls

1. It is assumed that running 50 14 × 17-inch (35 × 43-cm) films per gallon is a "normal" mix of films and that the volume is at least 25 to 50 14 × 17-inch (35 × 43-cm) films per day.
2. See the "Problems and Pitfalls" discussion under "Daily Photographic Quality Control of Mechanized Film Processors," below.

Acceptance Limits

The control or acceptance limits for daily processor control should be ± 0.10 for both the medium density and density difference. Until you are familiar with the procedures and have your processors in good control you may wish to use wider limits of ± 0.15 for the MD and DD but you should maintain the limit of + 0.05 for the base-plus-fog. If you use the wider limits initially you should be able to shift to the tighter limits within not more than 1 month after you start your quality control program.

Corrective Action

If you have difficulties with any of the above procedures, contact the technical service representative from the firm that manufactures your film and chemistry.

5.3. DAILY PHOTOGRAPHIC QUALITY CONTROL OF MECHANIZED FILM PROCESSORS

Purpose

To assure on a day-to-day basis that all photographic processors are operating at the same levels and producing consistent, high-quality films.

Equipment Needed

1. Sensitometer
2. Densitometer
3. Digital thermometer or metal-stem dial thermometer
4. Control emulsion

Procedure

1. Follow the manufacturer's start-up procedures every day.
2. Allow sufficient time for the processor temperature to stabilize—about one-half hour. Assure that the wash water temperature is adjusted properly, where appropriate.
3. Check the following:
   a. Solution temperatures
   b. Replenishment rates
   c. Water flow rates
   d. Dryer temperature
4. Run several clean-up sheets and check them for roller marks and scratches. (Use exposed but unprocessed film for cleanup sheets.)
5. Expose enough sensi-strips for a single day's use. If the film is a dual emulsion film expose a strip on both sides if you are using a sensitometer that only exposes one side.
6. Wait at least ½ hour but not more than 4 hours before running all of the sensi-strips in the processors.
7. Process the strips—two per machine, thin end leading, in the same location.
8. Zero and calibrate the densitometer.
9. Read the three density patches and the base-plus-fog level from the two strips (for sensitometers requiring two exposures) from each processor and average the pairs of readings.
10. Plot the DD, MD, and B + F on the control charts.
11. Analyze the control charts carefully.
    a. Are all three points within the control limits?
    b. Are there any apparent trends?

12. If any single point (or points) falls outside of the control limits, run two more strips and verify that your first readings were correct.

Problems and Pitfalls

Photographic processor quality control is probably the most difficult program to establish and operate properly. The photographic process is full of its own quirks, idiosyncracies, and pitfalls. Extreme care must be taken to follow the steps described exactly and to keep in mind all of the problems and pitfalls listed below. For further information and a more detailed discussion of photographic processor quality control and the associated problems, you should refer to the two-volume Bureau of Radiological Health publication on the topic (Gray, 1976, 1977).

1. Mercury or other liquid thermometers should never be used around photographic processors since the contents may contaminate the processor if the thermometers are broken. Digital thermometers or metal-stem dial thermometers are preferred.
2. The temperature in the developer tank should be taken in the same place each time. In addition, do not trust any thermometer that may be permanently installed in your processor since it may be more variable than your good quality control thermometer and it may not be accurately calibrated. (You can check the calibration of your thermometer against the standard thermometers used in the clinical laboratories.)
3. Many processors do not have adequate agitation of the solutions on the film's surface. This results in a directional effect caused by bromide drag. Bromide, a by-product of the development process, suppresses development and, if the dense end of a sensi-strip goes into the processor first, the larger quantities of bromide liberated will suppress the processing and the densities of the following strips.
4. Only a sensitometer should be used to expose your control strips. An x-ray generator is not repeatable enough to use for this purpose.
5. Sensi-strips aged more than a few hours may lose their ability to detect changes in the processor that may be apparent on freshly exposed radiographic or sensi-strips. However, it usually helps to age the strips for at least one-half hour after exposing them since this tends to decrease the amount of variability from strip to strip.
6. Film emulsion varies from batch to batch, and such variations may be considerable. Consequently, you should select enough film from the same emulsion batch to last at least 3 to 6 months. All of this film except the box that you are using should be stored, sealed in its original packaging, in a refrigerator or, preferably, a freezer in an area where you are sure it will not be exposed to scattered radiation, chemical fumes, or radioisotopes. [*Note:* Be sure to remove a box of film from the freezer or refrigerator at least 48 hours before you wish to use it. This allows the box sufficient time to come to room temperature.]
7. When it is necessary to change to a new emulsion batch, you must "cross-over" the old and new emulsions and adjust the control limits appropriately. This is done by exposing at least six sensi-strips on the old emulsion and six on the new emulsion. These strips are processed in a processor that is known to be in good control, their densities read, and the averages of the old and new emulsion values for the MD, DD, and B + F determined. If there is any difference in the old and new emulsions then the operating levels are adjusted appropriately.
8. In addition to a reduction in the sensitivity to changes in the process condition of an exposed sensi-strip, all photographic emulsions exhibit a certain amount of latent image failure. This means that the film appears to be less sensitive if it is processed a period of time after it is exposed, or it appears less dense overall. This can create problems not only in quality control, but on the clinical level if you use equipment with a film receiver and do not process the films frequently.
9. Low-volume processors, those machines processing less than 25 to 50 14 × 17-inch (35 × 43-cm) radiographs or their equivalent in an 8-hour period, are probably the most difficult of all processors to control properly. See the Procedure section on "Flood Replenishment" below.
10. Replenishment rates are provided by the manufacturer for a specific film-developer combination processed at a specific temperature and usually in a specific processor. In addition, the rates are provided for a specific mixture of film sizes for a set number of film sizes and for a set number of films processed in an 8-hour working day. If your conditions deviate from the ones specified by the manufacturer in any way, it will be necessary to adjust your replenishment rates—but only if your control charts indicate that the replenishment rates are either too high or too low. Watch your control charts closely for trends and only

make small corrections (15–20%) in your replenishment rates at any one time. After a correction has been made in the replenishment rates, monitor the processor for at least 1 week before making further changes.

11. In most areas, water filters are essential to assure optimum photographic processing. However, the filters become clogged, reducing the flow of wash water and the amount of water available to the temperature control system of the processor. A flowmeter located in the water line immediately before it enters the processor is essential. This should be monitored on a daily basis to assure that the water flow rate is that specified by the manufacturer of the processor.

Acceptance Limits

The acceptance limits on the DD and MD should be ±0.10 in density while the limit on the B + F should be +0.05. You may wish to use a slightly wider acceptance limit (±0.15 on the MD and DD) initially (for the first month) until you have all of your processors working in a stable condition.

Corrective Action

Corrective action is *required* if one or more data points falls outside of the control limits and *remains* outside of the control limits for a second set of test strips.

1. Be sure to verify the out-of-control condition with another set of sensi-strips *before* taking any corrective action.
2. Make the adjustments that you believe will bring the processor back into control.
    If control limits are exceeded check the following:
    a. Developer temperature
    b. Replenishment rates
    c. Water flow rates
    d. Water temperature (when appropriate)
    e. Recirculation
    f. Filters
    g. Batch mix dates
    h. Recent maintenance
    i. Film fog
    j. Transport time
    k. Control emulsion
    If trends are noted in the control charts check the following:
    a. Developer temperature
    b. Replenishment rates
    c. Change in the mix, types, and number of films being processed
    d. Proper mixing of replenisher
    e. Control emulsion age or fog (base-plus-fog tends to rise gradually as the film ages)
    f. Leaks or overflow from the fixer tank getting into the developer tank
    g. Gremlins
3. Make only one adjustment to the processor at a time.
4. After each change run another set of sensi-strips.
5. For future reference keep a log of the types of changes made (the amount the temperature was changed, for example), and the resultant change in the three control parameters.
6. When the processor is back in control, plot the new data points, circle all three of the points from the out-of-control strips, and record the adjustment made directly on the control chart in the space provided.

5.4. PROCESSOR CLEANING AND MAINTENANCE

Purpose

Processor maintenance is an essential part of the departmental QC program. In fact, it is virtually impossible to maintain an adequate processor QC program without processor maintenance. The purpose of processor maintenance is to assure that the processor is maintained in a clean, functional condition as intended by the manufacturer.

Equipment Needed

Discuss the needed equipment with the representative of the manufacturer of your processor.

Procedure

1. Establish and maintain processor maintenance logs. These must include information concerning the type of maintenance carried out (both preventive and repair maintenance) and cleaning, including the dates the work was done and who did the maintenance.
2. Clean cross-over racks every day immediately after the processor has been shut down. In addition, wipe all exposed surfaces with a damp cloth and assure that chemicals are not allowed to dry on any surface.
3. Processor racks should be cleaned and checked weekly. Flushing with fresh water and cleaning with a nonabrasive cleaning pad is sufficient. **Do not** use systems cleaner at this time.
4. Verify the condition of the processor after any maintenance and weekly cleanings using a set of sensi-strips.
5. If the processor goes out of control, suspect that some maintenance has been carried out and check to assure that everything was set back to the normal operating conditions.
6. LISTEN! Each processor has its own unique sound. Any change in sounds may indicate changes in the processor that may affect the quality of the radiographs produced.
7. Systems cleaner—*only as recommended by the manufacturer.* [**Note:** Always wear safety goggles when working with systems cleaner.]
   a. Never submerge the racks in the systems cleaner.
   b. Never mix the developer and fixer systems cleaner or use in the wrong tanks or on the wrong racks.
   c. Flush the tanks three times with fresh water after cleaning, running the recirculation pumps.
   d. Season the tanks and racks after using systems cleaner. This is done by filling the processing tanks with developer and fixer and allowing the processor to operate for approximately 10 to 15 minutes without processing any film. This chemistry is then drained from the tanks and the tanks refilled with fresh chemistry. This seasoning process helps eliminate any residual systems cleaner, which may adversely affect the chemistry over the next few days.
   e. Make a note indicating that systems cleaner was used on both the processor maintenance log and the control charts.

5.5. FLOOD REPLENISHMENT

Purpose

This modified method of processor replenishment may be required for low-volume processors (less than 25 to 50 sheets of conventional 14 × 17-inch (35 × 43-cm) radiographic film per 8 operating hours) in order to maintain stable processing levels. In addition, this method is usually needed in processors dedicated to processing of single emulsion nuclear medicine films, ultrasound imaging films, mammographic films, or 100-mm roll films, or the equivalent.

Equipment Needed

1. One 5-minute, 120-volt interval timer (about $35)
2. A 6-foot (180-cm) length of 4-conductor electrical cable
3. Strain-relief wire cable connectors
4. Electrician or qualified service engineer

Procedure

1. The timer must be installed by a qualified service engineer or electrician so that the replenisher pumps operate for 20 seconds out of every 5 minutes. (The replenisher pumps are no longer operated by the

microswitches connected to the entrance cross-over rollers.) This assures that approximately 780 ml of developer and fixer solution are added to the processor for each hour of operation.

2. After the timer has been installed, drain the chemicals from the processor and replenisher tanks and flush the tanks with fresh water, running the replenishment and recirculation pumps to assure that all old chemicals are purged from the system. (Be sure to remove the old developer recirculation filter, replacing it with a new one after you have flushed the system.)

3. Mix fresh developer replenisher and fill the replenisher tank.

4. Add 95 ml of developer starter (or the amount recommended by the manufacturer) to each gallon of developer replenisher in the replenisher tank and stir thoroughly.

5. Mix fresh fixer and fill the replenisher tank.

6. Operate the replenishment pumps until the developer (not the water that may be in the pumps and lines) starts to flow into the processor tanks.

7. Again drain and flush the processor tanks and then fill with the solutions from the replenisher tanks. [*Note:* *Do not* add more starter to the developer tank.]

8. Adjust the developer and fixer pumps to deliver 65 ml of developer for each 20 seconds the replenisher pumps are operating.

Problems and Pitfalls

1. This method will provide for a stable processor by replacing the total volume of chemistry in the processor every 16 operating hours (approximately). Consequently, your consumption of replenisher (both fixer and developer) will increase but the pay-back will be in higher quality, consistent films.

2. Every time you mix developer replenisher and add it to the replenisher tank, **it is essential that you add the developer starter as noted in procedure step 4 above.** This means that you are operating with the equivalent of fresh (not seasoned) chemicals at all times but, again, you will also have a stable processor since the developer will be replaced before it has a chance to become oxidized or deteriorate in any other way.

3. If the type of timer is different than the one mentioned above, set the replenisher flow rates so that you deliver approximately 780 ml of replenisher to the processing tanks every hour.

4. For specific instructions on the type of timer, how to modify the processor, and so forth, contact the technical representative from the company who manufactured your processor.

5. Be sure not to mix any more developer or fixer than you can use in 2 weeks since these chemicals will deteriorate in the replenisher tanks.

Acceptance Limits

The acceptance limits for films processed in a processor using flood replenishment should be the same as for any other processor (± 0.10 in density for MD and DD and $+0.05$ for the B + F).

Corrective Action

The corrective action required when the control limits are exceeded is the same as those for a processor operating with a normal replenishment system.

6 BASIC TESTS

In this first chapter on equipment tests we discuss some very basic tests that can be carried out with simple and inexpensive test tools. These tests are practical for a small office with only one piece of x-ray equipment or for larger facilities. These tests have one thing in common—they are easy to do, but they do provide basic information about the condition of your equipment. They are not, in most cases, as definitive as tests described later in this book, but they are a starting point.

VISUAL AND MANUAL QUALITY CONTROL CHECKS

These tests should be carried out in all x-ray facilities since they are just as applicable to a small facility as to a large facility. A check list is necessary (see the forms in Appendix A) to assure that all of the checks are made on a regular basis. Although many of the tests may seem very basic they all serve a purpose. For example, the High Tension Cable Check is required to assure that cables are not becoming cracked or frayed, which would present a potential hazard in terms of fire and possible injury to patients and technologists.

All of these tests are "pass-fail" tests, which means that either the equipment meets the standards or repair must be made by a qualified service engineer, or in some cases the QC technologist. These checks should be carried out before any other QC checks are made in each room every time QC tests are made.

IMAGE RECEPTOR SPEED

When you begin a quality control program, and even after a QC program has been in effect for some time,

it is not uncommon to find cassettes of varying types, i.e., different fronts and different manufacture, containing screens of different manufacture, speed, and age. These may be in general use in the department without compensation in exposure factors being made by the staff technologists, who may be unaware of the difference. This increases the variability in the quality of the radiographs produced and increases the number of repeat films, resulting in unnecessary radiation exposure to the patients while increasing the department's operating costs.

It may be necessary to segregate cassettes and screens of one type in a particular room in the department and color code those cassettes so that they are not inadvertently used in another area. If at all possible, a common type of cassette and screen should be used throughout the department since this decreases the potential for using the wrong cassette for the wrong exam.

If you decide to maintain two or more types of screens, then it is a good idea to use a different type of cassette for each screen type so that each is readily identifiable. This also helps in the darkroom if more than one film type is used since the darkroom or x-ray technologist loading the cassettes can easily identify the differences. (Ideally, you should strive to use the same screen-film-cassette combination throughout the department to reduce such potentials for error.)

SCREEN-FILM CONTACT

Whether your cassettes are old or new, they must be checked for screen-film contact on a regular basis. If any cassette appears to be damaged between regular checks, it should be checked immediately. Only if the screens are held in intimate contact with the film will you be able to obtain maximum definition in patient radiographs.

When you purchase new screens the screen-film contact tests should be carried out *prior* to acceptance of the new cassettes. As with any acceptance test, you should make the vendor aware that such tests are going to be carried out before complete payment will be authorized.

X-RAY FIELD–LIGHT FIELD CONGRUENCE

This test, also known as the nine-penny test, was first suggested by the personnel at the University of Wisconsin at Madison and requires the cheapest quality control test tool available—nine pennies. The purpose is to assure that the light field and x-ray field are properly aligned. It is simple but important in that many times the technologist thinks the appropriate area is being radiographed, as indicated by the light field, only to find out that the x-ray field is actually shifted an inch or two, resulting in a radiograph that does not include the area of interest to the radiologist. This often leads the technologist to use a larger than necessary x-ray field to compensate for the lack of congruence, resulting in an increased exposure to the patient.

BASIC HOMOGENEOUS PHANTOM TEST

For this test you may use either the patient equivalent phantom (PEP) described earlier or a 5-gallon cubitainer filled to the appropriate depth with water. In either case the purpose is to assure that the films pro-

duced are at the proper density and the entire radiograph is uniformly exposed. This test can also be used to compare different rooms in your department to assure that for the same patient a film of the same density will be produced for the posted technique in each room.

BASIC TOMOGRAPHY TEST

Tomographic test tools may cost hundreds of dollars but this test allows you to test the resolution, thickness of cut, and cut location of tomographic units with a tool that you can put together in your own department. Most tomographic units of the attachable type (not an integral part of the table) suffer much abuse and are seldom properly inspected by service personnel in routine checks. This simple test will allow you to assure that your tomographic unit is functioning properly.

STEP WEDGE TEST FOR GENERATOR LINEARITY

Now the test tools are becoming more expensive—an aluminum step wedge costs about $50. A wedge with 2- or 3-mm steps is required for this test, but with it you will be able to evaluate generator linearity. Linearity is important since it means that for the same mAs, regardless of the mA and the time stations selected, you will produce a radiograph with the same density. Many generators that have not been recently calibrated will produce results that are so variable that patient radiographs will range from acceptable to being too light or too dark for a diagnosis to be made.

PROCEDURES

6.1. VISUAL AND MANUAL QUALITY CONTROL CHECK

Purpose

To assure that the components in an x-ray room not normally evaluated as part of the QC tests, but that are visually apparent, are appropriately checked on a regular basis. This includes all x-ray equipment as well as equipment related to patient comfort and safety.

Equipment Needed

1. Check list
2. Tape measure
3. Carpenter's level

Procedure

Using the check list, visually and manually, check the following items, noting a pass by a check and a fail with an "F":

1. *SID indicator or marks*—Check the accuracy of the SID indicator using a steel measuring tape. Measure from the focal spot mark on the x-ray tube housing to the Bucky tray. If a mark is not present indicating the location of the focal spot, measure from a point 1 inch (2.54 cm) above the bottom of the tube housing. Also, check the accuracy of any measuring tape that may be built into the collimator. Assure that other distance indicator marks on the tube crane railings are in place and are accurate, e.g., the center mark for a wall-mounted film holder.
2. *Perpendicularity*—With the x-ray tube positioned in the standard position used for Bucky radiography, stand at the end of the table and then on one side, visually verifying that the collimator, x-ray tube, and crane appear to be perpendicular. If not, adjust or have this repaired before attempting alignment tests.
3. *Angulation indicator*—Use a level to make sure the tube and collimator are level when the angulation indicator reads 0°. Angle the tube in both directions and assure that the indicator is moving properly and not sticking in any position.
4. *Locks*—Check the function of all tube crane locks, assuring that they lock securely and unlock properly. Also, check the lock switch itself to assure that it is not broken.
5. *Field light*—Determine if the light works and is bright enough to be seen under normal operating conditions. Check for discoloration, dirt, and any other foreign matter on the underside of the collimator.
6. *Bucky center light*—Center the tube to the center of the cassette tray using the Bucky center light. Pull the overhead tube crane toward you and determine if its center corresponds to the position indicated by the Bucky center light, using the field light.
7. *High-tension and other cables*—Check all cables for frayed coverings, tight bends, and unsupported areas, and assure that none of the cables are pinched when the x-ray tube, crane, and table are moved to extreme positions. The stress relief fittings at the x-ray tube insert area should be intact and not kinked. Assure that any cables associated with foot switches are in good condition and that ground lines are intact.
8. *Overhead crane movement*—Move the tube crane system around the room and assure that it moves easily and quietly and does not encounter obstructions. Again, verify that cables do not bind or are not pinched during movement.
9. *Bucky lock*—Assure that the Bucky lock is functioning properly. (If the lock is not holding tightly, oscillation of the Bucky grid could cause the entire assembly to shift during the exposure, blurring radiographic detail.)
10. *Cassette lock*—Verify that the cassette lock holds the cassette firmly.
11. *Float and power top switches*—Check the function of the locks and smoothness of motion of the tops. Also, check that the switches are not loose or damaged.
12. *Measuring caliper*—Physically check the caliper and measure an object of known thickness.

13. *Step stool*—Inspect and then stand on the stool to assure that a solid step is provided and that the stool does not slide on the floor.

14. *Angulation indicator and center stop*—For tilting tables, place a level on the tabletop and assure the table is level in the center stop position when the indicator reads 0°. Check other stop positions if applicable.

15. *Foot board and shoulder rests*—Check the patient's foot and shoulder rests to ensure that they attach and remove easily. Also, pay particular attention to all locks to ensure that they will not come loose under the weight of a patient.

16. *Hand switch placement*—For the safety of the operator, the exposure hand switch should be mounted in a manner such that an exposure cannot be made if the operator is outside the control booth. (This is required by law in many states.)

17. *Window*—The operator's view from the control booth should not be obstructed in any way. [Windows should be a minimum of 24 × 18 inches (60 × 45 cm) with the long dimension in the vertical direction, and mounted on a 62-inch (158-cm) center.]

18. *Panel switches, lights, and meters*—Check the function of all the control panel switches, lights, and meters.

19. *Technique charts*—Assure that technique charts are present in the room and that they are the appropriate charts for the x-ray tube and the procedures normally done in the room.

20. *Overload protection*—Verify the function of the overload protection circuit for the specific x-ray tube(s) in the room (see pages 78–79).

21. *Locks*—Check the function of all the fluoroscopic tower locks, assuring that they lock securely and unlock easily.

22. *Power assists*—Assure that the power assist will move the fluoroscopic tower easily in all possible directions and that the motion stops when pressure is released from the switch or pressure-sensitive handle. These checks should be carried out with the table in both the horizontal and vertical positions.

23. *Motion smoothness*—Does the fluoroscopic tower move easily and quietly and not encounter interruptions?

24. *Switches, lights, and meters*—Check the function of all the lights, switches, and meters.

25. *Compression device or spoon*—Assure that the compression device moves in and out easily and quietly and is not damaged or splattered with contrast media. If a compression spoon is used, assure that it is located near the position of the radiologist during fluoroscopy and is not damaged or splattered with contrast.

26. *Fluoroscopic monitor*—Check the overall condition of the monitor, and verify that all electrical cords are intact and do not restrict the movement of the monitor. Assure that the switches on the monitor are functioning and intact and that the monitor face is clean.

27. *Fluoroscopic grid*—Check the function of the grid, making sure it moves in and out easily and that there is no grid cutoff or grid damage.

28. *Fluoroscopic timer*—Assure that the fluoroscopic timer is functioning and that an audible alarm sounds when the preset time (a maximum of 5 minutes) is reached.

29. *Fluoroscopic drapes*—Check the physical condition of the drapes, making sure they are not torn or damaged. Assure that the drapes move to their different positions with ease.

30. *Park position interrupt*—When the tower is in the park position, the x-ray generator should not be capable of producing radiation. Assure that the park position switch is working smoothly.

31. *Bucky slot cover*—Assure that the Bucky slot cover is present, is working smoothly, and covers the Bucky slot completely.

32. *Fluoroscopic shutters visible (high/low)*—Check the fluoroscopic shutters to assure that they are just visible inside the edges of the fluoroscopic image with the tower in the low and high positions.

33. *Gonad shields, aprons, and gloves*—Assure that these items are present and fluoroscopically inspect them for holes or cracks.

Problems and Pitfalls

1. On some older types of collimators, a special plastic sheet on the front of the collimator acts as a filter to reduce the amount of soft radiation reaching the patient. Therefore, it is important to assure that this material is present and that it is replaced with the same material (not Plexiglas).

2. Plexiglas and other plastic sheets in collimators may darken with age and exposure to radiation. These should be replaced with similar material.

Acceptance Limits

These are left to the technologist. Discuss problems with the service engineer. Many problems may not need immediate repair, but any item dealing with patient or staff safety should receive immediate attention.

Corrective Action

After all checks have been made, request service for the problem areas, and verify that corrections have been made in a reasonable time.

6.2. IMAGE RECEPTOR SPEED

Purpose

To assure that the image receptors (cassette-screen combination) used in a department may be used without altering exposure factors (i.e., are all the same speed).

Equipment Needed

Densitometer (visual comparison of film density may be used if a densitometer is not available)

Procedure

1. Inventory and sort all cassettes by cassette and screen type. Inspect mechanical integrity of cassette, i.e., latches, hinges, frames, and light seals. Inspect screens for dirt, scratches, worn spots, and yellowing due to age. Repair, clean, or discard any faulty cassettes before continuing this test.
2. Select one of the most common cassette and screen types for a standard.
3. Load the standard cassette and up to three other cassettes with film from the same box (cut to size if needed).
4. Place the cassettes on the x-ray table top with edges touching (Figure 6.1).
5. Identify the cassettes with lead numerals or markers.
6. Center the x-ray beam between the cassettes at the corner where all are touching.
7. Make an x-ray exposure that will produce a density in the range of 1.0 on the "standard" cassette-screen-film combination (approximately 70 kVp, 100 mA, $1/60$ sec at 100-cm SID).
8. Measure the density near the x-ray beam center on all films or view each film side-by-side with the "standard" on an evenly lit illuminator.

Problems and Pitfalls

1. X-ray film can vary in speed by $\pm 10\%$ between emulsion batches and sometimes more between boxes depending on age, storage, etc. For this reason, it is necessary to use film from the same box.
2. X-ray beam intensity varies because of the heel effect parallel to the anode-cathode axis of the x-ray tube, so it is essential to make the density comparison at the corner of the films that were closest to the center of the x-ray beam.
3. This test provides cassette-screen speed information at one kVp only. You should test cassettes at the kVp commonly used if it is low (e.g., for extremity work) or high (e.g., for GI studies).

Acceptance Limits

Density measurements should be within ± 0.05 of the "standard" or should not appear "significantly" different to the eye.

Corrective Action

Cassette and screen combinations that fall outside of the acceptance limits should be removed from general service or segregated and labelled in some readily identifiable way for special use.

6.3. SCREEN-FILM CONTACT

Purpose

To locate those cassettes that have poor screen-film contact.

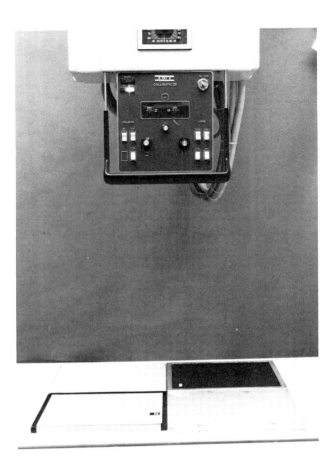

Figure 6.1. Image receptor speed test setup. Three cassettes are compared to a "standard" by exposing all four simultaneously, using the same type of film from the same box in each cassette. Note the lead identification numbers on each cassette. The densities should be compared only in the corner of the films that is closest to the central ray.

Equipment Needed

1. Wire mesh test object [15 × 18 inches (38 × 46 cm)]. Copper wire mesh with ⅛-inch (3-mm) spacing of the wires is preferred for use with ordinary cassettes and screens. For high-resolution imaging systems, such as are used for mammography, #60 copper mesh [60 wires per inch (25 wires per cm)] is preferred.
2. Densitometer

Procedure

1. Place the wire mesh test object and the screen-film cassette on the x-ray table top (Figure 6.2).
2. Collimate the x-ray beam to the cassette size.
3. Identify the cassette with lead numerals.
4. Radiograph the wire mesh phantom at factors of about 2 mAs at 70 kVp with a 100-cm SID.
5. Check to assure that a density of 1.5 to 2.0 is obtained on the film.
6. View the wire mesh radiographs in a dimly lit room on an x-ray viewbox at a distance of about 6 feet (2 meters). Areas of poor contact will appear darker than areas of good contact (Figure 6.3).

Problems and Pitfalls

1. Grossly over- or underexposed radiographs cannot be readily interpreted.
2. Artifacts from improper film handling during cassette loading are frequently seen. These may be ignored in interpretation of the contact radiographs but indicate a need to improve film loading techniques.
3. Freshly loaded cassettes may exhibit poor contact because of entrapped air. Wait a minimum of 10–15 minutes after cassette loading before making screen contact tests.

Acceptance Limits

1. Large central areas of poor contact indicate the need for corrective action.

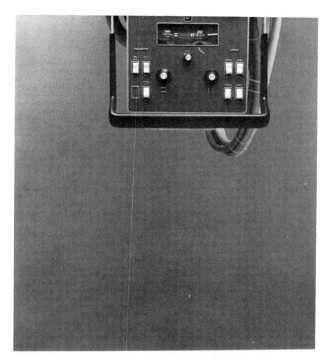

Figure 6.2. Screen-film contact test setup. An exposure is made with the test mesh on top of the cassette, with an identification number. The exposure should be such that a density of at least 1.5 is produced on the film.

Figure 6.3a. Radiograph of screen-film contact test showing acceptable results. In viewing the resultant films you should stand at least 6 feet (2 meters) from the viewbox. You are not interested in looking at the details of the mesh and in comparing the sharpness of the individual wires. Rather, you should look for areas of apparent increased density, indicating poor contact and also unsharpness. It is easier on your eyes to stand back and look for the dark areas than to view the film from a close distance and look for unsharp areas, and it is a lot faster.

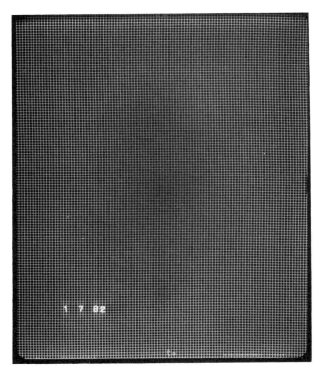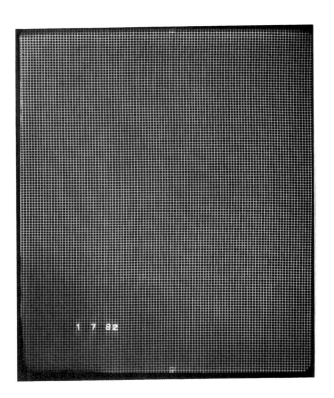

Figure 6.3b. Unacceptable contact is exhibited in this screen as a large dark area in the center of the radiograph of the mesh. This cassette should be repaired or replaced.

Figure 6.3c. Increased density is apparent in the lower left corner of this radiograph of the mesh. Although this indicates unsharpness it may be necessary to accept this since it occurs on the edge of the image, which it is hoped is outside of the major area of interest.

2. Small areas of poor contact along the edges or corners may have to be accepted.

Corrective Action

1. Cassettes occasionally can be repaired by re-arching (bending) the cover or springs.
2. Check the latches on those cassettes with corner or edge contact problems.
3. Rescreening with new pads may be a possible solution.
4. Replacement of cassettes that do not provide good screen-film contact is generally the best solution.

6.4. X-RAY FIELD–LIGHT FIELD CONGRUENCE

Purpose

To assure that the x-ray field and the light field are congruent.

Equipment Needed

1. One 10 × 12-inch (24 × 30-cm) cassette
2. Nine pennies
3. Lead letters, A and F (may be used rather than the ninth penny)

Procedure

1. Place a 10 × 12-inch (24 × 30-cm) cassette on the x-ray table top with its long dimension parallel to the long dimension of the table.
2. Center the light field to the center of the cassette at a 40-inch (100-cm) SID.
3. Manually collimate the x-ray beam to an approximate 6 × 8-inch (15 × 20-cm) field size.

4. Position two pennies in the center of each margin of the light field such that one entire penny is inside the light field and one penny is outside the light field. Place the ninth penny in the quadrant of the light field toward you and to your right as an orientation marker or place the lead "A" at the anode end of the x-ray tube and the "F" to mark the front of the x-ray table (Figure 6.4).
5. Place lead markers well inside the light field on the cassette to identify the room number and date.
6. Make a radiographic exposure using technical factors appropriate for a hand.
7. Process the radiograph and determine if the x-ray field is properly positioned (Figure 6.5).
8. Record the results in the QC room log.

Problems and Pitfalls

1. This test does not assure central x-ray beam perpendicularity.
2. This test does not assure that positive beam limitation (PBL) systems adjust to the proper cassette size.

Acceptance Limits

Federal guidelines for certified equipment allow ±2% of the SID for light field–x-ray field alignment. For a 100-cm SID, ±2 cm (1 penny) is acceptable. Light field–x-ray field alignment can and should be well within this amount. Alignment to ±1 cm (±0.5 penny) can reasonably be achieved.

Corrective Action

A service engineer should be called to align the light field to the x-ray field if acceptance limits are exceeded.

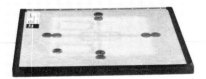

Figure 6.4a. X-ray field–light field congruence test setup. The nine-penny test uses the ninth penny to indicate the orientation of the cassette relative to the x-ray-light field.

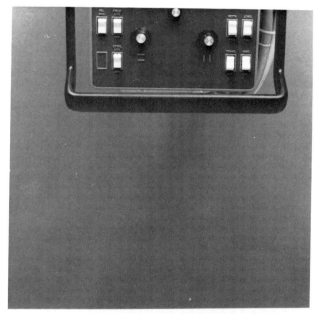

Figure 6.4b. The eight-penny x-ray field–light field congruence test uses lead letters to indicate the orientation of the film.

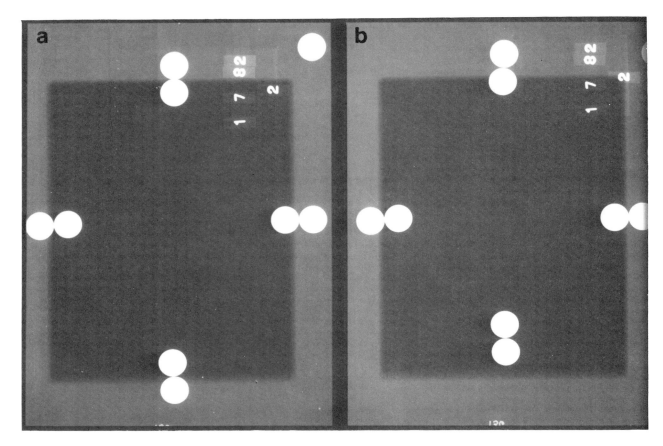

Figure 6.5. X-ray field–light field congruence test results. These radiographs should show the date, room number, and pennies. (a) Results where the x-ray field falls within half of a penny's distance from the center line are ideal. (b) If any side of the x-ray field exceeds the proper location by more than one penny (e.g., at the bottom of this image) a service engineer should adjust the collimator.

6.5. BASIC HOMOGENEOUS PHANTOM TEST

Purpose

To assure that the routine Bucky radiographs will be satisfactory at posted technical factors.

Equipment Needed

1. Patient equivalent phantom (PEP) [***Note:*** A water phantom made from a 5-gallon (20-liter) cubitainer may be used instead of the uniform density phantom; however, it is more difficult to work with. Fifteen cm of water will produce results similar to 15 cm of lucite.]
2. Densitometer (Visual comparison of film density may be used if densitometer is not available.)
3. Lead letters A and C

Procedure

1. Center the uniform density phantom on the x-ray table top.
2. Center the x-ray tube to the phantom.
3. Insert a 14 × 17-inch (35 × 43-cm) cassette transversely in the Bucky tray, center it to the phantom and central x-ray beam, and collimate the beam to the phantom (Figure 6.6). Identify, with lead letters, the anode and cathode ends of the phantom, as well as the room number and date.
4. Expose a radiograph using your posted technical factors for an anteroposterior view of a 21-cm lumbar spine and process the film. For example, with a three-phase generator, Kodak XL film and X-Omatic regular screens, a 16:1 ratio grid, and a 48-inch (120-cm) SID, use about 68 kVp and 65 mAs.

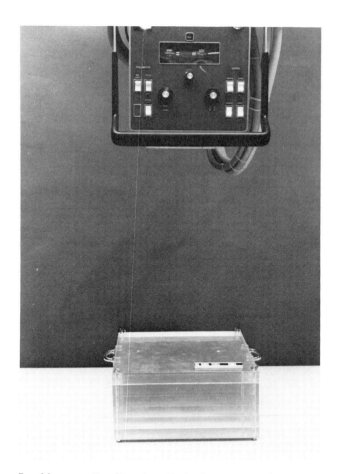

Figure 6.6. Basic homogeneous phantom test setup. The x-ray field should be centered and collimated to the edges of the phantom. A marker indicating the date and room number should be included.

5. Measure the film density in the center of the phantom. Visually compare the film density near the edges of the phantom image in a direction perpendicular to the anode-cathode axis (Figure 6.7).

6. If a densitometer is not available, visual acceptance limits can be established using two films, one exposed at +3 kVp and the other exposed at −3 kVp. These films should be made after the generator has been calibrated and after the processor has been optimized. On return visits, these films can be used to compare the density of the phantom film visually. The comparison should be done by placing the current phantom film on a viewbox between the two films originally exposed at +3 kVp and −3 kVp. If the density of the current film falls between the densities of the acceptance limit films, you may assume that radiographs of reasonable quality, in terms of density, will be obtained.

Problems and Pitfalls

1. Since this test evaluates the total system, it does not identify the exact cause of the problem. For example, if the density is too light or too dark, among other reasons the problem could be due to processing, generator calibration, or improper posted technical factors.

2. Expect to see density variations along the anode-cathode axis of the phantom because of the heel effect.

3. Problems caused by cassette and tray interference with motion of the Bucky grid are frequently not demonstrated unless a 14 × 17-inch (35 × 43-cm) cassette is used transversely, as for a routine pelvic examination.

Acceptance Limits

1. Ultimately, you will have to determine what the density, as measured in the center of this phantom radiograph, should be based upon technical factors that produce satisfactory images on patients with your screen-film combination. (The density measured in the center of the film should be about 1.2 ± 0.15.)

2. The film density in a direction perpendicular to the anode-cathode axis should not appear significantly different to the eye when viewed on an illuminator. If it does, Bucky grid cutoff due to nonperpendicularity of the x-ray beam, lateral decentering, or nonuniformity in the Bucky motion may be suspected.

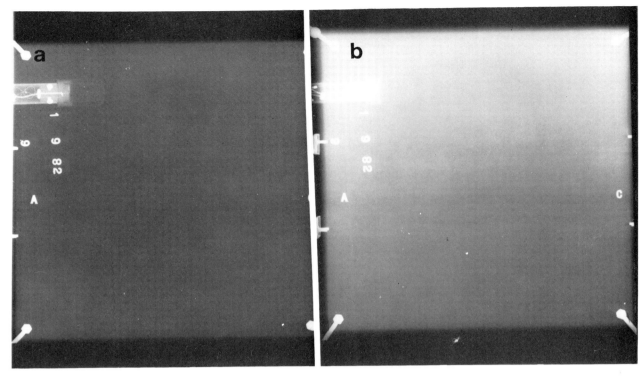

Figure 6.7. Basic homogeneous phantom test results. (**a**) A good film should appear relatively uniform in density, although you may anticipate some density differences parallel to the anode-cathode axis, especially at the anode end of the x-ray field. With the PEP the technique for a 21-cm lumbar spine film should produce a density of about 1.2 near the center of the film. (An ionization chamber shows in this radiograph and can be added to record the patient entrance exposure for this technique.) (**b**) The density variation perpendicular to the anode-cathode axis (indicated by the lead letters "A" and "C") that is apparent in this radiograph is not acceptable. This was caused by a grid–x-ray beam alignment problem.

Corrective Action

Appropriate adjustments should be made by a qualified service engineer.

6.6. BASIC TOMOGRAPHY TEST

Purpose

To assure that the tomographic cut level and thickness are correct and that the image sharpness is optimal.

Equipment Needed

Simple tomographic test phantom (Figure 6.8):

1. Cut a 30°–60°–90° triangular-shaped piece from a 2 × 4-inch (5 × 10-cm) piece of wood.
2. Attach a copper window screen of #40 mesh to the angled surface of the wood block.
3. Attach a small piece of copper wire or a straightened paper clip to the screen halfway up the block.
4. Attach a lead number to indicate the cut level.
5. Attach a thin lead sheet such as found in an old cassette or cardboard film holder to the base of the wood block.

Procedure

1. Place the simple tomographic test phantom on the tomographic table top (at a 45° angle to the tube-film motion if a linear tomographic system is being evaluated) and center it to the x-ray beam (Figure 6.8b).
2. Set the tomographic section level adjustment to correspond with the level of the wire marker.
3. Select the amplitude setting most commonly used for tomography.

Figure 6.8a. This basic tomography test tool can be simply constructed as described in the text.

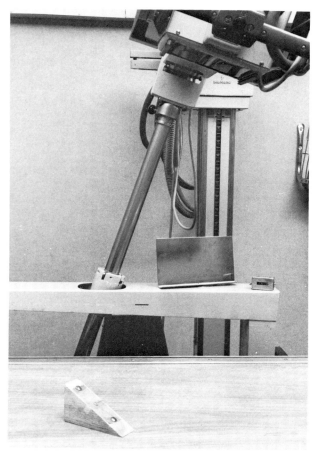

Figure 6.8b. Basic tomography test setup. Whenever this test tool is used to evaluate a tomographic system with linear motion the tool should be placed at 45° to the direction of motion.

4. Select the lowest mA available, 50 kVp, and the exposure time appropriate for the amplitude setting.
5. Make a tomographic exposure of the phantom.
6. Process and view the radiograph (Figure 6.9).

Problems and Pitfalls

1. Failure to position the test phantom at a 45° angle to tube-film motion on linear systems will result in incomplete blurring of the screen wires in the direction of tube-film travel.
2. Since the phantom is relatively radiolucent it may be difficult to select exposure factors that will not "burn out" the images of the test object. The addition of another thickness or thicknesses of cassette lead to the bottom of the phantom may be required.
3. Aluminum window screen should not be used because it offers insufficient attenuation of the x-ray beam to produce a useful image.

Acceptance Limits

Except for the tomographic section level, which should be within ±0.5 cm of the setting, this is not a highly quantitative test. If the in-focus image of the wire mesh does not coincide with the image of the wire indicator, measure the distance between the centers of these images and divide by 2 to determine the adjustment that must be made to the tomographic section level indicator. In-focus images of the wire mesh on the tomogram should appear sharp to the eye and there should be only one area that appears in focus. If there is more than one area in focus, the tomographic motion may not be smooth. On linear systems, there should be a zone of sharp

Figure 6.9a. Basic tomography test results. A properly functioning tomographic unit will produce one sharp area located near the indicated plane of cut with an increase in blurring as you move away from the plane of cut.

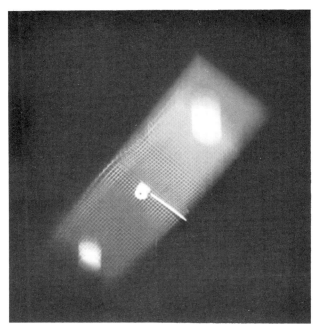

Figure 6.9b. Erratic motion of the tomographic unit will produce several areas that appear to be sharp at different levels with blurred areas in between. In addition, you can easily see multiple images of the tacks holding the screen, indicating that the x-ray tube was not moving smoothly.

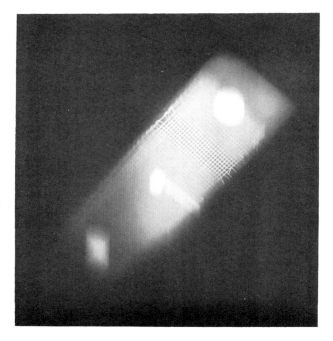

Figure 6.9c. In addition to good image quality you should assure that the tomographic unit is cutting at the indicated level. In this case the cut was quite a bit higher than indicated.

focus with a visible, although blurred, region on both sides. The thickness of the region in focus may be approximated by measuring the width of the mesh that is in focus and dividing by 2.

Corrective Action

Appropriate adjustments should be made by a qualified service engineer.

6.7. STEP WEDGE TEST FOR GENERATOR LINEARITY

Purpose

To simply check the mA station linearity of an x-ray generator.

Equipment Needed

1. Aluminum step wedge (one with 2- or 3-mm steps is preferred over a wedge with thicker steps)
2. Screen-film cassette, 10 × 12 inch (24 × 30-cm)
3. Fresh box of film
4. Lead sheet to block off one half of the cassette
5. Densitometer (visual comparison of film density may be used if a densitometer is not available)

Procedure—Step Wedge Calibration

1. Raise the x-ray tube to its maximum height.
2. Place a freshly loaded 10 × 12-inch (24 × 30-cm) cassette on the tabletop with the long axis of the cassette parallel to the length of the x-ray tube (Figure 6.10).
3. Mask off one-half of the cassette across its length with lead.
4. Place the step wedge on the cassette so it is in the central beam and perpendicular to the anode-cathode axis of the x-ray tube, thus avoiding problems introduced by the heel effect.
5. Collimate the beam to the step wedge.
6. Expose the step wedge at 80 kVp using the 100 mA station or the mA station on the generator closest to 100 mA at approximately 0.1 sec.
7. Move the step wedge to the other half of the cassette and mask the previously exposed area with the lead sheet.
8. Using the same factors make *two* individual exposures of the step wedge (i.e., a double exposure).
9. Develop and check the film (Figure 6.11a). The ideal exposure should exhibit each step of the wedge without the use of a bright light on the single-exposed wedge. If the film is under- or overexposed, repeat the exposures and change the exposure factors until an image is produced in which all steps on the wedge are seen on the single-exposed side.
10. Using a densitometer, select a step on the single-exposed wedge that has a density close to or slightly higher than 1.0 and mark it with a marking pen. On the double-exposed wedge, read the densities until the step that has the density closest to the 1.0 density on the single-exposed wedge is located. Once the match is found, mark it and count the number of steps between marks on the single- and double-exposed wedges to determine how many steps represent a 100% change in exposure. For example, if four steps separate the single- and double-exposure match, which represents a 100% change in exposure, then each step will represent about a 25% change.
    If you do not have a densitometer, cut the film so that the step wedge images can be placed side-by-side on a viewbox. On the single-exposed wedge select and mark a step that has a medium-gray density such as would be found in the soft tissue on an AP lumbar spine film. By sliding the double-exposed wedge past the single-exposed wedge, compare the densities with the selected step until the closest match is found, then count the number of steps to determine the number that yields a 100% change in exposure.

Procedure—Generator Linearity Test

1. Using the same cassette and film type used to calibrate the step wedge, make exposures at all the mA stations normally used on the generator. Keep the kVp constant and vary the exposure time to keep the mAs constant, e.g., at 80 kVp use 50 mA at 0.2 sec, 100 mA at 0.1 sec, 200 mA at 0.05 sec, and 400 mA at 0.025 sec.

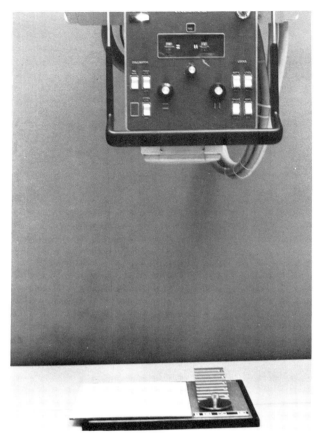

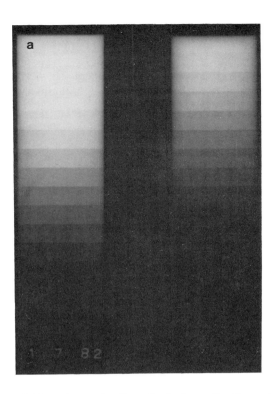

Figure 6.11a. Generator linearity test results. These two step wedges were produced as part of the calibration procedure with the wedge on the right receiving twice the exposure of the one on the left.

Figure 6.10. Generator linearity test setup. The step wedge should be placed directly under the central beam, and the remainder of the cassette covered with at least $1/8$ inch (3 mm) of lead. Note that this step wedge also contains a spinning top for checking the timing of single-phase generators. Room identification and date information must be included on the radiograph.

2. Use the method described in Procedure Step 10 above to compare the film density and determine how well the mA stations of your generator are calibrated (Figure 6.11b and c).

Problems and Pitfalls

1. Variation from this procedure can create problems that will falsely influence the results of this test.
2. Depending on the step wedge, variations in calibration of less than ±25% may not be detected with this test.
3. If a problem is found, you have no way of knowing the cause of the problem, i.e., exposure time, mA, or kVp.
4. This procedure must be done in a short period of time to prevent variation in film processing from influencing the test results.
5. Each time the test is performed, the single- and double-exposure initial film *must* be repeated because any drift in kVp will alter the densities and density differences from one step to another.

Acceptance Limits

The density of a step wedge image should match on the same step for all mA stations. A match on any other step will mean a variation of greater than ±25% (if there are four steps between the single- and double-exposure film matches), which is unacceptable.

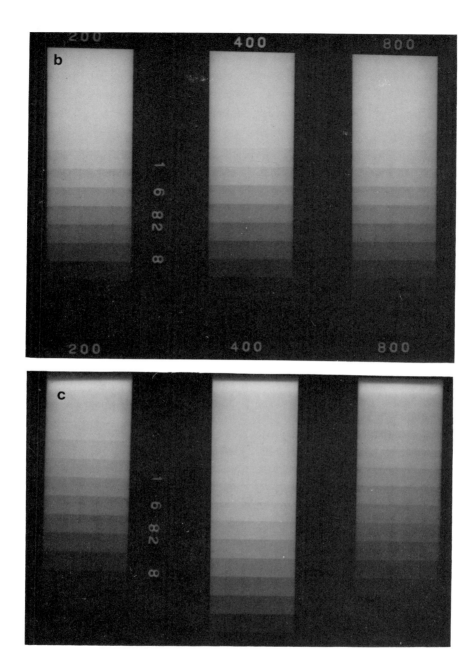

Figure 6.11b. Test results for one room before calibration, in which the wedge was exposed at 80 kVp and the same mAs but at 200, 400, and 800 mA as noted. There is a considerable difference in the density of the film produced at the 400 mA station. In comparing just these three images it is difficult to determine whether the 400 mA station is producing insufficient output or if the 200 mA and 800 mA stations are operating at a higher than normal output. (c) Test results produced in the same room with the same settings but after calibration. In this case, little variation in density is noted between the three mA station films.

Corrective Action

Have a qualified service engineer check the exposure time, mA, and kVp calibration.

7 ____ X-RAY TUBES
▋ AND COLLIMATORS

RATING CHARTS AND OVERLOAD PROTECTION

It may seem superfluous to spend time discussing x-ray tube rating charts, but it has been our experience that most problems associated with premature tube failures result from the appropriate charts not being properly used. This is particularly significant since it should normally be the responsibility of the quality control technologist to develop the technique charts for use in all x-ray procedure rooms.

X-ray tubes represent a significant investment since they range in price from about $5,000 to in excess of $15,000 for special procedure tubes. In addition to the cost of the tube, replacement means a considerable amount of downtime for a room, especially if x-ray tubes are not stocked by your institution or locally by the manufacturer.

Naturally, you would like to assure maximum life from every x-ray tube. This can be done by following the rating charts closely in developing technique charts and, whenever possible, not developing technique charts that require the x-ray tube to be operated in excess of 80% of the rated capacity of the tube or housing. Every technologist, including the QC technologist, should warm up the x-ray tube prior to use, following the manufacturers' instructions. If a room is not used continuously this means that the tube may have to be warmed up several times a day. These additional exposures will not shorten the life of the tube, but rather will reduce the possibility of premature failures caused by anode cracking when a cold anode is "hit" with a heavy technique.

Although overload protection is a function of the x-ray generator, it is included with the material on rating charts. The overload protection circuits should not allow the technologist to select techniques that exceed about 80% of the single exposure rating of the tube. If higher techniques can be selected tube damage can result, and if the generator limits you to techniques much less than 80% of the single exposure rating then the full capabilities of the generator and the x-ray tube cannot be realized. In either case the service engineer should adjust the overload protection circuit appropriately.

X-RAY TUBE FOCAL SPOT SIZE MEASUREMENTS

These measurements are particularly important during the acceptance testing of new x-ray equipment and whenever an x-ray tube is replaced. Although some firms may accept the results of the star resolution measurement for all sizes of focal spots, the National Electrical Manufacturers Association (NEMA) standard does specify that a pinhole camera must be used for focal spots larger than 0.3 mm nominal measurement (National Electrical Manufacturers Association, 1974). In addition, the standard specifies the use of dental x-ray film, which in combination with the pinhole camera results in techniques ranging up to 50,000 mAs, putting a severe load on an x-ray tube even if multiple exposures are made. A complete discussion of pinhole camera problems and modifications can be found in the literature (Gray and Trefler, 1980).

We acceptance-test all of our x-ray tubes using the star test pattern and an extremity cassette screen-film system. If the focal spot appears to be larger than specified we will then produce a pinhole image with the pinhole camera, again using the extremity cassette screen-film system, if the manufacturer will not accept the star measurement. If the focal spot still appears to be oversized then we will resort to the use of the NEMA-recommended pinhole camera and direct x-ray exposed film. However, it is far better to make arrangements with your manufacturer's representatives in ádvance so that they will accept the star pattern measurements as a means of acceptance testing.

Should x-ray focal spot measurements be made on an on-going basis for QC purposes? We do carry out the star pattern measurements as part of each room QC check since we have found a few significant changes in the size of the focal spot that have occurred before x-ray tube failures.

X-RAY FIELD, LIGHT FIELD, BUCKY ALIGNMENT, AND EXPOSURE CONSISTENCY

With the requirement for automatic collimators, tests for the alignment of the light field and x-ray field have become more important. Some institutions require that the edges of the collimators be visible on every film. Others add small pieces of lead to the edges of the collimator leaves so that these "tic" marks are visible on each radiograph. In any case the alignment must be checked to assure that only the appropriate film area is being exposed. All collimators should allow the technologist to cone *down* from the full-film size, even in completely automatic operation.

In addition to the above information, a dosimeter reading made at this time will provide the entrance exposure in air for the standard phantom (and average patient). This will allow you to compare patient exposure from room to room for consistency. In rooms with similar equipment, the exposures should be within fairly close levels, but it will be difficult to make comparisons if the equipment is different, if different tabletops are used, or if different screen-film combinations are used.

HALF-VALUE LAYER MEASUREMENTS

Half-value layer (HVL) measurements are extremely important, especially after any service that requires that the collimator be removed from the x-ray tube. The half-value layer, expressed in millimeters of aluminum, is not—we repeat, *is not*—the amount of aluminum in the x-ray beam. Instead, it is the amount of aluminum that is required to reduce the exposure to one-half of its original value, assuming the kVp and mAs remain fixed. This might sound like quite a technical definition but in reality the HVL is merely a

number that specifies the "hardness" of the x-ray beam. Figure 7.1 clearly shows that the HVL is not the same as the total aluminum filtration in the beam. In addition, you can see that, as the beam becomes harder (a higher HVL), more aluminum must be added to the beam to change the HVL by 0.1 mm as compared to the softer beam (lower HVL).

An increase in filtration (resulting in an increased HVL) for a fixed kVp has very little effect on the higher-energy x-rays present in the beam, but the increase in HVL indicates that more of the soft x-rays have been removed from the beam. Since the majority of softer x-rays in the beam will not be transmitted through the patient to form an image but will be absorbed by the patient, increasing the HVL will decrease the patient dose. For example, increasing the HVL from 2 mm to 3 mm of aluminum reduced the entrance exposure to the patient from 600 mR to 390 mR, a 35% exposure reduction (based on calculations, see Figure 7.2).

A close look at Figure 7.2 can provide useful insight into the effect of added aluminum filtration. This graph was plotted from data calculated using a computer simulation system. As it is easy to see, the addition of the first fractions of a millimeter of aluminum changes the entrance exposure to the patient dramatically, with the addition of more aluminum giving less, but still significant, exposure reductions. Note that this graph was plotted assuming that the density on the films was to be maintained at the same level after the beam passed through a 20-cm patient.

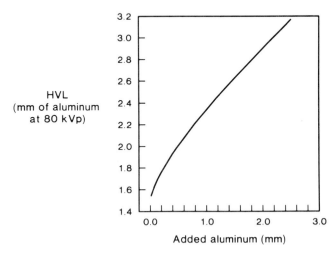

Figure 7.1. Half-value layer as a function of added aluminum. The HVL, although expressed in millimeters of aluminum, is a measure of the hardness, or softness, of the x-ray beam and is not the same as the added aluminum filtration. In addition, if the added aluminum is increased from 1.0 to 2.0 mm the HVL changes much less, by approximately 0.5 mm of aluminum.

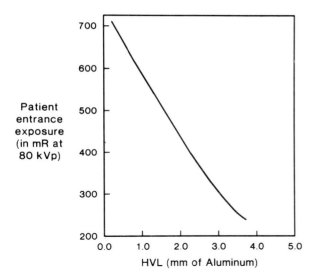

Figure 7.2. Patient entrance exposure as a function of HVL. The entrance exposure to the patient drops dramatically as the HVL increases since a higher HVL means less soft radiation, radiation that will be absorbed by the patient and not used to make an image. For this figure the patient exit exposure was kept constant, meaning that the same density was produced on the films.

Although this required a slight increase in the mAs as more aluminum was added, the entrance exposure was constantly reduced with added filtration.

Although the Bureau of Radiological Health requires that manufacturers ensure an HVL of 2.3 mm of aluminum at 80 kVp upon installation of the x-ray equipment, we feel that it is prudent to increase this to 3.0 mm of aluminum, for an exposure reduction of about 25% with no change in the density or film quality, and we have done this throughout our institution. (The service engineer should also assure that proper filtration is added to the beam upon replacement of an x-ray tube or collimator, but this may be neglected, so it is especially important to check the HVL after tube changes or removal of the collimator.) In fact, we have been able to match the HVLs of our tubes to 3.0 ± 0.2 mm of aluminum (at 80 kVp) with little difficulty.

The accuracy of HVL measurements when carried out by different people is important. Using the same data four individuals plotted the values on semi-log paper (as described in the protocol in this chapter) and obtained values of 3.68, 3.55, 3.60, and 3.60. This indicates that the plotting procedure is quite accurate and eliminates necessity for complicated calculations or computer analysis of the data. With different individuals making the measurements at different times, as well as plotting the data and determining the HVL, we have found that we can expect accuracies of ± 0.1 mm of aluminum.

Since the HVL indicates the "hardness" of the x-ray beam, and kVp will also affect the hardness of the beam, you must be sure that the kVp is measured and correct before making HVL measurements. As can be seen from Figure 7.3 a change of 2 or 3 kVp will result in a change of approximately 0.1 mm in the HVL (when measured at 80 kVp).

We have one final tip on measuring the HVL that we find useful. We normally set up our initial technique at 80 kVp and select the mAs so that we obtain an exposure reading of 300 mR. This assures that you have a high enough exposure to make the measurements accurately and also assures that your data can be plotted on semi-log paper where the scale is easy to read.

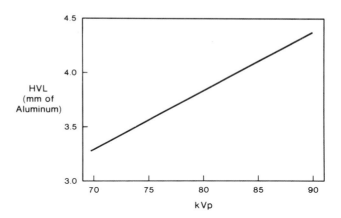

Figure 7.3. HVL as a function of kVp. Over this energy range the HVL does vary, although not rapidly, with kVp. Consequently, the kVp must be correct before determining the HVL in a diagnostic imaging system.

PROCEDURES

7.1. X-RAY TUBE RATING CHARTS

Purpose

To assure that departmental exposure techniques (combination of kVp, mA, and time) are within the ratings of the tubes and housings. During the production of x-radiation, a great deal of heat is produced at the surface of the x-ray tube's anode. It is essential that the rate at which this heat is produced is at a level that will not result in melting the surface of the anode and that the total quantity of the heat produced from a single or a series of exposures does not exceed the thermal capacity of the anode itself. In addition, it is essential that the rate of heat dissipation of the x-ray tube housing to its surrounding and its heat capacity be considered to avoid overheating with resultant damage to the rotor bearings and other structures within the x-ray tube.

Equipment

X-ray tube and housing rating charts for each type of tube and housing used in the department

Procedure—Single Exposure Rating

1. Select the single exposure rating chart for the specific x-ray tube used and for the conditions of use, e.g., focal spot size, single- or three-phase generator, 60 or 180 Hz stator rotation (Figure 7.4).
2. Refer to the technique chart for the room and determine the maximum exposure used for the thickest body part. A typical technique for a localized lateral view of the lumbar spine may be 100 kVp, 200 mA, and 1 sec, with a three-phase generator and a medium-speed screen-film combination.
3. Determine whether this technique is permitted by reference to the single exposure rating chart.

Problems and Pitfalls

1. There are as many as eight single exposure rating charts for each x-ray tube. It is essential that the correct rating chart be used. These eight charts include:

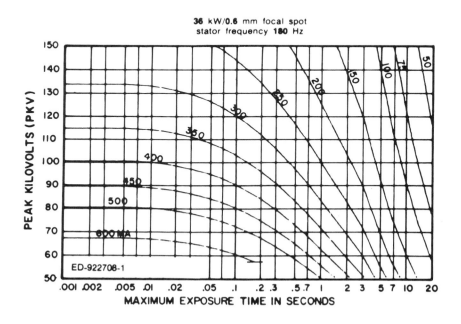

Figure 7.4. Single exposure rating chart for a 36-kW anode with a 0.6-mm nominal focal spot size with the anode operated at high-speed rotation on a three-phase, full-wave, rectified generator. Courtesy of Machlett Corporation.

	Small focal	Large focal
Single phase	60 Hz stator	60 Hz stator
	180 Hz stator	180 Hz stator
Three phase	60 Hz stator	60 Hz stator
	180 Hz stator	180 Hz stator

2. High mAs exposures may be permitted at low mA and long exposure times (200 mA, 1 sec), but may not be permitted at high mA and short exposure times (1,000 mA, 0.2 sec).
3. Operation of the x-ray tube within the single exposure rating limits does not prevent overheating the tube with a filming series.

Acceptance Limits

Most exposure techniques used with a specific x-ray tube must not exceed about 80% of the limits provided on the single exposure rating charts.

Corrective Action

Whenever possible, exposure techniques that exceed 80% of the single exposure ratings should be modified. It is usually possible to operate within the ratings by doing one or more of the following:

1. Use the large focal spot
2. Use high speed rotation
3. Reduce the mA and increase the exposure time
4. Increase the kVp and reduce the mA or time
5. Switch to a higher-speed screen-film combination

Procedure—Anode Thermal Characteristics

1. Select the appropriate thermal characteristics rating chart.
2. Determine the number of exposures and technique required for a study, e.g., a 10-exposure tomographic series at 70 kVp, 50 mA, and 6 sec.
3. Refer to the single exposure rating chart to determine if one exposure at the desired technique is permitted before proceeding. If not, modify the technique.
4. Compute the heat units for a single exposure and then multiply this value by the number of exposures in the series.

$$\text{Heat units (HU)} = \text{kVp} \times \text{mA} \times \text{time} \times 1.35$$

(The 1.35 factor applies to three-phase generators only.) For example,

$$70 \text{ kVp} \times 50 \text{ mA} \times 6 \text{ sec} \times 1.35 = 28,350 \text{ HU}$$
$$28,350 \text{ HU} \times 10 \text{ exposures} = 283,500 \text{ HU09}$$

5. Refer to the anode thermal characteristics chart and find the maximum number of heat units that may be safely stored in the anode. From Figure 7.5 you can see that the maximum is 135,000 HU. Consequently, the 10-exposure tomographic series, which generates 283,500 HU, cannot be completed without allowing time for the anode to cool between exposures.
6. Divide the maximum heat storage capacity of the anode by the heat units produced by each exposure to find the maximum number of exposures than can be made without waiting for cooling between exposures.

$$\frac{135,000}{28,350} = 4.76$$

In the example, four exposures can be made without waiting, but five cannot.

7. Multiply the number of heat units for each exposure by the number of exposures allowed in a series to determine the number of heat units stored in the anode.

$$4 \times 28,350 \text{ HU} = 113,400 \text{ HU}$$

8. Round off the values to 30,000 HU and 115,000 HU and determine the amount of time required for the anode to cool by 30,000 HU when 115,000 HU are stored. This is slightly less than 1 minute (Figure 7.5).
9. The 10–exposure tomographic series may be safely carried out within the ratings if 4 exposures are made in a series and the remaining 6 exposures made with 1-minute intervals between each exposure.

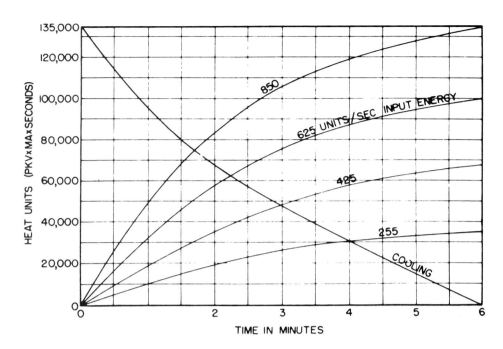

Figure 7.5. Anode thermal characteristic chart for the tube in Figure 7.4. Courtesy of Machlett Corporation.

Problems and Pitfalls

1. The above example assumes that the anode is cool (initially at 0 HU).
2. In general, a 6-minute period between patient procedures will allow the anode to cool sufficiently to start the set of exposures (4 exposures, then 1 each minute) again.

Procedure—Housing Cooling Chart

1. Select the appropriate housing cooling chart.
2. Note the number of heat units that may be safely stored in the x-ray tube housing, e.g., 1,250,000 HU in Figure 7.6.
3. The housing cools from its maximum storage of 1,250,000 HU down to about 800,000 HU in 15 minutes if the x-ray tube is equipped with an air circulator and in 30 minutes without a fan.

Problems and Pitfalls

1. It is essential that the single exposure rating chart and the anode thermal characteristic rating chart be referenced to assure that a single exposure and the proposed series of exposures are permitted.
2. Although the tube housing heat storage capacity is quite large when compared to the heat storage capacity of the anode, conditions that lead to exceeding the tube housing heat storage capacity can and do occur in:
   a. High-use radiographic and fluoroscopic situations
   b. High-use complex motion tomography
   c. Special procedures that involve fluoroscopy, filming, and cineradiography
   d. Frequent rotor starts (1600 HU per start)

Acceptance Limits

Exposure series that exceed the x-ray tube housing rating are unacceptable.

Corrective Action

1. Modifications of procedures may be required to allow sufficient time for the x-ray tube housing to cool.
2. If procedural modifications are not possible consider:
   a. Installation of an air circulator
   b. Replacement of the existing x-ray tube housing with a housing of greater heat storage capacity
   c. Replacement of the existing housing with a housing that is equipped with recirculating cooling system.

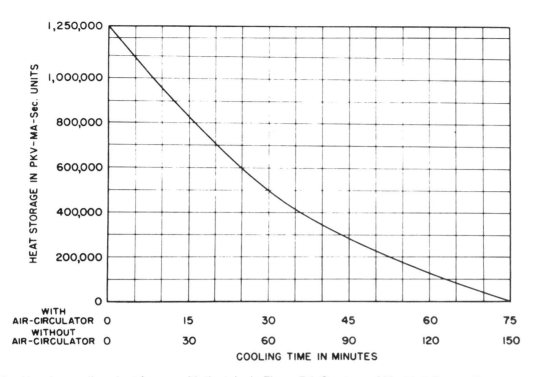

Figure 7.6. Housing cooling chart for use with the tube in Figure 7.4. Courtesy of Machlett Corporation.

Procedure—Angiographic Ratings

1. Select the proper angiographic rating chart (Figure 7.7).
2. Determine the exposure factors to be used for the individual exposures of the angiographic series, the number of exposures and the rate at which the exposures will be made, e.g., 2, 4, or 6 per second.
3. Refer to the x-ray tube single exposure rating chart to assure that technical factors are permitted.
4. Compute the number of heat units for a single exposure.
5. Compare the number of heat units computed in Step 4 to values in the angiographic rating chart to determine if the number of exposures planned in the series can be made without overheating the tube and housing.

Problems and Pitfalls

1. This procedure assumes that the x-ray tube and housing are cool.
2. In heavily used procedure rooms it will be necessary to determine both anode and housing heat storage conditions and allow an appropriate interval between filming procedures for cooling.

Acceptance Limits

The angiographic series must be within the angiographic rating.

Corrective Action

The desired combination of exposure factors, the number of exposures, and the filming rate will have to be modified if the maximum heat load exceeds the x-ray tube angiographic rating. This may be accomplished by:

1. Reducing the total number of exposures in the series
2. Changing to a slower filming rate
3. Increasing the kVp and reducing the mA and/or exposure time
4. Using a faster screen-film system

Procedure—Cine Radiographic Ratings

1. Select the appropriate cineradiographic rating chart.
2. Determine the number of heat units for a single-frame exposure.

EFFECTIVE FOCAL SPOT SIZE 0.60 MM
STATOR FREQUENCY 180 HERTZ

TOTAL NUMBER OF EXPOSURES

EXPOS. PER SEC	2	5	10	20	30	40	50	60
	MAXIMUM LOAD IN PKV X MA X SEC PER EXPOSURE (*)							
1	20500	13800	9000	5800	4400	3600	3100	2700
2	12600	9600	6800	4500	3400	2900	2500	2200
3	9200	7200	5800	3800	3000	2500	2150	1950
4	7200	5900	4800	3400	2700	2250	1950	1750
5	6000	5000	4100	3100	2450	2050	1800	1600
6	5100	4300	3600	2900	2300	1950	1700	1500
8	4000	3400	2950	2400	2050	1700	1500	1340
10	3300	2900	2500	2050	1800	1550	1380	1240
12	2850	2500	2150	1800	1600	1460	1280	1140

* SUBJECT TO LIMITATION OF THE SINGLE EXPOSURE RATING CHART
AS APPLICABLE TO THE INDIVIDUAL EXPOSURE OF THE SERIES

Figure 7.7. Angiographic rating chart for the same tube as in Figure 7.4. Courtesy of Machlett Corporation.

3. Assure that the single-frame exposure does not exceed the single exposure ratings for the x-ray tube.
4. In Figure 7.8, find the appropriate column under the heading "Maximum Duration of Cine Series in Seconds" and select the entry that corresponds to the "Pulse Length in ms." This value is the maximum allowable product of the kVp and mA for the length of the cine run selected and for the pulse length. [**Note:** This is not in terms of heat units (kVp × mA × time) but rather in terms of kVp × mA.]

    Example: Heat Units = 80 kVp × 100 mA × 0.004 sec = 32 HU. This obviously does not exceed the single exposure rating. Assuming a 20-sec cine run at 4 msec we find that the maximum allowable kVp × mA product is 20,000. The product for the combination we have selected is 80 kVp × 100 mA = 8000. This technique is acceptable.
5. If cine runs of lengths other than those given in the chart are anticipated it will be necessary to interpolate to determine the maximum kVp × mA combination.

Problems and Pitfalls

1. The cine radiographic rating chart must be selected properly, with consideration of the focal spot size, stator frequency, three-phase or single-phase generator, etc.
2. The ratings assume that the anode is starting from a cold condition. If previous cine runs have been carried out then it will be necessary to take the cooling characteristics of the anode into account.
3. You must also consider the housing cooling characteristics and heat loading capabilities to assure that the housing is not overheated. Remember that, especially for AP, the heat added to the tube and housing during fluoroscopy may reduce the loading characteristics significantly.
4. Most cine systems use some type of automatic exposure control, so it will be difficult to estimate the factors before the run. However, the technologist should have an idea of the maximum techniques used for specific patient thicknesses and can determine the maximum duration of the cine run, considering the pulse width, from this information.
5. Most cineradiographic rating charts assume a frame rate of 60 frames per sec. If the frame rate is 120 frames per sec, the values in the column labelled "Pulse Length" should be doubled, i.e., from 4 ms to 8 ms. If the frame rate is 30 frames per second, then the values in the column labelled "Pulse Length" should be cut in half.
6. You must be certain not to exceed the maximum mA as shown on the single exposure rating chart.
7. For more specific information on your x-ray tubes used in cine applications, contact the tube manufacturer.

69 /T4-0.60X - 60/180-1174JC

EFFECTIVE FOCAL SPOT SIZE 0.60 MM
STATOR FREQUENCY 180 HERTZ

DUTY FACTOR	PULSE LENGTH IN MS (*)	MAXIMUM DURATION OF CINE SERIES IN SECONDS							
		2	3	5	10	20	30	50	100
		MAXIMUM POWER IN PKV X MA (**)							
.015	.25	39000	39000	39000	38000	38000	37000	36000	33000
.030	.5	39000	39000	38000	37000	35000	34000	32000	29000
.060	1	38000	37000	36000	34000	32000	30000	27500	22500
.120	2	36000	35000	33000	30000	27000	24000	20500	15500
.240	4	32000	31000	28500	24500	20000	17000	13000	7800
.480	8	27500	25500	22000	17500	12000	9200	6400	3800

```
*   IN MILLISECONDS, FRAME RATE: 60 PER SECOND
    IF FRAME RATE IS DIFFERENT, ADJUST PULSE LENGTH CORRESPONDINGLY
    (HALF FRAME RATE = TWICE PULSE LENGTH AND VICE VERSA)

**  MA AS DETERMINED BY THE MA SELECTOR, NOT TO EXCEED THE MAXIMUM
    EMISSION CURRENT AS SHOWN ON THE SINGLE EXPOSURE RATING CHART

    DUTY FACTOR IS USED TO DETERMINE TOTAL HEAT UNITS OF CINE SERIES:
    HU = 1.35 X PKV X MA X SERIES DURATION X DUTY FACTOR
```

Figure 7.8.   Cine radiographic rating chart for the same tube as in Figure 7.4. Courtesy of Machlett Corporation.

Acceptance Limits

The techniques selected should at not time exceed the cineradiographic, single exposure, or housing ratings.

Corrective Action

1. If ratings are exceeded another technique must be selected.
2. If ratings are consistently exceeded consider using a faster film or having the service engineer open the aperture on the cine camera, adjusting your techniques accordingly. This will also require complete read-justment of the exposure control system.
3. If, after checking housing cooling charts, you find that the heat build-up in the housing is approaching the maximum it will be necessary to:
    a. Use less fluoroscopic time and/or reduce the length of the cine runs in all future cases
    b. Add a cooling system to the housing
    c. Improve the geometry of the x-ray tube-intensifier system
    d. Use a lower frame rate
4. Consider adding a tube heat monitor to your system. This will display the percentage of heat loading remaining. (This device also has an audible alarm that can indicate when you are approaching the maximum allowable loading.)

Procedure—Fluoroscopic Ratings

Most fluoroscopic units are equipped with systems that automatically adjust kVp and/or mA. Prior to proceeding with this section, it is necessary to observe actual operation to determine the usual operating level (kVp and mA), the maximum operating level, the amount of fluoroscopic time used on average per patient, the average time interval between patients, and the average number of factors for the spot films made during the procedures. The following instructions and examples assume that this has been done.

1. Select the appropriate rating charts:
    a. Fluoroscopic (Figure 7.5, graphs labelled heat units/sec input)
    b. Single exposure rating chart (Figure 7.4)
    c. Housing cooling chart (Figure 7.6)
2. Determine the usual and maximum heat unit/sec input rate.

3. Figure 7.5 shows that neither the usual nor the maximum heat unit/sec input rates stated will exceed the x-ray tube rating during 6 minutes of continuous operation.

Problems and Pitfalls

1. The fluoroscopic rating chart assumes that the anode is starting from a cold condition. If previous fluoroscopic examinations have been carried out, it will be necessary to take the cooling characteristics of the anode into account.
2. This test does not assure that the spot film exposures are within x-ray tube ratings. It is essential that the Single Exposure Rating and Anode Thermal Characteristics procedures be carried out to determine that the spot film exposures do not result in exceeding the x-ray tube ratings.
3. This test does not assure that the x-ray tube's housing rating will not be exceeded during a morning's fluoroscopic exams. Follow the Housing Cooling Chart procedure.

Acceptance Limits

The techniques selected should at no time exceed the fluoroscopic, single exposure, anode cooling, or housing ratings.

Corrective Action

1. If ratings are exceeded, another technique must be selected.
2. If anode cooling or housing ratings are routinely exceeded, consider:
   a. Extending the interval between patients
   b. Reducing the fluoroscopic time or number of spot films taken per procedure
   c. Installing a circulating fan and vent system to exchange the air inside the fluoroscopic table
   d. Installing a larger capacity x-ray tube

7.2. OVERLOAD PROTECTION

Purpose

To assure that the maximum exposure techniques that the x-ray generator overload-protection circuit will allow are within the 80% limitations of the x-ray tube rating chart.

Equipment Needed

Single exposure rating charts for the specific model of the x-ray tube

Procedure

1. Select the appropriate single exposure rating chart for your x-ray tube, focal spot size, type of generator, and anode rotational speed (for example, 0.6-mm focal spot, three-phase full wave rectification, and 180-Hz stator frequency).
2. Set the x-ray generator controls appropriately, e.g., to the small focal spot setting, the high speed rotor, and 100 kVp.
3. Refer to the single exposure rating chart and determine 80% of the maximum exposure time at 100 kVp allowable for each mA setting available on the generator control that can be used with the x-ray tube small focal spot. For example:

mA	Rated exposure time (sec)	80% rated exposure time (sec)
400	0.01	0.008
300	0.40	0.32
200	2.2	1.76

4. Set the generator controls to the "80% Rated Exposure Time" factors, one combination at a time, and observe the x-ray tube overload indicator.
5. If the tube protection circuit does not indicate tube overload, increase the exposure time until the tube overload circuit indicates an overload. DO NOT make an x-ray exposure.

6. If the tube protection circuit indicates a tube overload in Step 4, reduce the exposure time in steps at each mA setting to determine the point at which the tube overload protective circuit is set.
7. Repeat Steps 1 through 6 using values from the appropriate single exposure rating charts for the large focal spot.
8. Record the values in the QC room log.

Problems and Pitfalls

1. It is essential to check the function of the x-ray tube overload protection circuit on each mA station that may be used with each of the focal spots.
2. On x-ray generators that offer continuous control of mA, check the function of the tube overload protection circuit at the maximum obtainable mA with each focal spot and at approximately one-half and one-fourth of this value.
3. Overload protection circuits do not protect the tube from overheating that may occur from exposures made in a series.

Acceptance Limits

The x-ray overload protective circuit should indicate tube overload and prevent an x-ray exposure at about 80% of the x-ray tube rating and should function within ± 10% of that value.

Corrective Action

1. Immediate adjustment by a qualified service engineer is indicated if the overload protection circuit fails to indicate an overload for a combination of exposure factors that exceeds the single exposure rating.
2. Adjustment of the overload protection circuit by a qualified service engineer may be desirable if exposure factors of 80% of the x-ray tube's single exposure ratings cannot be obtained to avoid unnecessarily restricting the use of the equipment.
3. Function of the overload protection circuit should also be checked whenever the x-ray tube is changed.

7.3. X-RAY TUBE FOCAL SPOT SIZE MEASUREMENTS

Purpose

To assure that the x-ray tube focal spot size is within acceptable limits.

Equipment Needed

1. Star test pattern (1.5° or 2°; Figure 7.11a)
2. Screen-film extremity cassette, 8 × 10 inch (20 × 25 cm)
3. Lead letters, A and C
4. Clear plastic centimeter ruler
5. Pinhole camera test stand (Figure 7.9) with appropriate-sized pinholes
6. Small fluorescent screen
7. Spirit level
8. A 6× magnifier with reticle scale in 0.1-mm divisions

Procedure—Star Pattern Test for Focal Spots 0.3 mm or Smaller

1. Tape a star test pattern to the bottom of the collimator face plate while centering the star to the cross hair with the centering light or on a test stand (Figure 7.10).
2. Adjust the x-ray tube mount to the center, perpendicular position.
3. Place the image receptor on the x-ray table top. Set the focal spot–to-film distance to 24 inches (60 cm) and collimate the beam so that the total test pattern is included in the field.
4. Place the lead letters A and C on the film holder to denote the anode and cathode orientation of the x-ray tube.
5. Expose the radiographs using technical factors of 75 kVp and half the maximum rated mA at 0.1 sec for each focal spot. Use an exposure time appropriate to obtain 10–15 mAs.

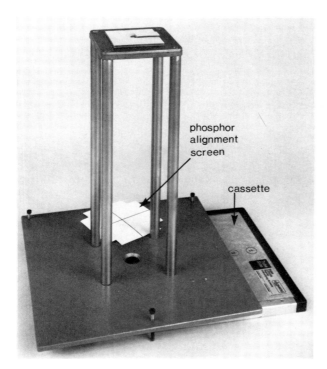

Figure 7.9. A commercially available pinhole camera has been modified by the addition of a large leveling base, which also allows the use of an 8 × 10-inch (20 × 25-cm) extremity cassette system. In addition a lead rubber mask has been placed on top of the camera to attenuate the radiation that passes through the large alignment holes and to eliminate an artifact produced as a result of poor fitting of the pinhole assembly. For further details of the modifications see Gray and Trefler (1980). (Reproduced with permission from: Gray, J. E., and Trefler, M. 1980. Pin-hole cameras: Artifacts, modifications, and recording of pin-hole images on screen film systems. *Radiologic Technology* 52:277–282.)

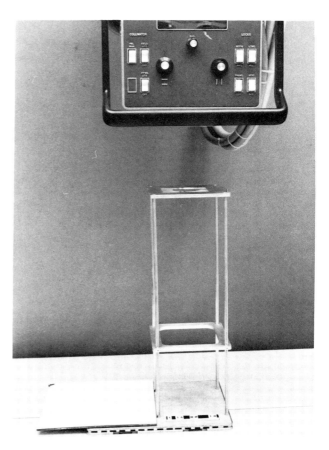

Figure 7.10. X-ray tube focal spot size star measurement test setup. The star test target (see Figure 7.11) is placed on top of the stand and an image is produced using an extremity cassette system. Images made with both the large and small focal spot can be placed on the same sheet of film.

6. Measure the total diameter of the star pattern image on the radiograph. This dimension should be about 90 mm ± 2 mm, assuming a 45-mm star target.

7. Starting at the outside edges of the star test pattern and in the same direction as the anode-cathode axis, move toward the center of the image and make sharp lead pencil marks on both sides where the bars first disappear (Figure 7.11b). Repeat the procedure in the other direction, i.e., 90° to the anode-cathode axis.

8. With a clear plastic ruler, measure and record the distance between the pencil marks made in Step 7 and record these dimensions with respect to the anode-cathode axis.

9. Compute the focal spot size. The width is determined by the measured dimension along the anode-cathode axis and the length is computed from the dimension measured at 90° to the anode-cathode axis. For a 2° star, the focal spot size is:

$$\frac{\text{Diameter of blurred area}}{28.65 \left(\dfrac{\text{Diameter of star image}}{45 \text{ mm}} - 1 \right)}$$

For a 1.5° star, the focal spot size is:

$$\frac{\text{Diameter of blurred area}}{38.2 \left(\dfrac{\text{Diameter of star image}}{45 \text{ mm}} - 1 \right)}$$

Figure 7.11a.   Contact radiograph of star test target made of 0.05-mm thick lead with 2° angles for the bars and spaces.

For example, the distance between the blurred regions of a 1.5° star target along the anode-cathode axis is 15 mm, giving a focal spot width of:

$$\frac{15 \text{ mm}}{38.2 \left(\dfrac{90 \text{ mm}}{45 \text{ mm}} - 1 \right)} = 0.39 \text{ mm}$$

10.   Record the results in the QC room log.

Problems and Pitfalls

When the star pattern radiographs are viewed it is frequently observed that the star images are first lost and then reappear toward the center of the image. This is known as false resolution. Ignore this reappearance. For the purpose of these measurements, the first point at which star images cannot be resolved is the point of interest.

Acceptance Limits

The National Electrical Manufacturers Association (NEMA) specifies that focal spots with a nominal size of 0.3 mm or less should be measured with a star pattern. The measured size may be 50% greater than the nominal, or stated, size and still be within specifications. This means that a 0.3-mm focal spot may be as large as 0.45 mm when measured using the star technique and still be considered as a 0.3-mm focal spot.

For focal spots larger than 0.3 mm, NEMA requires that the focal spot measurements be made with a pinhole camera for acceptance testing purposes. However, some manufacturers may agree to the use of the star target measurement for acceptance testing of focal spots larger than 0.3 mm. This should be discussed with the vendor prior to tube purchase and the acceptance limits should be established at this time. At our institution, we do use star target measurements, and our acceptance limits are those specified by NEMA for the pinhole measurements except that the 0.7 correction factor (see the following pages) is not applied.

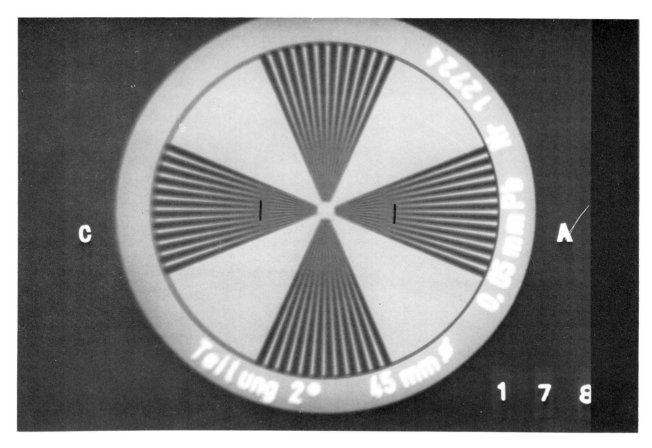

Figure 7.11b.   Star target image made under the geometry described in the text with a 0.6-mm focal spot. Measurements should be made of the first blur patterns, moving in from the outside of the star, where the bars first disappear.

Procedure—Pinhole Camera Measurement for Focal Spots Larger Than 0.3 mm

1. Place the pinhole camera test stand on the x-ray tabletop (or other means of firm support) and align the locator holes to the anode-cathode axis of the x-ray tube (Figure 7.12).
2. Check the test stand for perpendicularity and level with the spirit level.
3. Center the x-ray beam to the pinhole camera and adjust the pinhole-to-film distance and x-ray tube focal spot–to-film distance to obtain the proper enlargement factor. For focal spots 2.5 mm in size or smaller the enlargement factor should be 2.0 (pinhole-to-film distance equal to 60 cm and the focal spot–to-pinhole distance equal to 30 cm). For focal spots larger than 2.5 mm the enlargement factor should be 1.0 (pinhole-to-film distance equal to 40 cm and the focal spot–to-pinhole distance equal to 40 cm).
4. Place the small fluorescent screen on the camera base plate.
5. Set a radiographic exposure technique of about 75 kVp, 50 mA, and 2 sec or use the fluoroscopic mode if available.
6. Turn off all room lights and view, on the fluorescent screen, the location of the images projected from the center and the supplemental locator holes. Shift the test stand to assure that the three holes are centered to the cross-hairs on the fluorescent screen.
7. Insert the pinhole of the size appropriate for the focal spot to be measured:
    a. Use 0.030 mm for focal spots smaller than 1.0 mm
    b. Use 0.075 mm for focal spots from 1.0 mm to 2.5 mm
    c. Use 0.100 mm for focal spots larger than 2.5 mm
8. Expose the extremity cassette at factors of 75 kVp, and one-half the maximum rated mA at 0.1 sec. About 50 mAs will be required.
9. Process and view the pinhole image and check that the density of the pinhole image is in the range of 0.8–1.2 above the density of the unexposed film, or is of a reasonable density.

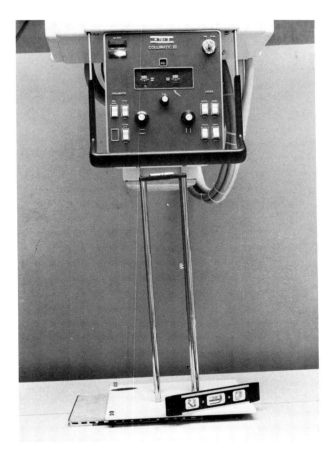

Figure 7.12. X-ray tube focal spot size pinhole measurement test setup. The pinhole camera top plate, containing the pinhole, should be leveled, as has not yet been done in this figure. With the appropriate modifications an extremity cassette may be slid under the camera and multiple exposures can be made on one film.

10. When a satisfactory pinhole camera radiograph has been obtained, measure the image of the focal spot as follows:
    a. Use a magnifying lens with a built-in graticule with 0.1-mm divisions and a 6 × magnification.
    b. Measure the x-ray image in two directions, i.e., parallel to and perpendicular to the anode-cathode axis. Divide the measurements obtained by the enlargement factor in Step 3 to obtain the dimensions of the focal spot. An additional correction factor of 0.7 is applied as a multiplier to the measured dimension made parallel to the anode-cathode axis.

Problems and Pitfalls

1. Misalignment of the pinhole with respect to the anode-cathode axis and the central beam of the x-ray tube can alter the measurements.
2. The focal spot size may change with mA and kVp; therefore, it is essential that measurements be made as specified.
3. Expect to see two areas of density in the pinhole camera image separated by a lesser-exposed central portion (Figure 7.13).
4. The manufacturer may require the use of direct x-ray exposed film instead of an extremity cassette system for acceptance testing.

Acceptance Limits

The National Electrical Manufacturers Association (NEMA) specifies that focal spots with a nominal size of 0.3 mm or less should be measured with a star pattern. For focal spots larger than 0.3 mm NEMA requires that the focal spot measurements be made with a pinhole camera for specification and acceptance testing purposes. For focal spots smaller than 0.8 mm the measured size may be 50% greater than the nominal size. For focal spots from 0.8 mm to, and including, 1.5 mm the measured size may be 40% greater than the nominal size. For focal spots greater than 1.5 mm, the measured size may be 30% greater than the nominal size. (All pinhole measured sizes are those obtained after applying the 0.7 multiplication factor to the dimension parallel to the anode-cathode axis.)

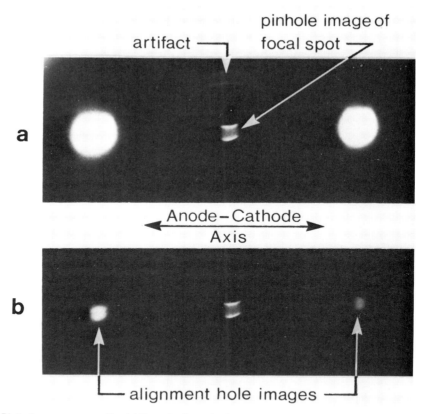

Figure 7.13a and b. Pinhole camera results. (a) Result of producing a pinhole camera image without the lead rubber cover described in the literature. (b) After placing the lead rubber on the top plate of the camera the artifact is eliminated and the exposure through the alignment holes is reduced, making the measurement of their separation, and hence determination of the magnification, easier. (Reproduced with permission from: Gray, J. E., and Trefler, M. 1980. Pin-hole cameras: Artifacts, modifications, and recording of pin-hole images on screen film systems. *Radiologic Technology* 52:277–282.)

Corrective Action

There is nothing that can be done to correct an oversized focal spot. It is essential to repeat the test if the focal spot is found to be oversized to assure that the measurements are correct. If the focal spot is oversized, request replacement of the x-ray tube by the vendor.

7.4. X-RAY-LIGHT FIELD, X-RAY FIELD, BUCKY ALIGNMENT TESTS, AND EXPOSURE CONSISTENCY

Purpose

1. To assure that the x-ray field and the light field are congruent and that the automatic collimation system adjusts to the cassette size used, or that the film size indicators of a manual system are accurate. Also to assure that the patient entrance exposure is similar from room-to-room.
2. To assure that the central x-ray beam is perpendicular to the table.
3. To assure that the x-ray field is centered to the cassette and to the cassette tray.

Equipment Needed

1. Collimator alignment template marked from center to edge in either centimeters or inches
2. X-ray beam alignment test tool
3. One 10 × 12-inch (24 × 30-cm) single screen extremity or mammographic cassette [**Note:** If a single screen cassette is not available, a conventional cassette with the front screen blocked with a totally blackened sheet of x-ray film will produce similar results.]

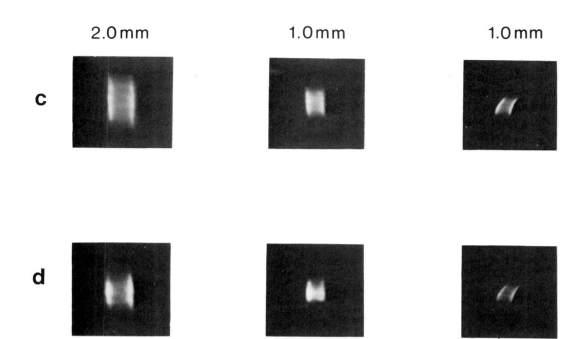

2.0 mm   1.0 mm   1.0 mm

c

d

Figure 7.13c and d.   Pinhole images of three focal spots with nominal sizes of 1.0 and 2.0 mm made on (**c**) dental x-ray film and (**d**) an extremity cassette system. (Reproduced with permission from: Gray, J. E., and Trefler, M. 1980. Pin-hole cameras: Artifacts, modifications, and recording of pin-hole images on screen film systems. *Radiologic Technology* 52:277–282.)

4.   One 8 × 10-inch (20 × 25-cm) cassette
5.   Several straightened paper clips, or solder strips
6.   Spirit level
7.   Lead letters, A and F
8.   One sheet of scrap film for each cassette size to be evaluated
9.   Patient equivalent phantom (PEP)
10. Direct readout dosimeter

Procedure—Light Field, X-ray Field Alignment, and Perpendicularity

1.   Set the x-ray tube to the transverse center position at the most commonly used SID.
2.   Stand at the end and then the side of the table and visually inspect the x-ray tube and collimator assembly for perpendicularity and centering to the tabletop. If problems are found, correct them before continuing.
3.   Place the alignment template on top of the 10 × 12-inch (24 × 30-cm) single screen cassette, and center the cassette and template to the center line of the table, or to the collimator if the tabletop is not marked (Figure 7.14).
4.   If the unit being tested has a tilting top or a curved top, the template with cassette should be checked with a level both longitudinally and transversely to assure it is level.
5.   Place the x-ray beam alignment test tool in the exact center of the template (Figure 7.14).
6.   Adjust the collimator light field to the light field alignment marks on the template.
7.   If the light field is centered to the template and one or more of the edges of the light field are not on the corresponding field marks, place straightened paper clips, or solder strips, on the edges of the light field to denote their location.
8.   Place the lead letter "A" to denote the anode of the x-ray tube, and the lead letter "F" toward you to denote the front of the x-ray table, along with the date and room number.
9.   Make a radiographic exposure at the factors of approximately 65 kVp and 10 mAs. [***Note:***   Do not move the cassette-template combination or the x-ray tube.]
10. Securely lock an 8 × 10-inch (20 × 25-cm) cassette in the Bucky tray and center the tray to the Bucky tray centering light.

Figure 7.14. X-ray–light field alignment and x-ray beam perpendicularity test setup.

11. If your system has positive beam limitation (PBL), close the tray and allow the system to automatically adjust to the cassette in the Bucky tray. If your system has manual collimation, adjust the field size to the appropriate film size using field size indicators of the collimator. [**Note:** Make sure the indicator corresponds to the SID being used.]

12. Expose *both* cassettes at approximately 65 kVp and 10 mAs.

13. Process both radiographs to determine beam alignment, x-ray field–light field alignment, and sizing.

14. The twice-exposed *tabletop film* is used to determine the central ray perpendicularity, collimator x-ray field–to–light field alignment, and x-ray field size of the PBL system or field size indicator of a manual system. The film from the *Bucky tray* is used to determine Bucky tray film centering, and for comparison with the tabletop film to determine PBL system or field size indicator accuracy (Figure 7.15).

15. The x-ray field–to–light field alignment is determined by measuring the distance between the image of the inscribed light field alignment marks of the template and the edge of the x-ray field (Figure 7.15).

16. The method of determining the central ray perpendicularity will vary somewhat with the manufacturer of the alignment test tool. In most cases the perpendicularity is checked by measuring the deviation between the upper (magnified) bead and the bead or ring at the bottom of the test tool.

17. To determine PBL system misalignment, or field size indicator accuracy, place both the tabletop and Bucky tray film in the same orientation side by side on a viewbox. First, determine the maximum area of the Bucky tray film by observing the outermost image of the measuring scale (inches or centimeters) seen on the alignment template along all four dimensions of the film. Then with a felt-tip pen mark the corresponding numeric information onto the scale imaged on the tabletop film. Using this scale, or a ruler, measure the difference between the area imaged on the Bucky tray and tabletop films to determine the total misalignment.

18. To assure that the film in the Bucky tray is centered to the x-ray beam, visually check for squareness to the collimator alignment template. Then using the measuring scale of the template, measure the distance from the center of the template to all four edges of the Bucky tray film.

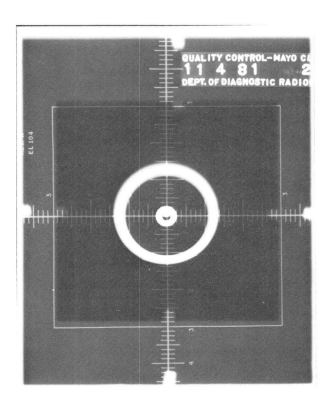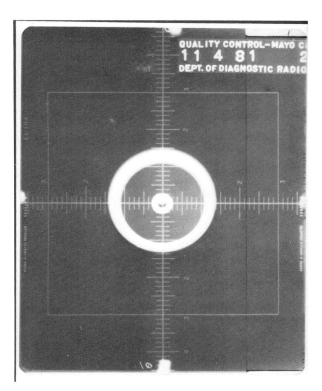

Figure 7.15a. Acceptable x-ray–light field alignment and x-ray beam perpendicularity test results. Left film from tabletop; right film from Bucky tray.

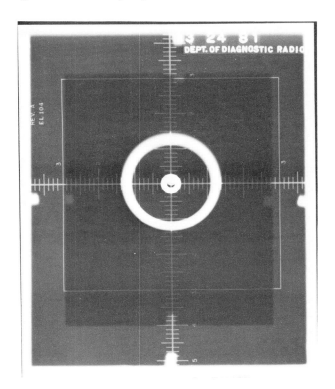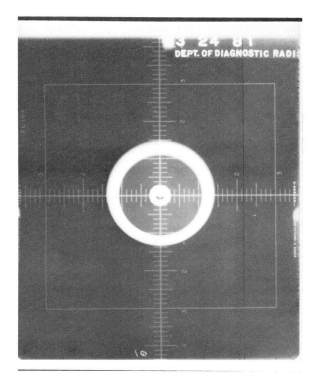

Figure 7.15b. X-ray beam perpendicularity is acceptable but the lower collimator leaf extends out too far (left film) and the film from the Bucky tray (right) indicates that the cassette was not centered properly.

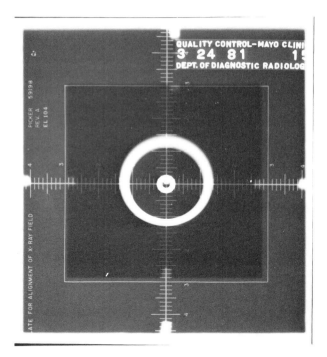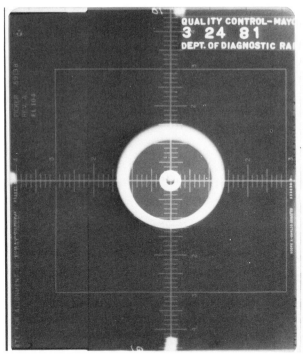

Figure 7.15c. This would be an acceptable result except that the x-ray beam perpendicularity exceeds acceptance limits. Left film from tabletop; right film from Bucky tray.

19. Record the collimator light field–to–x-ray field, PBL or film size indicator, and Bucky tray film alignment in millimeters in the QC room log. A simple "pass" or "fail" for central ray perpendicularity should also be recorded.

Problems and Pitfalls

1. The field edges of the projected light field are fuzzy with some collimators. This makes it difficult to exactly adjust the light field.
2. Balancing the film density between the tabletop and Bucky tray films may be difficult, particularly if a conventional cassette with the front screen blocked is used. If your department has several different screen-film speed combinations, use a higher-speed combination in the Bucky tray and a slower combination on the tabletop.
3. The image of the collimator template will be somewhat magnified on the film exposed in the Bucky tray. This magnification is a result of the divergence of the x-ray beam so the procedures previously described will be accurate, but measurements from the scale of the template will not match the actual size of the film.

Acceptance Limits

1. Federal guidelines allow ±2% of the SID in collimator light–to–x-ray field and PBL system misalignment (e.g., a 100-cm SID would allow ±2 cm) for certified equipment in x-ray field–light field alignment and sizing. However, a ±1-cm acceptance limit is reasonably achievable and is recommended for most modern equipment.
2. The edge of the radiation field should be within ±1 cm of the template markers denoting the location of the light field edges. This should include field edges that do not align with the template marks.
3. For both automatic (PBL) and manual collimation, the maximum area exposed on the tabletop film should be within ±1 cm of the maximum area of the Bucky tray film.
4. The film from the Bucky tray should be centered within 1 cm in all directions from the center of the template and should be square to the alignment template.
5. The image of the upper bead (magnified) should fall within 5 mm of the lower bead or ring, particularly if a high-ratio Bucky grid is in use.

Corrective Action

Resizing of field size and alignment of the light field–x-ray field and/or perpendicularity by qualified service engineers is required if acceptance limits are exceeded.

Procedure—Field Size vs. Cassette Size for PBL Systems.

1. Set the x-ray tube at the SID used for Bucky radiography.
2. Make sure the PBL selector is set to automatic mode.
3. Insert the size of cassette commonly used in the Bucky tray lengthwise and then transverse. Check visually that the changes in the light field size occur with cassette size and that the size of the light field is appropriate by comparing the light field size with an appropriate sized sheet of scrap film placed on the tabletop.
4. Record the results in the QC room log.

Problems and Pitfalls

1. Make sure that the light field to x-ray-field alignment is acceptable by the collimator template or the nine-penny test before doing this test.
2. Due to x-ray beam divergence, the field size at the film during actual Bucky radiography will be slightly larger than as measured on the x-ray tabletop. For this reason, the light field should be slightly smaller than the scrap film sheet.

Acceptance Limits

Federal guidelines for certified equipment allow a variation of $\pm 2\%$ of the SID. Thus, a ± 2-cm variation in field size is acceptable. However, a ± 1-cm variation is reasonably achievable, and should be the acceptance limit for most modern equipment.

Corrective Action

A service engineer should be called in to readjust the PBL system if acceptance limits are exceeded.

Procedure—X-ray Beam, Bucky Grid Motion and Centering, Image Receptor Alignment, and Exposure Consistency

1. Place the x-ray tube in the transverse center position.
2. Place solder strips on the x-ray tabletop aligned to the light field cross-hairs and tape them in position (Figure 7.16a).
3. Place the patient equivalent phantom on top of the solder strips, center the phantom to the light field, and place the small dosimeter chamber above and in contact with the top of PEP, close to the center (Figure 7.16b).
4. Insert a 14 × 17-inch (35 × 43-cm) cassette transversely in the Bucky tray.
5. Allow the automatic collimator to set the field size. On manual systems, collimate the x-ray beam to the cassette size.
6. Make a radiographic exposure using the factors appropriate for a 21-cm AP view of the abdomen from the technique chart in the room.
7. Record the results (Figure 7.17) and the dosimeter reading in the QC room log.

Problems and Pitfalls

1. The x-ray field–light field alignment test must be done before this test.
2. This test serves to identify whether or not a problem exists, but is nonspecific as to cause.
3. Expect density variation across the phantom image along the anode-cathode axis because of heel effect.
4. Problems caused by cassette tray interference with Bucky motion are frequently not demonstrated unless a 14 × 17-inch (35 × 43-cm) cassette is used transversely.
5. Some Bucky grids have many flaws that may cause artifacts. Replacement of the grid may be the only way to correct such artifacts.
6. Some tabletops may also contain flaws, or residual contrast media on the table or grid may produce artifacts.
7. The dosimeter must be positioned in the same location each time, both along and perpendicular to the anode-cathode axis, to assure consistent results.

Figure 7.16a.   X-ray beam, Bucky grid motion and centering, and image receptor alignment test setup. Lead solder strips should be placed on the tabletop, centered to the collimator cross-hairs, and then the PEP placed on top of the strips.

Acceptance Limits

1. The radiograph should show that the lead solder strips are centered to the cassette within ± 1 cm and the radiograph should appear evenly exposed across the transverse dimension.
2. For rooms using similar generators, tubes, collimators, tabletops, and screen-film combinations, the entrance exposures to the phantom should be within ± 10%. If there is a greater variation, you should investigate the cause, paying particular attention to the HVL, output of the x-ray tube, and any other factors that may affect the exposure to the patient. If rooms do not use similar equipment, then exposure variations will be greater than noted above. However, you should investigate the reason for these variations and consider differences in the tabletops, HVLs, collimator design, x-ray tubes, and any other factors that may affect the output of the x-ray generator and the patient exposure.
3. Three-phase and single-phase generators should produce similar exposures to the patient if the techniques for the single-phase generators are set approximately 10 kVp higher than those for the three-phase generators. This will also result in similar HVLs for the same radiographic projections, and the resultant films should appear identical, assuming that the mAs has been changed to match film densities.

Corrective Action

An evaluation and correction of the grid alignment, centering, and Bucky motion by a qualified service engineer is in order if excessive density variation (greater than ± 0.10) is found transversely on the test film.

7.5.   HALF-VALUE LAYER (HVL) MEASUREMENT

Purpose

To assure that the permanently installed filtration at the x-ray tube is maintained at an appropriate level to help minimize patient exposure.

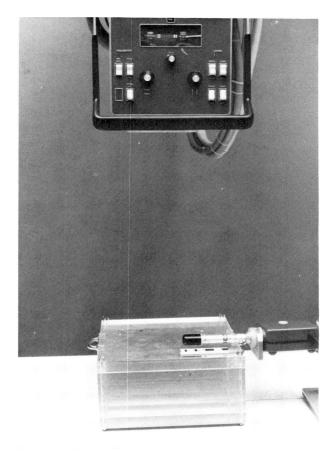

Figure 7.16b. A direct-readout dosimeter and date-room identification marker should be placed in the lower corner of the phantom as shown.

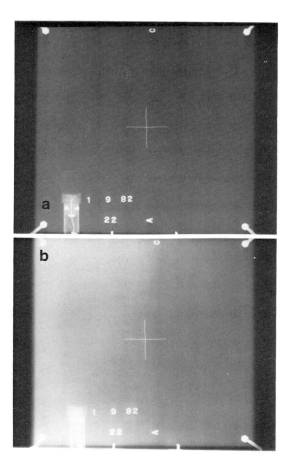

Figure 7.17. X-ray beam, Bucky grid motion and centering, and image receptor alignment test results. (a) The film densities should be uniform and on the order of 1.2 above base-plus-fog levels for a 21-cm lumbar spine technique. Some change in density will be noted along the anode-cathode axis. (b) This film is exceptionally light, in addition to the fact that the densities are not uniform, indicating a grid alignment, centering, or Bucky motion problem.

Equipment Needed

1. Dosimeter
2. Known thickness of aluminum (1100 alloy):
   a. Four pieces 6 × 6 inch × 1.0 mm thick (150 × 150 × 1 mm)
   b. One piece 6 × 6 inch × 0.5 mm thick (150 × 150 × 0.5 mm)
   c. One piece 6 × 6 inch × 0.25 mm thick (150 × 150 × 0.25 mm)
3. Lead sheet
4. Test stand (Figure 7.18)
5. Semi-logarithmic graph paper

Procedure—Overtable Radiographic and Fluoroscopic Tubes

1. Center the lead sheet on the x-ray tabletop with the test stand on top of the lead sheet (Figure 7.18a).
2. Place the dosimeter chamber on top of the lead sheet directly under the test stand.
3. Set the x-ray tube to a 36-inch (90-cm) source-to-tabletop distance and center the x-ray field through the opening on top of the test stand to the dosimeter chamber below, making sure the entire chamber will be included in the x-ray field.

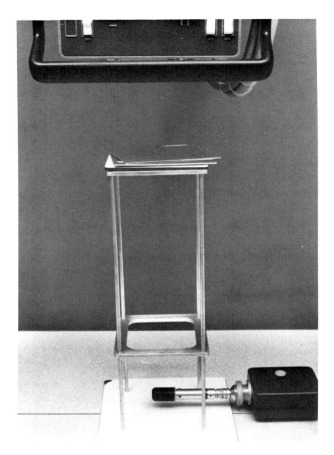

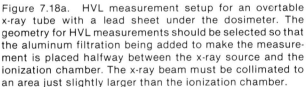

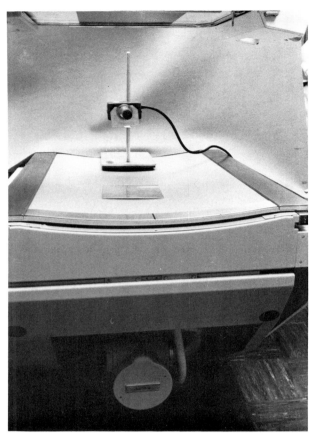

Figure 7.18a. HVL measurement setup for an overtable x-ray tube with a lead sheet under the dosimeter. The geometry for HVL measurements should be selected so that the aluminum filtration being added to make the measurement is placed halfway between the x-ray source and the ionization chamber. The x-ray beam must be collimated to an area just slightly larger than the ionization chamber.

Figure 7.18b. HVL measurement setup for an undertable x-ray tube with the aluminum filtration placed directly on the table and the intensifier raised as far from the ionization chamber as possible.

4. The HVL is measured at a given kVp setting. For general x-ray equipment one HVL measurement at 80 kVp will be sufficient. Mammographic equipment should be measured at 30 kVp if film is used or at 50 kVp for xeroradiography.
5. Set the kVp and use a 0.10-sec exposure with sufficient mA to produce a reading of about 300 mR on the dosimeter.
6. Make one radiographic exposure and record the reading on the graph paper.
7. Proceed to make three additional exposures with 2.0, 3.0, and 4.0 mm of aluminum placed in the x-ray beam on top of the test stand. Plot the individual values for each of these exposures on the graph paper (Figure 7.19). Do not change the technique for the four exposures.
8. Draw a straight line through the three points on the graph corresponding to the exposures made with the 2.0, 3.0, and 4.0 mm of added aluminum.
9. Draw a horizontal line from the point corresponding to one-half of the original exposure (150 mR in this example) to the line drawn through the three exposure points on the graph. Draw a vertical line from that point to the lower horizontal scale and read the HVL (in mm of aluminum) off that scale. For the example shown, the HVL is 2.7 mm of aluminum (Figure 7.19).
10. Record the results in the QC room log.

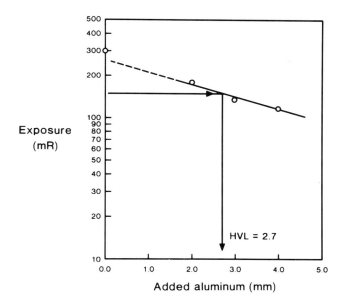

Figure 7.19. HVL data on semi-logarithmic graph paper. The graph paper used for this plot should have a logarithmic scale on the vertical axis. A solid line is drawn between the three points representing 2, 3, and 4 mm of added aluminum. This line will probably not connect with the measurement made with no added aluminum.

Procedure—Undertable Fluoroscopic Tubes

1. Raise the image intensifier tower to its maximum height, and support the dosimeter chamber halfway between the tabletop and the tower. Use fluoroscopy to place the chamber in the center of the fluoroscopic beam, and collimate so the beam will be smaller than the 6 × 6-inch (150 × 150-mm) aluminum sheets when they are placed on the tabletop in the beam. The aluminum sheets must be placed *under* the chamber when measuring the HVL on an undertable tube (Figure 7.18b).
2. Adjust the radiographic spot film device to the *manual* mode and set the kVp to 80. Adjust the mA and time to a setting that will produce a reading of about 300 mR on the dosimeter.
3. Proceed to make the four exposures (refer to Steps 6 and 7 in the overtable tube procedure above).
4. Plot the data in the same manner as for overhead tubes. [**Note:** If a manual time cannot be set on the fluoroscopic unit, the HVL can be measured as follows: manually set 80 kVp and adjust the mA so a reasonable image is obtained, then set the dosimeter to the "exposure rate" mode and operate the fluoroscope long enough to allow the mR rate reading to stabilize. The four readings obtained in this mode will be "exposure rates" rather than a given exposure value. The kVp and mA must be locked, or manual mode used, to check the HVL using the exposure rate mode.]
5. Record the results in the QC room log.

Problems and Pitfalls

1. The entire dosimeter chamber must be in the x-ray beam. When placing the sheets of aluminum in the beam, be sure that the entire beam is intercepted by the 6 × 6-inch (150 × 150-mm) sheet. Once selected, the technical factors must not be altered for the four exposures.
2. The kVp should be checked before measuring the HVL to ensure that it is within acceptance limits.
3. When measuring the HVL on mammographic equipment (at 30 kVp), place 0.25, 0.50, and 1.00 mm of aluminum in the beam for the measurements.
4. The aluminum used for HVL measurements should be type 1100 and should be located halfway between the x-ray source and the ionization chamber to assure accurate results.

Acceptance Limits

Federal and many state regulations specify minimum required HVLs at various kVp values (Table 7.1). If the HVL is measured at 80 kVp for conventional equipment and at 30 kVp for mammographic equipment, this will assure compliance. Although the minimum required HVL at 80 kVp is 2.3 mm of aluminum, we suggest that this should be increased to at least 3.0 mm of aluminum (but no more than 3.5 mm), thereby reducing the dose to the patient without affecting the radiographic quality.

Table 7.1. Half-value layers required by the Radiation Control for Health and Safety Act of 1968 (Bureau of Radiological Health, 1980)

kVp	HVL for radiographic units	HVL for dental units
30	0.3	1.5
40	0.4	1.5
49	0.5	1.5
50	1.2	1.5
60	1.3	1.5
70	1.5	1.5
71	2.1	2.1
80	2.3	2.3
90	2.5	2.5
100	2.7	2.7
110	3.0	3.0
120	3.2	3.2
130	3.5	3.5
140	3.8	3.8
150	4.1	4.1

Corrective Action

Additional aluminum filtration must be added to the x-ray tube–collimator combination by a qualified service engineer if the acceptance limits are not met. If additional aluminum is added, remeasure the HVL and record the new value in the QC room log.

8 X-RAY GENERATORS

Although the x-ray generator is the most complicated piece of conventional radiographic equipment, there is no need to be concerned with its complexity nor be "afraid" of evaluating it (see Thompson, 1978; Rausch, 1981). It is easy to make noninvasive tests that not only will tell you if the generator is performing properly, but will also assist the service engineer in quickly repairing or recalibrating the components that are not performing properly. For example, you could tell the service engineer that the generator is "shooting light," and that you have verified this by making a radiograph of the PEP. If this is all the information the engineer has, he must check the kVp, timer, and mA calibration as well as the linearity, repeatability, and phototimer accuracy. However, using the tests described in this chapter you will be able to determine the nature of problem with the generator and the engineer will be able to make the appropriate adjustments in much less time.

It is very important to verify the calibration of the x-ray generator with your test tools after the engineer has completed his work, *before he leaves,* and, most importantly, make a radiograph with the PEP to assure that the problem has been corrected. In fact, if you work closely with the engineer you can make the tests before he disconnects his test equipment so that if other adjustments are required they can be made with a minimum of additional effort.

kVp CHECK

The kVp can be checked to an accuracy of 1 or 2 kVp using a modified Ardran and Crookes cassette, which is available from most x-ray vendors and has been described in detail in the literature (Jacobson et al.,

1976). Although the test film produced with this cassette can be evaluated visually, accurate and repeatable results can only be obtained by using a densitometer to read the patches on the film.

In some cases your test results may not agree with the measurements made by the service engineer, but this is usually because of differences in the kVp waveform. The test cassette determines the effective or average kVp, whereas the test devices used by most service engineers determine the true peak of the waveform. If there is a significant amount of ripple or a small spike on the waveform the results obtained with the test cassette will be lower than those obtained by the engineer.

Electronic kVp test devices that measure the output of the x-ray tube are now available. These are much more rapid to use although they are more costly than the test cassette. If you obtain one of the electronic test devices, follow the manufacturer's instructions very closely.

EXPOSURE TIMING AND X-RAY OUTPUT WAVEFORMS

The exposure time you set on the x-ray generator must be accurate and repeatable if you wish to obtain properly exposed radiographs each time an exposure is made. Older generators using low mA values and long exposure times are not as sensitive to small variations in exposure time, but the new, high-powered generators being used with high-speed screen-film systems must be able to time exposures accurately down to a few milliseconds. The spinning top or motorized synchronous top timers are suitable under somewhat limited conditions, whereas the more sophisticated dosimeters offering timing features as well as the electronic pulse counter–timer systems offer much more flexibility.

Ideally, the x-ray output waveform should be a perfect square pulse with the leading and trailing edge rising and falling instantly (Figure 8.1a). However, this is seldom the case and makes the measurement of the x-ray exposure time quite difficult. If the voltage rises and falls slowly (Figure 8.1b), exactly where on the waveform do you measure the exposure time?

Most engineers measure the exposure time at a point that is 70% of the peak value of the waveform. Since this is measured on the *input* to the x-ray tube it is necessary to measure the output waveform at a level of about 50% of the peak value. Both the dosimeters with built-in timers and the electronic timers allow for this adjustment.

The waveform itself provides a considerable amount of information about the function of the x-ray equipment (Figure 8.2). For example, are all three phases of the generator producing the same output? Is there a high-voltage spike on the waveform indicating arcing or other problems? Is the output stable during the exposure? Many problems can be diag-

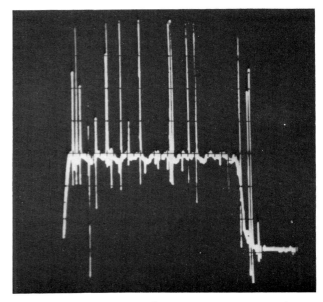

Figure 8.2a.   Excessive spikes on x-ray output waveform.

nosed from these waveforms; consequently, we feel that the waveform should be monitored as part of the QC room check. This requires the use of a solid-state detector and a storage oscilloscope. In place of the solid-state detector some dosimeters now offer, as an option, an output that provides a signal proportional to the waveform. It is important to remember that the waveform you record from the output of the x-ray tube will be different from the kVp waveform the engineer looks at, since the output waveform contains information about the kVp and mA as well as the exposure time and any effects that may result from cable capacitance (a problem encountered at low mA

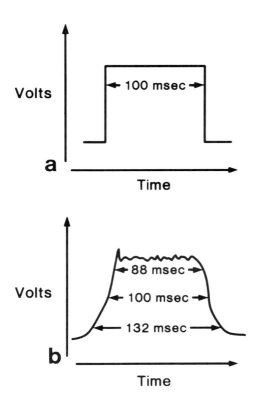

Figure 8.1.   X-ray output waveforms. (a) Schematic drawing of a "perfect" waveform, which you will never see. (b) Typical waveform that creates difficulty in measuring the exposure time.

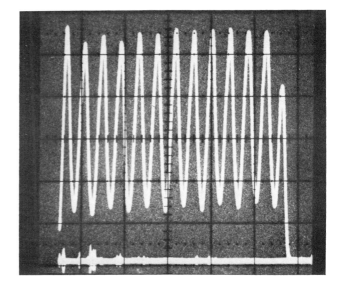

Figure 8.2b.   One of three phases missing in x-ray output waveform.

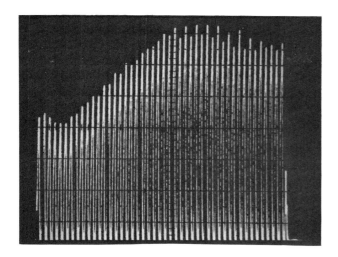

Figure 8.2c. Output waveform of a single-phase unit that is not stable with time.

values when long cable lengths are required between the generator and the x-ray tube).

A standard set of waveforms at various kVp and mA values should be recorded with a camera and placed in the QC room log, clearly labeled as to the date, kVp, mA, and exposure time as well as oscilloscope settings used. It is not necessary to photograph and record waveforms each time you evaluate the room, but the images of the waveforms on the storage oscilloscope should be compared to the standard set in the QC room log to assure that no changes have occurred.

The x-ray output waveforms have been one of the most valuable tests we have used in troubleshooting x-ray equipment problems. They have provided valuable insight to both our QC technologists and our service engineers concerning problems that could not have been diagnosed in any other way. Consequently, we feel that the evaluation of the output waveforms is an essential part of any quality control program.

mR/mAs

The output of an x-ray tube varies with kVp, mA, and exposure time, so in order to better compare the output and reduce the number of variables in the exposure measurement it is convenient to determine the mR/mAs—the exposure output per mAs input to the tube. This can be measured in two locations: in air (above the PEP), or under the phantom. Many service engineers prefer to determine the mR/mAs in air since the measurements are much more sensitive to small changes in the x-ray tube output (the phantom will filter out a significant proportion of the soft x-ray out-

put). However, we have adopted as our standard the measurement of the mR/mAs under the phantom since this more closely represents the radiation as seen by the screen-film combination.

Regardless of where the mR/mAs is determined, it provides a quick check on the consistency of the output of the x-ray system. Only a dosimeter and phantom are required to determine if the output of the x-ray tube is the same as it-was when the room was last evaluated. However, the mR/mAs does *not* provide specific information concerning any changes in output that may have occurred, such as changes in the kVp, mA, or timer calibration, although inferences may be made. It does provide a quick way to evaluate the linearity and repeatability of the generator and provides an additional tool for the QC technologist to use in evaluating the performance of the x-ray systems in general.

In quality control, we do have *noninvasive* methods to determine the exposure timer accuracy and the accuracy of the kVp calibration, but we do not have a simple and accurate way to check the mA calibration of a generator. However, by using mR/mAs measurements, along with exposure time and kVp measurements, you can make some assumptions, or inferences, about the mA calibration. If an mA station appears to be providing an output, as measured in terms of the mR/mAs, that is different than that of the neighboring mA stations, and the exposure time and kVp measurements are within acceptance limits, then you may assume that the calibration of that particular mA station may be incorrect.

STUDY OF EFFECTS OF CHANGES ON mR/mAs

A series of measurements were made under a PEP to evaluate the effect of various changes on the mR/mAs values. In addition, it was necessary to determine the correlation between changes in the mR/mAs values and our acceptance limits for film density variation so that we could determine the amount of variation in mR/mAs that would be acceptable in the diagnostic setting. All measurements for this series were carried out on the same three-phase generator in cooperation with our service engineers using a Machlette Dynalyzer to determine the actual kVp, mA, and exposure time for each exposure.

First we wanted to determine the effect of added filtration on the mR/mAs values. The collimator was removed and 1, 2, 4, and 6 mm of type 1100 aluminum were added to the x-ray tube port, with measurements being made both under the phantom and in air. The collimator was then replaced and additional measurements made adding 1 and 2 mm of type 1100 aluminum (in addition to the inherent filtration of the collimator). All measurements were made at 80 kVp dialed with Dynalyzer readings ranging from 78.9 to 81.2 kVp.

As expected, the mR/mAs measurements made under the phantom were less sensitive to changes in the filtration of the x-ray beam than those made in air (Figures 8.3 and 8.4). In addition, it is apparent that the data on both figures are consistent for measurements made with and without the collimator in place. The in-air mR/mAs values dropped 36% with the addition of 2 mm of aluminum (with 2 mm already in the beam), whereas the change for measurements under the phantom was only 19%.

Another series of measurements compared the changes in mR/mAs in air and under the phantom with changes in kVp. Figures 8.5 and 8.6 show that measurements made under the phantom are more sensitive to changes in kVp than those made in air. For example, a change of 3–4 kVp is required to obtain a 10% change in mR/mAs as measured in air, whereas a change of only 2 kVp will produce the same change in mR/mAs values as measured under the phantom. The majority of photons transmitted through the phantom are higher energy, and it appears as if these have a predominate effect on the measurements.

In the final series, we wanted to determine the relationship between changes in mR/mAs measured through the phantom and film density (Figure 8.7). A variation of ±10% in mR/mAs readings produced a change in density of ±0.12, a level that we feel is acceptable in the clinical setting. When an mR/mAs measurement is made under the phantom, all technical factors are being considered, including kVp, mA, and time. Consequently, if you assume that the error

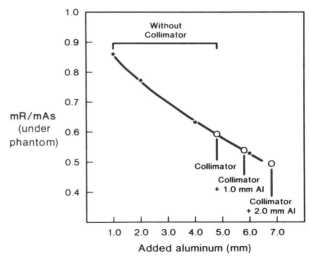

Figure 8.4. mR/mAs as a function of added aluminum filtration (with exposures measured under the PEP).

in output due to calibration is equally divided among all three factors, then a change of ±6% would be allowed in each. However, we are still interested in the total change in output, regardless of how the change is apportioned among the factors—if we see more than 10% variation in x-ray output under the phantom, it is time for generator calibration.

USE OF mR/mAs MEASUREMENTS

Although mR/mAs measurements are the only method we can use to infer mA calibration, the mR/mAs measurements can be used in other ways. For example, we can determine:

Repeatability—the ability of the generator to reproduce the same exposure for the same technique.

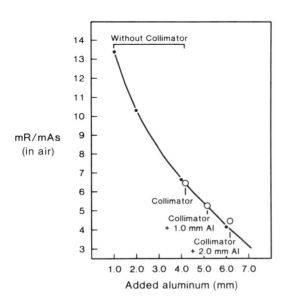

Figure 8.3. mR/mAs as a function of added aluminum filtration (with exposures measured in air).

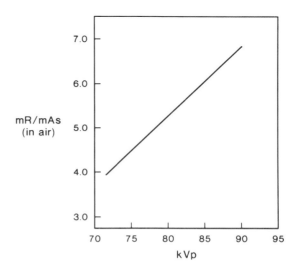

Figure 8.5. mR/mAs as a function of kVp (with exposures measured in air).

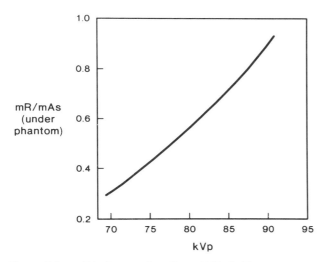

Figure 8.6. mR/mAs as a function of kVp (with exposures measured under the PEP).

Linearity—similar generator output for the same kVp and mAs regardless of the mA station used.

Room-to-Room Consistency—helps to assure that x-ray rooms using similar generators and tubes produce the same output so that the same technique charts may be used.

As an example of the room-to-room consistency, consider our 10-room general radiographic section. These rooms have the same type of generators and x-ray tubes. All 10 rooms have the same technique charts, which results from the fact that the mR/mAs output (at 80 kVp) for each room is within ±7%, which is better than our ±10% acceptance limit. Phantom film densities, measured over a 2-week period, showed density variations of ±0.14 (at a density of 1.0 above the base-plus-fog). This density

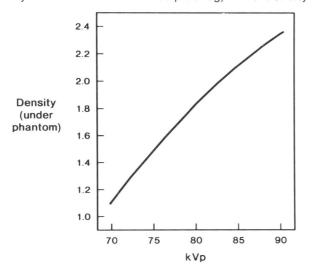

Figure 8.7. Film density for films exposed through the PEP as a function of kVp.

spread is wider than we would like to see, but it does include all sources of variation, such as film processing (±0.10), manufacturing film speed variations (±0.10), and all of the inherent variations in the generators. It must be noted here that variations of this magnitude in film density are acceptable to our radiologists for clinical purposes. Another point worth noting is that it is necessary to limit the variation of each component of the imaging process to ±0.10 in density since, in practice, all of the variables may add together, resulting in larger variations in the total system than are seen in any of the individual components.

Comparing mR/mAs measurements for equipment by different manufacturers is a rather difficult problem. In general, we have found similar results for all single-phase generators, all three-phase, six-pulse generators, and all three-phase, twelve-pulse generators, but there are some exceptions. The use of smoothing circuits by some manufacturers, or capacitive smoothing resulting from long, high-voltage cable lengths (especially at low mA values) will change the mR/mAs measurements. In general, we have seen slightly higher mR/mAs measurements with American-made equipment as compared to European equipment, but this is a general statement, and we have not made measurements on all of the various American or European equipment. Three-phase, six-pulse generators will have mR/mAs outputs less than three-phase, twelve-pulse generators. This again is related to the amount of ripple in the x-ray waveform.

Capacitor discharge equipment will have different mR/mAs measurements depending on the mAs used. This is because the kVp is continuously dropping during the exposure with this type of equipment. Capacitor discharge units, using a 1-microfarad capacitor, will drop 1 kVp for every 1 mAs used for exposure. For example, if 80 kVp is set on a capacitor discharge unit, the actual kilovoltage will be 80 kVp at the beginning of the exposure but will drop to 70 kVp at the end of a 10-mAs exposure.

It becomes obvious that mR/mAs measurements can be valuable in comparing equipment. However, you must only compare such measurements on similar equipment and never expect the mR/mAs measurements to be the same on single-phase, three-phase six-pulse, three-phase twelve-pulse, and capacitor discharge generators.

The x-ray output may also vary for the same generator as the x-ray tube ages. This usually results from the surface of the anode becoming roughened with use, which tends to reduce the amount of radiation emitted by the tube. Contrary to popular opinion, this decrease in output is usually not due to increased deposition of tungsten in the x-ray tube, since the HVL does not change and the thickness of the tungsten layer deposited is insignificant relative to the energy of the x-rays used in diagnostic radiology. For newly installed x-ray tubes, the mR/mAs measurements may be higher at first, dropping slightly (a few percent) to a stable level in a short period of time. Slight decreases will then become apparent, but for the most part, these changes are minor and do not affect the density of the films produced. However, for older tubes, we have found mR/mAs measurements 20–25% below normal, even after repeated efforts by our service engineers to assure proper generator calibration. Replacement of the x-ray tube will normally resolve this problem. If you experience similar problems, it would be valuable to make your mR/mAs measurements along with your service engineer to assure that the generator calibration is correct while the measurements are being made. This way you can be assured that the output of the x-ray tube is at fault, and, considering the cost of replacing x-ray tubes, it is certainly worth the extra effort!

Off-focus radiation, or extra-focal radiation, will also affect the mR/mAs measurements. It has been shown that the off-focus radiation can be as much as 25% of the total radiation in the x-ray beam (Rao, 1966; Weaver et al., 1975; Thomas et al., 1981). In addition, image degradation can be noted in terms of decreased contrast and decreased resolution due to off-focus radiation. The amount of off-focus radiation can vary from tube to tube for the same brand and model of tube and with different models of collimators.

Once sufficient data have been collected, mR/mAs measurements are very useful for troubleshooting purposes. You can use mR/mAs measurements to quickly confirm or rule out generator miscalibration or component failure by comparing the data with data collected during past QC room checks for the specific unit in question.

mR/mAs measurements can be misleading in some instances. For example, it is possible for the kVp and mA calibrations to drift in opposite directions and yield an mR/mAs measurement that is within the acceptance limits. Therefore, in troubleshooting a room it is reasonable to check the kVp at one station in question and also to do a quick timer-check to verify your conclusions before calling a service engineer.

mR/mAs MEASUREMENT ACCURACY

In order to collect reliable mR/mAs measurement data, great care must be taken to design a procedure that is easily reproduced. (It is then necessary to strictly follow that procedure each time the measurements are made.) All factors, such as distance, control of backscatter, and x-ray field size, must be specified and the same factors used each time. In addition, it is very important to use the same method of setting the kVp, mA, and exposure time, i.e., these must be dialed in the same manner each time. With care and consistency, the mR/mAs measurements will provide valuable data for a QC program, but *care* and *consistency* are essential in order to minimize potential errors that will lead to erroneous data.

Our procedure for determining mR/mAs starts with the use of a 36-inch (90-cm) source-to-tabletop distance. This distance is measured with a tape measure each time, rather than relying on the SID indicator of the tube crane. If the mark indicating the position of the focal spot in the x-ray tube housing is not visible, we assume the focal spot is located 1 inch (2.5 cm) up from the bottom edge of the housing end cap. Even if the focal spot is not located at this point, and we have no way of knowing with many tubes, the measurements are done the same way each time for consistency. The only time we deviate from this procedure is when we are dealing with an x-ray tube with a fixed SID, and, for comparative purposes, we can correct for this difference using the inverse square law.

Our mR/mAs measurements are made with the dosimeter chamber under the phantom and the x-ray field size set so that the entire 12 × 12-inch (30 × 30-cm) area of the PEP is irradiated. If it is not possible to cover the entire phantom, the mR/mAs measurement data cannot be used for comparison purposes with measurements made when the entire phantom is irradiated, since the amount of scattered radiation measured by the ionization chamber will be different.

To control backscatter, a 12 × 12-inch (30 × 30-cm) sheet of 1/8-inch (3-mm) thick lead is placed under the phantom and ionization chamber. This assures that differences in tabletop construction and supporting structures, as well as Bucky trays, do not produce different amounts of backscatter.

kVp, mA, and exposure time are always selected in a consistent manner. Normally, mA selection with push buttons should not create problems. However, kVp and time selection with dials (continuously variable scales) and even kVp selection with push buttons may not be repeatable unless you approach the setting of interest in the same manner each time. For example, if we are going to set 80 kVp on the generator control panel, first 70 kVp is set, whether using a dial or push button–type selector. Next, the selector is *slowly* moved to 80 kVp, with care taken not to pass the 80 kVp point on the selector. If the kVp selection is made with push buttons, the kVp should be set first at a value of at least 10 kVp below the kVp desired and then increased in 1-kVp steps until the desired kVp is reached. This technique should be used not only for mR/mAs measurements but for all measurements and for clinical radiography.

Before undertaking mR/mAs measurements for our QC program, we carried out several tests to determine the accuracy of these data. In order to determine the repeatability of the dosimeter, a sequence of six sets of exposures were made, with three individual exposures in each set. These were made at 30-minute intervals without moving any of the components and without changing the technical factors. The variation in exposure measurement was found to be ±1.4% (2 standard deviations). This variability includes some generator variation over time, but the variation in each set of three exposures was minimal (less than a fraction of a percent).

To determine the repeatability of measurements due to changes in the equipment setup, one individual made measurements once a day for 5 days, making one three-exposure set of measurements each day with the same generator, technical factors, and measurement equipment. This resulted in mR/mAs measurement variability of ±5.6% (2 standard deviations).

In order to determine the amount of variability introduced by different individuals, the four authors, using the same procedure, made six sets of three individual exposures each within 1 hour, taking down the complete equipment setup and changing the technical factors each time. The mR/mAs measurement variation was found to be ±2.0%, ±2.3%, ±3.6%, and ±8.8% for each individual's measurements. The variation of all of the mR/mAs measurements made by the four individuals in 2 days was ±15.6% (2 standard deviations).

As you can see from these data, the variability of the particular instrumentation used to make the measurements is minimal. The short-term setup variabilities for each of the four authors (six sets of exposures in 1 hour) show the importance of extreme care in the setup procedure. The ±2.0 to ±3.6% errors are probably acceptable, but the ±8.8% error is unacceptable considering our acceptance limits of ±10%. The long-term variability of 5.6% (5 sets of measurements in 5 days by one person) probably includes some generator variation, but again it points to the necessity for extreme care in the setup procedures. It also provides some assurance that the data from one visit to the next are accurate to within approximately ±6%. However, these data do support the necessity of repeating the measurements, including the complete setup procedure, if the data are at all in question.

The variability of ±15.6% in mR/mAs measurements among the four authors does indicate that having one individual making the measurements is ideal. Unfortunately this is not always possible, but for maximum accuracy and efficiency a minimum number of well-trained individuals should be making the measurements.

LINEARITY AND REPEATABILITY

Many times a technologist may wish to reduce the exposure time (e.g., for small, uncooperative children or older patients that cannot hold their breath) and must increase the mA proportionally in order to do so. Although the same mAs may be selected, the output of the tube may be different and the resultant radiograph is less than satisfactory. This is especially true when the highest mA stations are used. The linearity test determines the output of the x-ray tube, using mR/mAs, for various mA and timer station combinations. Unless the output is maintained within close tolerances, it will not be possible to interchange mA and time combinations, even at the same mAs, and produce consistent quality radiographs.

The Bureau of Radiological Health, through federal regulations, requires that all new x-ray equipment maintain linearity of ±10% from mA station to mA station. This means that if your x-ray generator has six mA stations it would be possible to have linearity of ±50% and still meet the federal requirements. We have found that the linearity can be maintained to ±10% over the entire working range of the generator (e.g., from 100 to 600 mA) regardless of the number of mA stations, not only from station to station. In fact, we have found that it is necessary to maintain the linearity to this tighter standard in order to eliminate problems and repeat radiographs as the technologists change from one mA station to another.

kVp and linearity are only part of the problems in x-ray generator calibration. If the generator is not repeatable then optimal kVp calibration and linearity will be of little value. When we speak of repeatability we do not mean that the output of the tube is the same if you make three exposures in a row at the same technique—most generators can do this without much difficulty. However, a generator must be repeatable within reasonable limits every time you change technique and then come back to the same kVp, mA, and exposure time. This especially becomes a problem as generators age and the mechanical components begin to wear.

You may find that with some older, as well as some newer, generators you may have to approach the kVp setting you desire from the same direction each time and slowly; e.g., if you want to obtain 80 kVp you may have to dial down to 70 kVp first and approach 80 kVp slowly. In many generators, this problem cannot be corrected, but if you advise the technologists of this problem they can set the techniques properly each time and obtain consistency in their radiographs.

With a proper evaluation of the x-ray generators you can be assured that they are calibrated properly and you will be better able to diagnose problems that may previously have gone uncorrected. In addition, some problems that may not be easily or inexpensively corrected (a new generator may be the only solution) can be identified and it may be possible to work around those problem areas.

PHOTOTIMER EVALUATION

Phototimers are considered by many to be one of the best innovations in radiography, whereas many others consider them the component that causes the most difficulty. With phototimers patient positioning becomes more critical since a slight mispositioning, which may be acceptable diagnostically, can result in a significant change in the exposure of the radiograph. Although they have their problems, phototimers are here to stay.

The evaluation of phototimers must include the consideration of many factors. What is the backup time, i.e., what is the maximum time the system will allow before terminating the exposure? If the backup time is too short you will produce radiographs that are too light on heavier patients. If the backup time is too long you may be unnecessarily exposing a patient if, for example, the kVp is set too low. What is the shortest exposure that the phototimer can accurately time? With high-mA generators and new high-speed screen-film systems the phototimers must work in the range of milliseconds accurately and repeatably.

Can the phototimer be properly compensated for the screen-film combination you are using in your department? Many systems will show excessive changes in density over the working kVp ranges since the sensitivity of the intensifying screens to radiation is not the same as that of the detectors used in the phototimers.

In general, the new phototimers available today can perform quite adequately, but it is still essential to evaluate them on a regular basis. In addition to being concerned about kVp, mA, and conventional timer

calibration when problems arise, you must also consider the possibility that the phototimer itself is not functioning properly. It is also necessary to measure the phototimed exposure to the PEP regularly since if the kVp drifts you can still produce adequate radiographs (the phototimer will compensate for changes in the x-ray tube output), but the exposure to the patient will increase significantly if the kVp decreases and the contrast will become degraded if the kVp increases.

Phototimers may make the staff technologists' job easier but for the QC technologist, phototimers mean more work, more measurements, and more potential problems, all of which can be handled following the procedures outlined in this chapter.

MAMMOGRAPHY AND XERORADIOGRAPHY

Mammography and xeroradiography are two areas that require particularly close attention for several reasons. First of all, these procedures do deliver a relatively high dose to a radiation-sensitive organ. Second, the imaging requirements are probably the most demanding in diagnostic imaging since both minute particles of calcium and low-contrast masses must be faithfully reproduced. Finally, there has been an extensive amount of public concern over mammography and xeroradiography and these patients tend to question the radiologist and technologist concerning the exposure from this exam as well as the necessity for it.

Since radiographs are made with extremely low energy radiation, it is essential to use the appropriate instrumentation. Dosimeter chambers designed for conventional radiography will filter out much of the softer radiation used in mammography and xeroradiography, giving a false, low reading. Likewise, specially designed phantoms must be used to provide information about the ability of the system to produce consistent, high-quality mammograms and xeroradiograms.

TECHNIQUE SELECTION FOR GENERATOR QUALITY CONTROL

All techniques selected for the purpose of evaluating the generator, whether for acceptance or for QC testing, should be those typically used in the clinical setting. Most manufacturers state broad acceptance limits for kVp and mA since they are expected to maintain those limits over the entire range of the generator. Consequently, by selecting the working range appropriately, it is possible to maintain the generator calibration to much tighter standards than those specified by the manufacturer. For example, our institution maintains kVp calibration to better than ± 2 kVp between 60 and 120 kVp, as compared to manufacturers' specifications that sometimes run as wide as ± 5% plus 2 kVp (i.e., ± 7 kVp at 100 kVp).

The mA stations that should be evaluated as part of the QC program should include those used clinically plus one station on either side. For example, if a room is only used at 200 and 400 mA, then 100, 200, 400, and 600 mA should be evaluated.

kVp, in most instances, should be evaluated at 60, 80, 100, and 120 kVp, although the 120-kVp station may be ignored if 100 kVp is never exceeded on the technique chart. Likewise, the mR/mAs should be evaluated at the same kVp and mA values. For units used for mammography, the measurements should be made at the low kVp values of interest clinically. Most importantly, kVp, mA, and exposure time should be evaluated over a *range* of values that encompass the factors used clinically.

The linearity should be determined at the kVp where the generator is most heavily used. For exam-ple, on a generator used in general radiography, a kVp range of 60 to 100 kVp may be used. The majority of the work will be done at approximately 80 kVp so the linearity should be evaluated at this level. However, if the generator is also heavily used at lower or higher kVp values, the linearity should be checked in these areas as well.

It is not necessary that each of the technique combinations used produce the same mAs for the mR/mAs evaluation. In many instances, one or more of the combinations will produce a different mAs, but by dividing the exposure (in mR) by the actual mAs, the resultant mR/mAs for various combinations can readily be compared.

The mAs values to be evaluated (as well as the mA stations) should be typical of the operating range in the particular room. For example, if the room typically operates from 10 to 100 mAs, then 50 to 60 mAs should be used for measurements.

PROCEDURES

8.1 kVp CHECK

Purpose

To assure that the x-ray generator is producing the kVp as indicated on the control panel.

Equipment Needed

1. kVp cassette, 8 × 10-inch (20 × 25-cm) film
2. Two sheets of lead [4 × 9-inch (10 × 23-cm) and 9 × 9-inch (23 × 23-cm)]
3. Densitometer

Procedure

1. Place the kVp cassette on the x-ray table with the long axis of the cassette parallel to the anode-cathode axis of the x-ray tube. Center the x-ray tube to the cassette using a 36-inch (90-cm) source-to-tabletop distance (Figure 8.8).
2. Set the generator to the mA at which the kVp values will be checked.

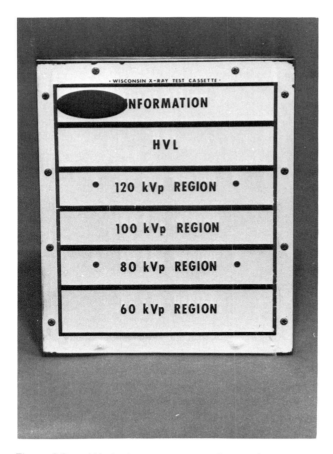

Figure 8.8a. kVp test cassette, sometimes referred to as the modified Ardran and Crookes cassette. The HVL region of the cassette is unreliable and should not be used for HVL measurements (the HVL should be measured using a dosimeter and aluminum filters, see pages 90–94).

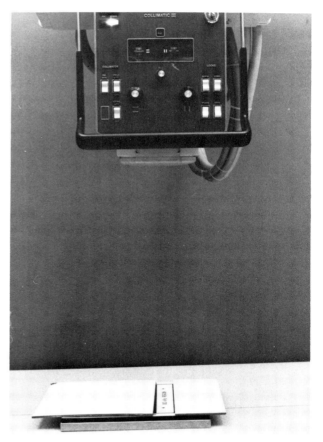

Figure 8.8b. kVp check test setup. Although it may be possible to collimate to the kVp region of interest on the cassette, 1/8-inch (3-mm) of lead should be used to cover the remainder of the areas.

3. Make four radiographic exposures on the appropriate area of the cassette at 60, 80, 100, and 120 kVp. Adjust the time (not the mA) so that a density of about 1.0 (no less than 0.50 nor more than 1.50) is produced on the film in the test region. Be sure to place lead sheets on the cassette to block out the regions of the cassette that are not being exposed (Figure 8.8b).

Approximate mAs techniques*

kVp	Single phase	Three phase
60	500	400
80	75	40
100	15	10
120	12	8

*Using Kodak XL film and a 36-inch (90-cm) SID

4. If the kVp is checked at more than one mA station, expose lead numbers indicating the mA used for the exposures on the information region of the cassette and then process the film.

5. Each kVp region on the film contains two columns of dots (Figure 8.9). Using the densitometer, find a density in the left column that matches the density in the right column. The density of the dots in the right column will generally be uniform; these are referred to as reference dots. The dots in the left column will show a density gradient. A density "match" should occur at one of the 10 steps. If an exact density match is not found, you must interpolate between the steps for best accuracy. For example:

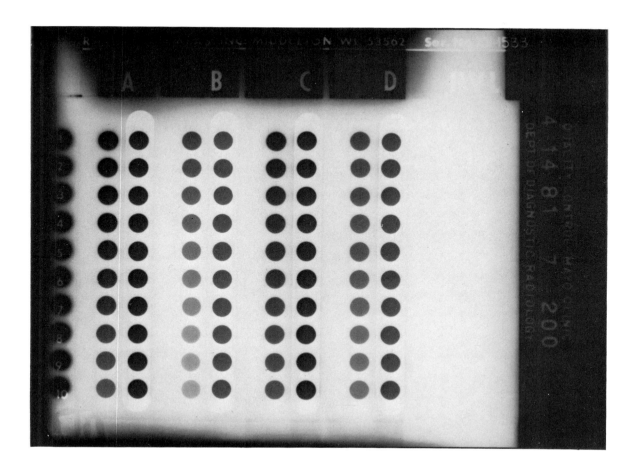

Figure 8.9.   kVp check test results. The densities must be in adjacent patches using a densitometer; visual matching will not suffice. It is also necessary to interpolate to determine matches if the match falls between two specific density patches.

	Density of step	Density of reference dot
Step 5	1.10	1.05
Step 6	1.03	1.05

$$\text{Match Step} = 5 + \left[\frac{1.10 - 1.05}{1.10 - 1.03}\right] = 5 + \frac{.05}{.07} = 5.7$$

6. After the match step has been determined for each of the kVp regions, refer to the calibration charts that the manufacturer provides with each cassette to determine the kVp (Figure 8.10). [**Note:** There is a separate chart for each kVp region and there is a separate line on each chart for single- and for three-phase generators.] If, for example, the image in Figure 8.9 from the 60 kVp region of the cassette was obtained from a three-phase generator and the match occurred at step 5.7, then the kVp would be 59.
7. Record the results in the QC room log.
8. To ensure that the kVp compensation is working properly, the kVp should be measured at the minimum, middle, and maximum mA stations *normally used* on the generator.

Problems and Pitfalls

1. The HVL should always be measured after assuring that the kVp is correct.
2. The major cause of kVp variation is calibration. Some generators maintain their calibration well and others drift constantly. It is important to note that a change in kVp may not always show as a change in film density because changes in the mA will often compensate for the change in kVp.
3. Since the kVp affects the radiographic contrast, it must be checked to assure that it is within acceptance limits.
4. Other major causes of variations in kVp are line voltage drops and electrical component failure.
5. On some generators, the kVp may measure 5-8 kVp low at high mA settings. This results from the higher percentage of ripple that is present at high mA stations plus, possibly, poor compensation. Since the cassette averages the tube output, lower kVp readings may be obtained from the cassette.

Acceptance Limits

The kVp on a properly calibrated generator can be maintained within ± 2 kVp. A variation of more than ± 5 kVp requires calibration by a qualified service engineer.

Corrective Action

A qualified service engineer should recalibrate the generator if it does not meet the acceptance limits. Be sure to measure the kVp with the cassette after calibration and *before* the service engineer leaves.

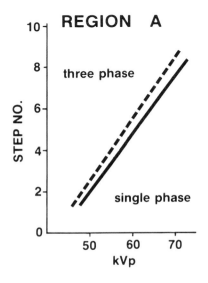

Figure 8.10.   Typical kVp test cassette calibration curve.

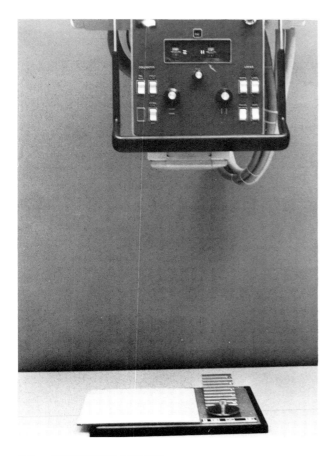

Figure 8.11. Exposure timing test setup for manual spinning top. This spinning top is incorporated into a step wedge, but some are available without the wedge.

8.2. EXPOSURE TIMING

Purpose

To assure that the x-ray generator is producing the exposure time as set on the control panel.

Equipment Needed

1. One of the following: manual spinning top, motorized synchronous top (also known as the mAs-timer test tool), a dosimeter with a timer readout, or timer–pulse counter device
2. Screen-film cassette (for spinning and synchronous tops)

Procedure—Manual Spinning Top (Single-Phase Units Only)

1. Determine the exposure needed to produce a radiograph in which the dots produced from the hole in the spinning top will be visible.
2. Place the top on a cassette and manually start it spinning (Figure 8.11). (The exposure is made while the top is spinning.)
3. Make radiographs of the spinning top at $1/5$, $1/10$, $1/20$, and $1/30$ sec using the same mA. Other times can also be checked as long as the dots do not overlap.
4. Process the films.
5. On each radiograph, count the dots (Figure 8.12) and determine the exposure time by dividing the number of dots by 120 if the generator is full-wave rectified or by 60 if the generator is half-wave or self-rectified. For example:

<table>
<tr><td>Full-Wave Rectification</td><td>Half-Wave or Self-Rectification</td></tr>
<tr><td>$\dfrac{12 \text{ dots}}{120} = 0.10 \text{ second}$</td><td>$\dfrac{6 \text{ dots}}{60} = 0.10 \text{ second}$</td></tr>
</table>

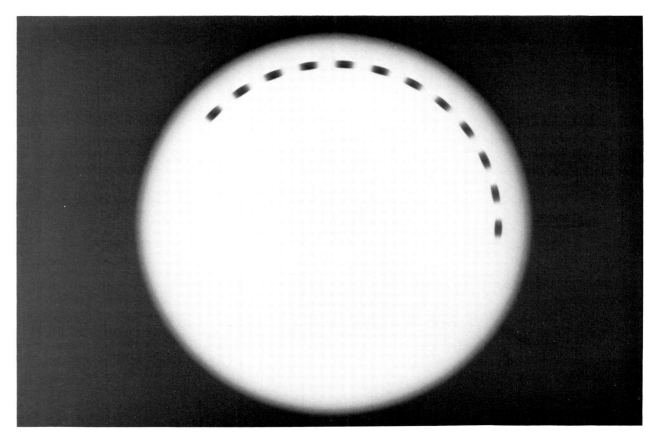

Figure 8.12.   Exposure timing results for manual spinning top. The number of pulses, or dark spots, is counted to determine the exposure.

[***Note:***   Be sure you know what type of rectification is used. Half-wave or self-rectification produces 60 dots (pulses) per second and full-wave produces 120 per second.]
6.   Record the results in the QC room log.

Procedure—Motorized Synchronous Top (for Single-and Three-Phase Units)

The motorized synchronous top functions similarly to the manual spinning top with the exception that it is turned using a synchronous electric motor. The device also contains a copper step-wedge for determining mAs reciprocity.

1.   Place the unit on one half of an 8 × 10-inch (20 × 25-cm) cassette and plug the timer in (Figure 8.13). Be sure to place lead on the other half of the cassette so that side can be used for a second exposure. [Three images of the tool can be made on a 10 × 12-inch (25 × 30-cm) cassette.]
2.   Determine the exposure needed to produce a radiograph of acceptable density.
3.   Make four exposures using the same mAs, one at each of the following times: $1/5$, $1/10$, $1/20$, and $1/30$ sec.
4.   Process the films.
5.   Using the protractor provided, measure the length of the trace made on the film for each of the exposures to determine the exposure time (Figure 8.14). The measured exposure time should be within the acceptance lines shown on the protractor. If exposure times other than the above are checked, measure the angle of the trace using the section of the protractor indicating exposure time. (Generator timers that are in fractions can be converted to milliseconds by dividing the numerator by the denominator as follows: $3/20$ second = 0.150 seconds = 150 milliseconds.)
6.   Record the results in the QC room log.

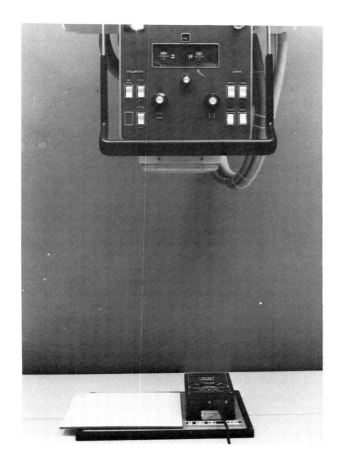

Figure 8.13.   Exposure timing test setup for motorized synchronous top.

Procedure—Dosimeter or Timer Device (for Single- and Three-Phase Units)

Many of the currently available dosimeters have an added feature that allows the measurement of exposure times. The dosimeter or timing device is the most accurate method of determining exposure times since the actual length of time that the radiation is emitted from the x-ray tube is measured. In addition, this method of measuring exposure times is faster since radiographs are not required. On some devices different threshold levels can be set, allowing exposure times to be measured at any point across the output waveform.

1. Place the dosimeter or timing device on the x-ray table on top of a sheet of lead (Figure 8.15).
2. Center the x-ray beam and collimate to the chamber.
3. Set any exposure time on the generator and make an exposure.
4. Record the results in the QC room log.

Problems and Pitfalls

1. The manual spinning top cannot be used on three-phase generators. Neither the manual nor the electric spinning tops will measure long exposure times (greater than ½ sec). When using a dosimeter or electronic timing device, always set the threshold to the same level each time the exposure times are checked. (We recommend that the threshold be set at the 50% level.) It is not necessary to check all the exposure times on the generator for a routine QC check. Four timer stations, two short and two long, should be sufficient to ensure that the generator timer is working correctly.
2. For generators that use a premagnetization circuit, the low-energy radiation produced may or may not fall below the 50% level. If the exposure time is 12–15 msec longer than expected, increase the threshold level to 80% and repeat the measurement. At this point, the time should drop to near the expected time. In addition to the premagnetization pulse, other abnormalities in the x-ray waveform may affect the time measurements.

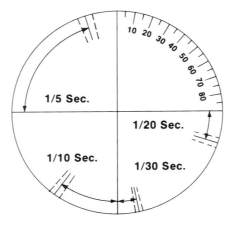

TIMER PROTRACTOR

Figure 8.14a. Timer protractor used to determine actual exposure timing test results for motorized synchronous top. This device can be used for both single-and three-phase generators. The dotted lines represent the minimum and maximum limits for the exposure time.

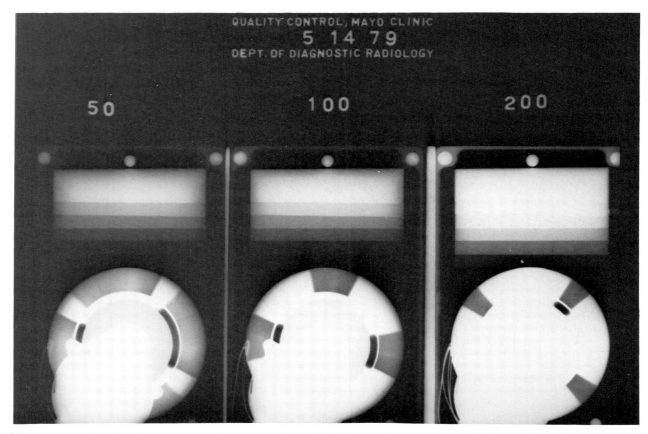

Figure 8.14b. A typical film produced at exposure times of $^1/_5$, $^1/_{10}$, and $^1/_{20}$ second and 50, 100, and 200 mA, respectively. Note that the mAs is constant but the step wedge exposure at the 200 mA station is significantly lighter than the other two. If the exposure time is correct (according to the protractor), this would suggest that the mA calibration is not correct, or that the compensation circuit is not operating properly.

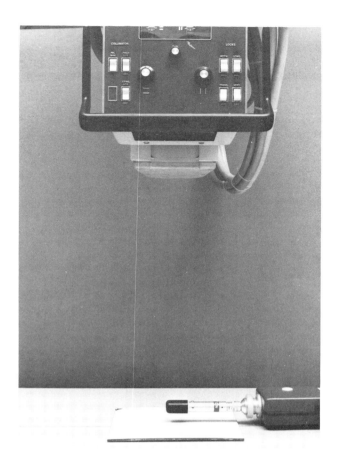

Figure 8.15. Exposure timing test setup for dosimeter or timing device. The ionization chamber of a direct readout dosimeter with the timing function or the timing device should be placed on a sheet of lead. In addition, it is essential to use only the conventional small ionization chamber since larger chambers often exhibit extreme capacitive effects, giving incorrect exposure times.

Acceptance Limits

For single-phase generators using the manual spinning top, we suggest the following:

Time	Pulse
$1/5$ sec	24 = ± 1 dot
$1/10$ sec	12 = ± 1 dot
$1/20$ sec	6 = ± 0 dots
$1/30$ sec	4 = ± 0 dots

When using the motorized spinning top the time should fall within the lines drawn on the protractor for the $1/5$, $1/10$, $1/20$, and $1/30$ time stations. For times other than these the acceptance limit should be ± 5%. The ± 5% acceptance limit is also used for the dosimeter or timing device, except in single-phase equipment where each x-ray pulse is equal to 8.4 msec. As an example, at $1/10$ sec, or 100 msec on single-phase equipment 5% will equal 5 msec, but most timers cannot terminate during an x-ray pulse. All times should be within ± 5% of that indicated on the generator.

Corrective Action

A qualified service engineer should be called to recalibrate the timer stations on the generator if it does not meet the acceptance limits. Be sure to check the timer after each calibration and *before* the service engineer leaves.

8.3. X-RAY WAVEFORM MONITORING

Purpose

To evaluate the actual output waveform from an x-ray generator–tube combination to determine if problems exist.

Equipment Needed

1. Storage oscilloscope
2. X-ray detector such as a solid-state detector that can provide a voltage output proportional to the x-ray flux, a photodiode intensifying screen combination, or a dosimeter that has an analog waveform output capability
3. Oscilloscope camera and Polaroid film

Procedure

1. Place the x-ray detector about 50 cm from the x-ray source and in the direct beam, but not in a position where it would interfere with test procedures (Figure 8.16).
2. Connect the detector to the oscilloscope with the BNC connectors and a coaxial cable.
3. Set the trigger levels so that the oscilloscope triggers on the leading edge of the x-ray waveform and not on electronic noise before this (i.e., noise caused by the contactors from the stator motor, etc.).
4. Set up the storage oscilloscopes so that the waveform covers most of the vertical portion of the screen (by varying the voltage per division control) and horizontally by varying the time per division control.
5. Visually monitor every exposure measurement you make during your check of the room.
6. Photographically record any waveforms that do not appear normal. Be sure to record all pertinent information on these photographs, including the oscilloscope settings, the technique that produced the waveform, and any other data that you think may be helpful to the service engineer in isolating the problem.
7. Watch for (Figure 8.17):
   a. Three-phase equipment that has an output that looks similar to single-phase equipment (one or two phases may be missing; Figure 8.17c).
   b. Spikes or valleys in the waveform that are more than a few percent higher or lower than the waveform itself (Figure 8.17d).
   c. Waveforms that appear considerably different, for whatever reason, from the other waveforms that the machine produces.
   d. Waveforms with excessive ripple. Single-phase equipment should have peak heights that are very close to each other. Three-phase equipment should have a minimum amount of variation between the peaks and valleys in the waveform. The percentage of ripple can be determined by measuring the distance of the peaks of the waveform from the baseline (the maximum height) and the distance of the valleys of the

Figure 8.16a. X-ray waveform monitoring test setup. The detector is a small box containing solid-state detectors with its output passing through the BNC connector.

Figure 8.16b. The detector should be placed about 50 cm from the x-ray source to avoid saturation of the detector. We place the detector on top of the PEP and monitor waveforms during all exposures made with the PEP.

waveform from the baseline (the minimum height) and dividing by the average waveform height using the following formula:

$$\frac{\text{Maximum Height} - \text{Minimum Height}}{\left(\dfrac{\text{Maximum Height} + \text{Minimum Height}}{2}\right)} \times 100\% = \% \text{ ripple}$$

For example, if we assume that the maximum height measured is 38 mm and the minimum height is 32 mm, then we obtain

$$\frac{38 - 32}{\left(\dfrac{38 + 32}{2}\right)} \times 100\% = 17\%$$

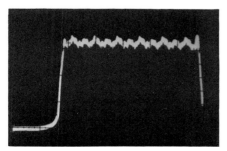

Figure 8.17a. Normal three-phase x-ray output waveform.

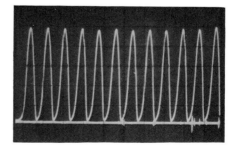

Figure 8.17b. Normal single-phase x-ray output waveform

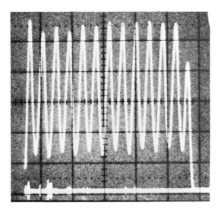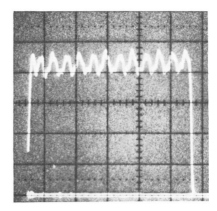

Figure 8.17c. Three-phase waveform with one phase missing *(left)* and after service *(right)*.

8. Mount the pictures of the baseline and aberrant waveforms in the QC room log along with all of the data concerning how they were produced.

Problems and Pitfalls

1. You may have difficulty in setting the trigger levels of the oscilloscope so that the scope triggers on the leading edge of the waveform. Ask the representative from the firm that you purchased the scope from to assist you or ask your x-ray equipment service engineer for assistance.
2. Most detectors that are available today are not sensitive enough to evaluate fluoroscopic equipment.

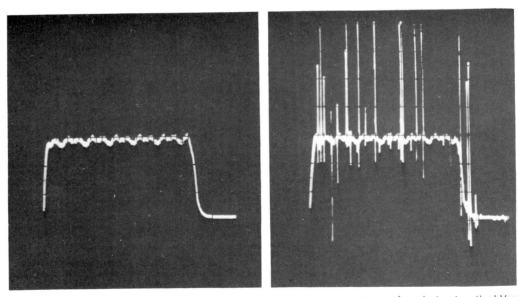

Figure 8.17d. The spikes on the waveform on the right were apparent on the output waveform but not on the kV waveform the service engineer produced *(left)*. However, after further investigation it was determined that the spikes were present on the mA waveform as measured by the service engineer. The output waveform measured with the solid-state detector includes both mA and kVp waveform information, whereas the service engineer normally only looks at the kV waveform. This is another case where you may be measuring something different than the service engineer measures. It is essential to work together to sort out such problems.

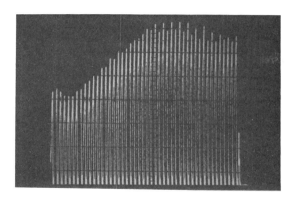

Figure 8.17e. This single-phase generator in a dental section required service to correct a problem with the filament stabilization circuit.

3. Don't photograph every waveform, just the unusual ones. (On new equipment, or the first time you check any room, record one waveform at each mA station for the QC room log.)
4. Don't try to verbally describe the appearance of an aberrant waveform to the service engineer. Either provide him with the original or a photocopy (Xerox copies are very good).
5. If the x-ray detector saturates, you will obtain a waveform with a very flat top. Saturation occurs when the detector receives too high a radiation flux level. To avoid this, move the detector further away from the x-ray source.

Acceptance Limits

1. Any waveform that you think deviates from a normal waveform should be shown to the service engineer. With experience, you will be able to diagnose the possible problems from the waveforms, but work closely with the service engineer and rely on his diagnosis. You should point out any deviation from normal since small changes that occur infrequently may be indicative of a major problem that is in the process of developing and may have serious consequences if allowed to persist.
2. In theory three-phase, twelve-pulse waveforms should have about 5% ripple, but most of these will actually exhibit ripple of the order of 10–15%. Any three-phase, twelve-pulse system with ripple in excess of 20% should be further evaluated by a service engineer to determine the cause. Three-phase, six-pulse equipment will probably have ripple in excess of 15%, but ripple in excess of 25% indicates potential problems and a need for corrective action. Single-phase equipment has 100% ripple, but all of the peak heights should not vary by more than 10%, and ideally this variation should be much less.
3. In some cases of excessive ripple, the cause may be an inherent flaw in the design or construction of the high-tension transformer or generator that cannot be corrected. However, the knowledge of the percentage of ripple will help in troubleshooting other problems such as apparent problems in kVp calibration. The kVp cassette measures the effective or average kVp, so with a considerable amount of ripple the cassette measurement will be lower than that made by the service engineer using a voltage divider and reading the true peak kilovoltage. Also, high ripple will result in lower tube output, in terms of mR or mR/mAs, as compared to systems exhibiting less ripple.

Corrective Action

If you detect problems with x-ray output waveforms, it will be essential to call in the x-ray service engineer since the problems that affect these waveforms must be corrected internally in the x-ray generator and its associated components.

8.4. REPEATABILITY, LINEARITY, AND mR/mAs OUTPUT

Purpose

1. *Repeatability*—To assure that the exposure received for the same mA, time, and kVp is the same from exposure to exposure.
2. *Linearity*—To assure that similar exposures are obtained for the same mAs and kVp, regardless of the exposure time and mA used.

3. *mR/mAs Output Consistency*—To assure that the average radiation output of like systems is consistent from room to room.

Equipment Needed

1. Direct readout dosimeter
2. mAs/timer test tool (alternate procedure)
3. Screen-film cassette and film (alternate procedure)
4. Patient equivalent phantom (PEP) with base
5. Sheet of 12 × 12-inch (30 × 30-cm) lead

Procedure—Repeatability, Linearity, and mR/mAs Output Using the Direct Readout Dosimeter

1. Place the sheet of lead in the center of the x-ray table with the phantom and base directly on top of the lead.
2. Place the large chamber in the opening beneath the phantom, making sure the chamber is in the exact center of the phantom (Figure 8.18a).
3. Set the x-ray tube at a 36-inch (90-cm) source-to-tabletop distance, center the tube to the phantom, and collimate to the edges of the phantom (Figure 8.18b).
4. A complete set of measurements will be made in order to collect all of the data necessary for this test, as shown in Table 8.1.
5. Make radiation exposure measurements at 60 kVp and at four mA stations using the same mAs and record the data (use mA and time combinations typically used in this room). [**Note:** Be sure to set the techniques carefully, dialing slowly *up* to the technique desired.]
6. Repeat Step 5 at 100 kVp, using the same mA and time combinations, and record the data.
7. Make measurements at 80 kVp. Since you will also use the data to determine the generator repeatability, three exposures will be needed at each mA and time combination. Record each individual reading (Table

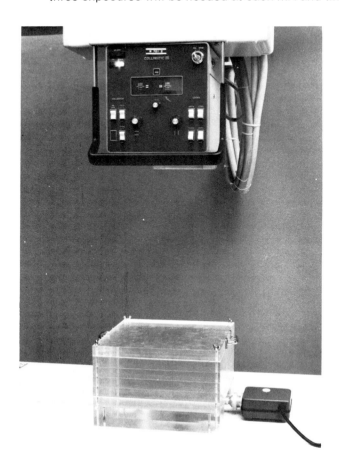

Figure 8.18a. Repeatability, linearity, and mR/mAs output test setup. PEP on the base with the dosimeter properly positioned. A sheet of lead must be placed under the phantom base.

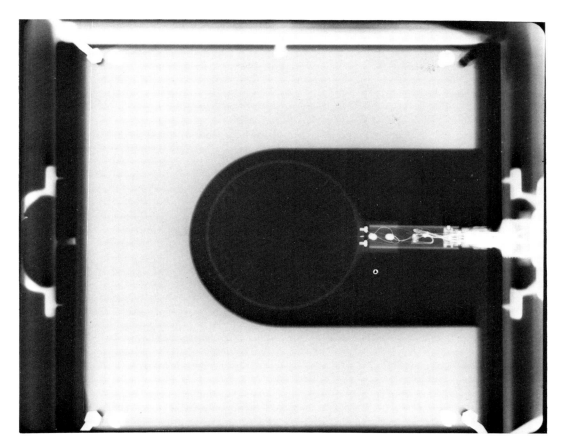

Figure 8.18b. Repeatability, linearity, and mR/mAs output test setup. It is essential to cone to the edge of the phantom and to assure that the ionization chamber is centered to the x-ray beam and the phantom.

8.1). [**Note:** Do *not* set the techniques as you did for the above measurements. Before each exposure, change the technique and then go back to the desired technique, but do *not* dial the technique in the same way, i.e., dial up one time, dial down the next. The reason for this is to determine how repeatable the generator is when used under normal operating conditions.]

8. Determine the average of the three measurements made at each mA and time setting at 80 kVp and enter the data in the table (Table 8.1).

9. The repeatability is then calculated for each of the mA-time combinations at 80 kVp using the formula

$$\frac{\left(\dfrac{\text{Maximum mR} - \text{Minimum mR}}{2}\right)}{\text{Average mR}} \times 100\% = \% \text{ Repeatability}$$

Table 8.1. mR measurements for repeatability, linearity, and mR/mAs output

| (40 mAs) | | 60 kVp | 80 kVp | | | | 100 kVp |
mA	Time		1st exposure	2nd exposure	3rd exposure	Average	
100	0.40	7.98	30.0	30.2	28.9	29.7	67
200	0.20	6.86	31.1	31.5	31.8	31.6	65
400	0.10	7.23	27.2	32.0	30.6	29.9	60
800	0.05	6.95	34.0	34.1	34.3	34.1	62

For example, at 400 mA and 0.10 seconds,

$$\frac{\left(\dfrac{32.0 - 27.2}{2}\right)}{29.9} \times 100\% = 8.0\%$$

The resulting repeatabilities are 2.1%, 1.1%, 8.0%, and 0.4% at the 100, 200, 400, and 800 mA stations, respectively.

10. The mR/mAs values are next determined by dividing each mR reading in Table 8.1 by the mAs (in this case 40 mAs). Record the mR/mAs in a table such as Table 8.2. [**Note:** At 80 kVp the mR/mAs is determined using the *average* mR value from the three readings for each mA-time combination.] For example, at 80 kVp, 100 mA, and 0.40 seconds,

$$\frac{29.7\ \text{mR}}{40\ \text{mAs}} = 0.74\ \text{mR/mAs}$$

11. Determine the average mR/mAs value at 80 kVp (Table 8.2). For example,

$$\frac{0.74 + 0.79 + 0.75 + 0.85}{4} = 0.78\ \text{mR/mAs}$$

12. Determine the linearity for each kVp station using the formula

$$\frac{\left(\dfrac{\text{Maximum mR/mAs} - \text{Minimum mR/mAs}}{2}\right)}{\text{Average mR/mAs}} \times 100\% = \%\ \text{Linearity}$$

For example, at 80 kVp

$$\frac{\left(\dfrac{0.85 - 0.74}{2}\right)}{0.78} \times 100\% = 7.1\%$$

The resulting linearities are 8.3%, 7.1%, and 5.7% at 60, 80, and 100 kVp, respectively.

13. Enter the repeatability, linearity, and mR/mAs data in the QC room log.

Problems and Pitfalls

1. The x-ray tube should be checked for overheating since a large number of exposures are being made in a short period of time. (You should be familiar with the tube loading and cooling charts for the rooms, so overheating the tube should never occur during a QC check.)

2. The sheet of lead is placed under the phantom and dosimeter to obtain standard backscatter conditions. Tabletops made by different manufacturers may have different backscatter characteristics, thus altering the dosimeter readings. Standard backscatter conditions assure more accurate mR/mAs output comparisons of all radiographic rooms in the department.

3. The mR/mAs measurements should be made using the focal spot or spots that are used in the room.

4. Follow a strict procedure with regard to the phantom position and the x-ray tube, the chamber position within the phantom, and the distance from the x-ray source to the tabletop. This will produce more consistent and accurate results.

Table 8.2. mR/mAs (calculated from data in Table 8.1)

mA	Time	60 kVp	80 kVp	100 kVp
100	0.40	0.20	0.74	1.68
200	0.20	0.17	0.79	1.63
400	0.10	0.18	0.75	1.50
800	0.05	0.17	0.85	1.55
Average		0.18	0.78	1.59

5. Never use the overhead distance indicator. Always measure the distance accurately, using a *tape measure*. The overhead distance indicator can be incorrect.
6. Always approach the technique setting slowly, dialing up to the desired setting (except for the repeatability measurements). This assures consistency in the results.
7. Always evaluate the generators closely following the test protocol.
8. The use of pen-type dosimeters is not recommended for this test of generator performance. Pen-type dosimeters are not accurate and cannot reliably be used for QC purposes.
9. It is essential that kVp measurements be done before initially performing this test to establish baseline values. If the kVp calibration exceeds acceptance limits, the mR/mAs data will be inaccurate.

Acceptance Limits

1. The repeatability should be maintained within ± 5% and the linearity should be less than or equal to ± 10%.
2. The average mR/mAs output at 80 kVp from each room should be within ± 10% for all rooms. However, the output from different generators does vary somewhat. For example, only single-phase generators (full-wave rectified) should be compared, only three-phase, six-pulse generators should be compared, and only three-phase, twelve-pulse generators should be compared. In addition, generators made by different manufacturers may exhibit different output. If the output can be maintained to within ± 10% for like rooms, then the same technique charts will produce diagnostic-quality films from those rooms.
3. The individual mR/mAs values, as recorded in the QC room log, will provide valuable data in troubleshooting problems. For example, if a room is said to be "shooting light," a check of the mR/mAs values at the present time with those recorded in the log book will indicate if the generator output is lower than acceptable, and what mA and time stations are at fault.
4. It is also important to review all of the resultant data from this test since changes can occur in the repeatability, linearity, or individual mR/mAs values, independent of each other. In other words, the repeatability may exceed acceptance limits while the linearity is still acceptable, or the individual mR/mAs values may exceed acceptable limits while the repeatability and linearity are acceptable.

Corrective Action

A service engineer should be called to recalibrate the generator if these tests indicate that it is outside of acceptance limits.

Alternate Procedure for Linearity Using the Motorized Synchronous Top

1. If the timing has already been checked using the motorized synchronous top and found to be acceptable, the mA calibration can be interpreted from the wedge pattern that is also imaged on the film.
2. Check the step wedges from the various mA stations and determine if the steps on each pattern are the same density (Figure 8.19). For the most accurate results, read the densities with a densitometer. If the generator is properly calibrated, the densities should be within ± 0.1 in density.
3. Record the results in the QC room log.

Problems and Pitfalls

1. Variability in film batches and processing conditions can increase the error between checks.
2. Numerical values and percentage variations cannot be obtained from this test.
3. It is difficult to check the generator at high kVp and mAs techniques because the test tool will be overpenetrated. However, a sheet of aluminum can be placed over the test tool to obtain proper film density.

Acceptance Limits

The density should not vary by more than one step on the wedge or ± 0.10 if read with a densitometer.

Corrective Action

If the linearity is found to be outside of the above limits, a service engineer should be called to correct the problem.

8.5. PHOTOTIMER EVALUATION

Purpose

To assure that the exposure is being terminated at the proper time after a predetermined quantity of radiation has been detected.

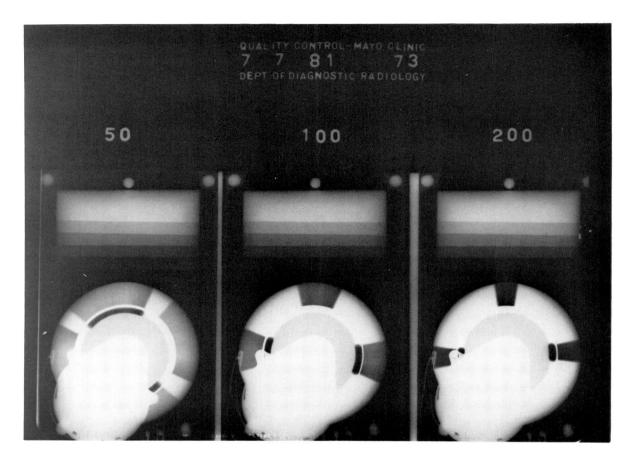

Figure 8.19a.   Acceptable density variation in generator linearity test results using the motorized synchronous timer.

Equipment Needed

1. Homogeneous patient equivalent phantom (PEP), plus two additional 1 × 12 × 12-inch (2.5 × 30 × 30-cm) sheets of Plexiglas
2. Densitometer
3. Single cassette to be used for all exposures and film from the same batch
4. Direct readout dosimeter
5. Two sheets of 1/8-inch (3-mm) lead, 12 × 12-inch (30 × 30-cm)

Procedure—Conventional Phototimed Systems

1. Set the x-ray tube at the normal working distance and center the tube to the table and cassette.
2. Place four sheets of Plexiglas from the PEP in the light field and cone slightly inside the dimensions of the phantom (Figure 8.20). (The phantom must be centered to the phototiming sensors.)
3. Use the center sensing area and make three exposures on three different films using the same cassette at 60, 80, and 100 kVp, keeping the mA constant. (Use the mA that is typically used in the room.) Remember to use the *same cassette* for all exposures. This will entail processing the film after each exposure.
4. Place four more sheets of Plexiglas on top of the original four and repeat the exposures at the same three kVp values and at the same technique using the same cassette and film from the same emulsion batch.
5. After the sixth film has been processed, read the densities of the films (in the same area) with the densitometer. [**Note:**   You should also check the system at different mA stations and with the different sensing areas to assure that the entire system is working properly.]
6. Record the results in the QC room log.

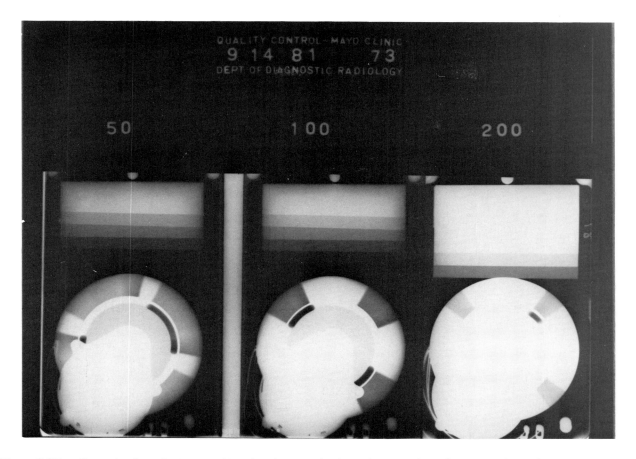

Figure 8.19b.   Generator linearity test results using the motorized synchronous timer. Density variation for the various mA stations exceeds acceptable limits.

Procedure—Photofluorospot (PFS) Film Units and Automatic Chest Units

1.   The procedure described above is used to check these units using the same thicknesses of Plexiglas and three different kVp values.
2.   On fluoroscopic systems that vary the PFS kVp, the kVp should be set to the manual mode.
3.   On automatic chest units, three and then six layers of Plexiglas should be used to better simulate the chest.

Problems and Pitfalls

1.   Assure that the Plexiglas is covering the phototimer sensors and that the radiation field is coned to the Plexiglas.
2.   Care must be taken to use only the screen-film system for which the unit has been calibrated.
3.   The exposure time required may be shorter than the minimum response time of the system if high kVp and/or mA techniques are used.
4.   On PFS film and chest systems, make sure the systems are being checked in the typically used kVp and mA ranges.
5.   This test of the phototiming system may not entirely reveal calibration problems. Consequently, all the tests described in this chapter should be done to ensure optimal calibration and operation of the system.

Acceptance Limits

The densities of the six radiographs from a given system should be within ± 0.10 of each other. The average densities of the six radiographs from one check to another should be within ± 0.20 of each other. The larger variation accepted in this latter case is to allow for processor and film batch variations.

Corrective Action

If the densities exceed the above limits, a service engineer should be called to calibrate the system.

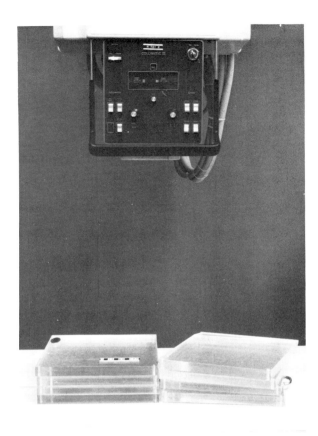

Figure 8.20. Phototimer evaluation test setup. Center the first four sheets under the x-ray tube and directly over the phototimer detectors. Be sure to include date, room, and technique information on each film.

Procedure—Backup Timer Check

It is important to assure that the backup timer is functioning and the backup time does not exceed that specified in federal regulations. If the phototimer should fail, the backup timer must terminate the exposure.

1. Remove the Plexiglas and place at least two sheets of ⅛-inch (3-mm) lead over the detector field so that *no radiation reaches the detectors.*
2. Place the small chamber on the dosimeter and place the dosimeter (or electronic timer) in the center of the x-ray beam in front of the lead sheets (Figure 8.21). Set the dosimeter to the time-measuring mode.
3. Make an exposure at a standard technique with the system in the phototiming mode.
4. The exposure should terminate after the preset backup time is reached.
5. Read the backup time on the dosimeter.

Problems and Pitfalls

Be sure that the phototimer sensors are completely covered by the lead.

Acceptance Limits

The backup timer should terminate the exposure so that a total exposure of 600 mAs is not exceeded.

Corrective Action

If the backup time can be exceeded, the equipment should not be used in the phototiming mode until a service engineer has corrected the problem.

Procedure—Minimum Exposure Time Check

The minimum exposure time is checked to record the shortest time at which the phototiming circuit will function. There are no minimum limits for exposure time; however, it is of value to know and record the minimum time so that techniques are selected using at least twice the minimum, even for thin patients.

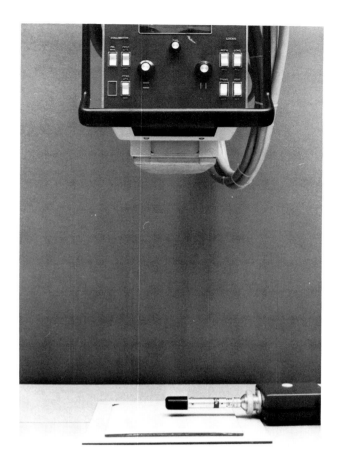

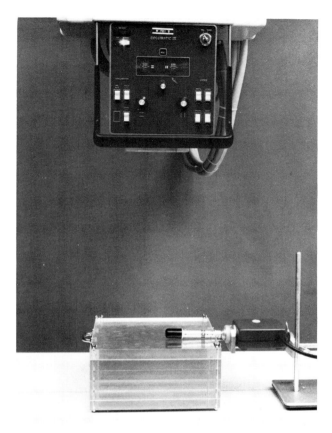

Figure 8.21. Backup timer check test setup. At least two sheets of ⅛-inch (3-mm) lead should be used to cover the phototimer detectors completely.

Figure 8.22. Minimum exposure time check test setup.

1. Place six sheets of Plexiglas over the detectors.
2. Place the dosimeter chamber (or electronic timing device) in the beam with the dosimeter set to the exposure time reading mode (Figure 8.22).
3. Make an exposure at a standard technique and note the exposure time.
4. Remove one sheet of material and make another exposure, again noting the exposure time.
5. The exposure time should be reduced for each sheet of material that is removed.
6. Keep removing the sheets of material until the minimum time is reached, i.e., when the time no longer changes as sheets of material are removed.
7. Record this value in your QC room log.

Problems and Pitfalls

1. In some cases, the minimum time may not be reached with just one layer of Plexiglas in the beam. In this case, leave the last sheet of Plexiglas in the beam and make additional exposures increasing the kVp by increments of 5 until the minimum time is reached. Record both the minimum time and kVp used in the QC room log.
2. It is necessary to use the $1 \times 12 \times 12$-inch ($2.5 \times 30 \times 30$-cm) sheets of Plexiglas in this and the previous phototimer tests to assure that sufficient scattered radiation is introduced to simulate patient scatter conditions.

Acceptance Limits

There are no established limits for this test. However, make sure that the system will produce the minimum time as described in the manufacturer's specifications.

Corrective Action

A service engineer should check the system if the phototiming circuit cannot produce the minimum exposure time as described in the manufacturer's specifications.

8.6. MAMMOGRAPHY AND XERORADIOGRAPHY

Purpose

To provide consistent, high-quality mammograms and xeroradiographs with minimum exposure to the patient.

Equipment Needed

1. Full set of QC test tools
2. Low-kVp cassette (30–50 kVp)
3. Number 50 or 60 copper mesh for screen contact
4. Direct readout dosimeter with low-energy ionization chamber
5. Mammographic phantom

Procedures

1. All the components of a mammographic system should be checked exactly as in any other radiographic system and the same acceptance limits apply.
2. Check the half-value layer (HVL) at a kVp typically used for mammography and xeroradiography. Place 0.25, 0.50, and 1.0 mm of aluminum in the beam since the HVL will be much lower than in a conventional radiographic system. In addition, be sure the compression device, and any other devices that are normally in the x-ray beam, are in position while the HVL is checked.
3. Measure the kVp with the low-kVp cassette (sometimes referred to as the mammography cassette).
4. Check the screen contact of cassettes or vacuum bags regularly using a number 50 or 60 copper mesh.
5. Establish and outline an easily reproduced procedure controlling the mA, kVp, and target-to-film distance for radiographs of a mammographic phantom. Make radiographs of the phantom on a regular basis and observe the test objects in the phantom to ensure optimal resolution. Record the film density and resolution information in the QC room log.
6. Make sure the xeroradiographic cassettes are checked and cleaned at least once each week and that the proper maintenance is performed regularly on the charger and processor units.

Problems and Pitfalls

1. Because of the complexity and potential radiation hazard of mammography, it is wise to work closely with a qualified diagnostic radiologic physicist to establish a QC program on mammographic or xeroradiographic systems.
2. Because of the low-energy x-ray beam used for mammography, conventional ionization chambers will not provide accurate readings. Special thin-window, low-energy mammographic chambers can be obtained for most dosimeters. All measurements made on mammographic and xeroradiographic equipment should be made with the mammographic chamber.
3. Since the standard phantom cannot be used to check the linearity, repeatability, and mR/mAs output on mammographic and xeroradiographic systems, these measurements should be made in air. Be sure to closely follow your procedure with regard to such things as the chamber position in the beam for each subsequent QC check.

Acceptance Limits

The acceptance limits for conventional generators apply. Phantom procedures should consistently reproduce the test objects in the phantom. The film density from the phantom should remain within ±0.15 on each QC check if the processor is in control.

Corrective Action

1. Consult a diagnostic radiologic physicist if questions arise regarding the use of the equipment.
2. Call a qualified service engineer for equipment problems.

9 FLUOROSCOPIC EXPOSURE CONTROL AND IMAGE QUALITY

Fluoroscopic imaging systems are by far some of the most complex systems in the radiology or diagnostic imaging department. Most hospitals and the majority of service engineers do not have the appropriate equipment to properly set up and evaluate video systems. In general, there is a significant lack of understanding in the field of radiology concerning how video systems work and the associated problems. Even more significantly, many manufacturers provide video systems that do not conform to the EIA Standard RS-170 (Electronics Industries Association, 1957). This standard specifies the shape and composition of the video waveform. If a system does not meet these standards, then it may be impossible to interface it with generally available video equipment, e.g., with ¾-inch videotape recorders or TV monitors other than those provided by the fluoroscopic system manufacturer. In addition, much of the equipment that is needed to evaluate video systems must be presented with a standard signal, specified by RS-170, to function properly.

Without going into detail about the specifics of video systems and how they function and differ, we provide the QC technologist with sufficient information to carry out quality control checks on this equipment. Ideally, to set up and evaluate video systems, you need a video waveform monitor and video signal generator. Since these are not commonly available in most hospitals (in fact, most manufacturers do not supply their service engineers with this type of equipment at the present time), we will describe tests that will provide the maximum amount of information with tools that are commonly available. If you are interested in delving further into video systems evaluation, a video engineer (usually affiliated with televi-

sion facilities, both commercial and private) may be able to provide additional assistance and insight.

Although it is possible to use pen-type dosimeters for the evaluation of fluoroscopic systems, we would recommend the use of a direct readout digital dosimeter. Pen dosimeters are much less accurate than direct readout dosimeters, are usually rate dependent, and require that you measure the exposure time and calculate the exposure rate from the time and total exposure received. This latter problem is compounded by the fact that most fluoroscopic systems do not stabilize at the actual exposure rate immediately, causing a significant error in the measurements.

FLUOROSCOPIC IMAGE SIZE AND BEAM LIMITATION

Most fluoroscopic imaging systems do not provide the radiologist with a television image of the entire input and output phosphor of the image intensifier tube. In some instances, this is intentional since the outer edges of the image intensifier exhibit many forms of image degradation including brightness fall-off and loss of resolution. In other cases, an inappropriate lens may have been chosen to couple the intensifier to the video camera or the scan size may be improperly set on the video camera. This test will allow for the determination of the exact area being imaged and allow the QC technologist to assure that all fluoroscopic systems in the department are producing images of a similar size.

Although the federal government provides regulations concerning the amount of collimation error allowed relative to the image intensifier, these regulations, like all of the federal regulations, deal only with the condition of the equipment when it is initially installed. However, many states do have requirements that must be met and are usually similar to those set out by the federal government x-ray equipment certification regulations (Bureau of Radiological Health, 1980). In addition, the collimation must be adjusted and functioning properly to assure that the patient is not receiving unnecessary radiation exposure. This will ultimately reduce the amount of scatter radiation that the technologist and radiologist are exposed to in the examining room and will improve image quality.

MAXIMUM FLUOROSCOPIC EXPOSURE RATE

The maximum fluoroscopic exposure rate setting is important in two respects. First, if the maximum rate is set too low, then adequate radiation will not be available to penetrate larger patients in the AP projection nor will it be available to penetrate most patients in the lateral or oblique positions. Second, if the rate is set too high, then the patient and staff will be receiving unnecessarily high radiation exposures, especially in the lateral projections or when a bolus of barium may be obscuring most of the photodetector area. Again, the federal regulations do not impact directly on the radiology department, only on the original equipment installer. However, we prefer to recommend the federally prescribed maximum radiation levels since these have been found to be quite adequate in our practice and also since many states have adopted the federal x-ray equipment certification levels as state laws.

STANDARD FLUOROSCOPIC EXPOSURE LEVELS

To maintain optimum fluoroscopic image quality over an extended period of time, it is necessary to assure that the radiation levels reaching the image intensifier (and the patient) are consistent. In addition, the quality of the radiation (kVp) must be in a reasonable range with sufficient mA to produce an image with acceptable image noise. In many instances, the standard exposure rate is increased by the service engineer if the radiologist complains of a slightly noisy or mottled image. Consequently, many institutions find that their standard fluoroscopic exposure rate approaches the maximum fluoroscopic exposure rate, providing adequate fluoroscopy for the normal patient in the AP position but resulting in severely degraded images for the heavier patient or any patient in the lateral position. The appropriate balance of technical factors and video system adjustments

will assure that good-quality fluoroscopic images can be maintained at reasonable exposure rates for all but the extremely obese patient. A few patients, because of their size, cannot be adequately imaged with fluoroscopic systems without exceeding the maximum fluoroscopic exposure rates and exposing the patient and staff to high levels of radiation.

Another goal of a good quality control program in regard to fluoroscopic image systems is to provide a good-quality image at a minimum exposure level. However, adjusting exposure levels requires a good service engineer familiar with fluoroscopic systems and perhaps the advice of a diagnostic radiologic physicist. The adjustment requires the proper and delicate balancing of the kVp, mA, video gain, and optical aperture size. For example, you can reduce the exposure to the patient by increasing the camera gain and/or opening the camera aperture. However, this will result in a noisy image, with the noise being primarily quantum mottle. Another approach would be to increase the video camera gain to a maximum value but set the aperture at a reasonable level. In this case, the image will also be noisy, but the noise will result primarily from the electronic noise in the video system. In addition, if the camera is set at maximum gain, the automatic gain control will not be able to provide additional gain to compensate for the low radiation levels transmitted through an obese patient or most patients in the lateral position, thereby limiting the diagnostic information available. Consequently, by correctly selecting the proper technical factors, aperture, and gain, you can provide an image of reasonable quality at a reasonable exposure while allowing the system sufficient gain to compensate for a radiation-starved image with large patients.

Another point to consider is the elimination of grids for fluoroscopic procedures and for the production of PFS films on all patients, and for making conventional spot films in pediatric areas. In most instances where high-contrast information is present in the diagnostic image (e.g., GI studies and hip pinnings), it is possible to eliminate grids and realize a dose reduction of up to two times (Gray and Swee, 1982). In making spot films, this allows for a reduction in exposure time, which may result in better images because of decreased peristaltic motion.

AUTOMATIC BRIGHTNESS CONTROL (ABC), AUTOMATIC DOSE CONTROL (ADC), AND AUTOMATIC GAIN CONTROL (AGC)

Confused? You are not alone! Many people think that all of these controls do the same thing, i.e., provide automatic control of the exposure, and hence of the brightness, of the final image. ABC and ADC are systems that automatically adjust the kVp and/or mA in a fluoroscopic imaging system to maintain sufficient radiation for a quality image. Since these controls are tied to the x-ray generator, it is necessary to have servo mechanisms that adjust the technical factors, a sometimes slow process especially if you are going from low to high kVp or mA. In addition, the maximum fluoroscopic exposure rate is preset so that the kVp and mA cannot exceed a certain level.

The AGC, on the other hand, is an automatic *gain* control that is an integral part of the video camera and does not affect the technical factors nor the exposure to the patient. With AGC an image will be produced even after the fluoroscopic system has reached the maximum exposure level through obese patients or in lateral projections. In this case the gain is increased, making a brighter image than would normally be possible, although the noise in the image is also increased. However, the tradeoff is that you obtain an image where the TV monitor normally would be dark. Also, in a situation where the kVp and/or mA servo mechanisms have not yet driven to the proper level, the AGC will change the camera gain to present a reasonable image while the technical factors are changing (the AGC can react in milliseconds, whereas most servo mechanisms adjust much more slowly).

In most instances, the AGC either works properly or is not functioning at all, so the tests to determine if it is functioning are quite simple. The only difficult thing is getting the system set up properly in the first place.

TV MONITORS AND VIDEOTAPE AND VIDEODISC RECORDERS

A large proportion of service calls concerning fluoroscopic image quality involve the adjustment of the TV monitor. In many cases, this is the correct approach, but in other cases it is not. It is easy to adjust the monitor to correct for problems in other parts of the system, but this does not produce good quality fluoroscopic images. For example, if the video signal from the system is too low, you can increase the brightness and contrast settings of the monitor and produce a viewable image. However, this increases the apparent mottle and electronic noise, which is sometimes compensated for by increasing the standard operating exposure level, thus also increasing the exposure to the patient and staff.

In some cases, the brightness and contrast are misadjusted during use and it is difficult to readjust the settings to produce a pleasing image. This is best done by using a standard phantom and should not be done during patient studies. Many TV monitors have inadequate black level clamping, which causes difficulty in adjusting the contrast and brightness. In this case, if you adjust the contrast, the brightness may drift and adjustments in the brightness may change the contrast. Consequently, both controls must be adjusted simultaneously. This can be avoided by requesting a good-quality TV monitor with black level clamping. (It is interesting that, when you spend $200,000 to $300,000 on a fluoroscopic suite, the salesman often offers a less expensive TV monitor to save a few dollars. This is really a false savings since good quality black and white monitors cost about $1500, a fraction of the cost of the room.)

Videotape players offer a real challenge in diagnostic radiology. The inexpensive units using ¾-inch cassette tapes have a significantly lower bandpass than the video systems used for fluoroscopic systems, so that reduced image quality can be expected from taped images. The newer, small format recorders, designed for home use, have even lower bandpass and should *not* be used in diagnostic radiology or any area of diagnostic imaging (such as ultrasound). Also, almost all videotape recorders available at prices less than $5,000 do not have a means of viewing a single field with reasonable quality nor do they have the potential for slow motion replay. Note that when you are viewing a still image from a videotape recorder, the image is displayed in the field mode, i.e., only half of the TV scan lines are displayed. Therefore, in addition to a loss in resolution from a lower bandwidth, a stop-frame image from a videotape recorder has decreased vertical resolution since only half of the scan lines are being used.

If a videotape recorder is to be used in diagnostic imaging, then a good-quality black and white monitor should be purchased for replaying videotapes. Color TV monitors, such as those used for home viewing, are extremely limited in the amount of detail that can be displayed. In addition, a reasonable black and white image cannot be properly viewed on a color monitor because of the phosphor dot size and/or overlay mask used in making the CRT.

Videodisc recorders are available with the ability to provide instant replays, just like those used for professional football game broadcasts. Normally, the image can be replayed in real time (30 frames per second), or at slower frame rates and even in stop-action mode. Some of these devices are also available with removable discs, although the discs cost about $150 each.

Videodisc recorders all have one major limitation—most cannot record more than 600 TV frames, or the equivalent of 20 seconds of video imaging at 30 frames per second. However, the slow motion and stop-action capabilities may be beneficial in diagnostic imaging and the image recorded on videodisc could then be transferred to videotape if a permanent video record is required. Both videotape and videodisc recorder images can be recorded on a multiformat or video hard-copy camera to provide a permanent hard-copy image.

FLUOROSCOPIC IMAGE NOISE

The noise in fluoroscopic images can come from two sources—electronic noise and quantum mottle or noise. In a well-designed and properly calibrated fluoroscopic imaging system, the predominant noise should be quantum noise. It is important to determine which type of noise is limiting the capabilities of the system. If electronic noise is the culprit, a complete recalibration of the system is probably required.

IMAGE LAG

Lag in television images is best described as a smearing of the image when the camera is rapidly panned past an object or the object is rapidly moved past the camera. Lag is also sometimes referred to as comet tailing. Lag is much greater in vidicon camera tubes as compared to the plumbicon tubes or other newer types of tubes. However, some of the newer vidicon tubes do exhibit lag characteristics similar to plumbicons, and plumbicon tube lag can be greater than that of vidicons if they are not set up properly. The primary reason for lag in a new plumbicon is a lack of light reaching the imaging surface of the tube. This can be corrected by opening the optical aperture of the camera system or by increasing radiation levels to the input of the image intensifier. However, most camera tubes will show an increase in the lag with time, becoming objectionable near the end of their useful life.

The amount of lag that is acceptable will depend on the radiologist viewing the image and the use of the fluoroscopic system. A system used for imaging orthopedic procedures, such as hip pinnings, can operate with relatively long lag, whereas a system used for placing the electrodes of a pacemaker in the heart will require a camera tube with a minimum amount of lag.

Although lag has a detrimental impact on the overall quality of the image because of its smearing effect, it can also be beneficial. Increasing lag will

tend to integrate frames of the video image and thereby reduce the apparent level of the quantum mottle. This may be beneficial where low doses are more important than imaging of rapidly moving objects. In such cases, the vidicon should be the image tube of choice.

SETTING AND MAINTAINING CINE AND PHOTOFLUOROSPOT (PFS) FILM CAMERA EXPOSURES

Like all radiographic systems, the cine and PFS camera systems require attention to assure that the exposure levels remain constant. However, cine systems produce exceedingly high exposure rates (on the order of 50–75 R/min and higher) so that they warrant particular attention. Most people assume that PFS film exposures are relatively low. This may be the case if you are filming the abdomen without barium, but these exposures may be quite high (on the order of 2 to 6 rads) if the photodetector is located over a bolus of barium and the system is attempting to penetrate the barium (Gray and Swee, 1982). Consequently, both cine and PFS filming devices should be checked frequently to assure they are producing proper film densities at reasonable exposure levels. In addition, since most of these systems operate with some type of automatic exposure control or photo-timing device, there is an increased possibility of system problems.

FLUOROSCOPIC, PHOTOFLUOROSPOT FILM, AND CINE RESOLUTION

Resolution is directly related to the sharpness and detail in a diagnostic image. These systems are affected by focal spot size, imaging geometry, optical focus (two optical chains for each system), electronic focus of the image intensifier, and (in the case of fluoroscopy) the electronic focus of the video camera. A shift in focus of any one of the elements will degrade the image quality and resolution; if more than one element is not properly focused, the resultant image will be significantly degraded. However, many times systems may drift out of focus and the loss of information will go unnoticed if it happens slowly over a long period of time. Periodic, quantitative checks are necessary to avoid significant degradation in image quality of this nature.

LOW-CONTRAST FLUOROSCOPIC TEST

Resolution normally refers to the ability to discern the presence of two or more small, high-contrast objects in close proximity. Another important test of an imaging system involves its ability to image single, low-contrast objects. Where high-contrast resolution will be rapidly degraded by slight changes in focus, it will not be affected by increases in either electronic or quantum noise. Low-contrast images may be less affected by drifts in focus but will be significantly degraded by minor increases in noise. (In fact, slight defocus may even improve the detection of low-contrast objects since it helps to reduce the noise by integrating its effect.)

Because of the different applications of diagnostic imaging systems, it is essential that all imaging systems in diagnostic use be evaluated both for high-contrast resolution and to determine the low-contrast imaging ability.

VIDEO WAVEFORM MONITORING

Video systems are some of the most complex pieces of equipment in a diagnostic imaging department and require specific tests and test instrumentation for proper setup and maintenance. The video waveform monitor is a device similar to an oscilloscope that allows the display of individual TV lines or groups of TV lines directly from the video camera. The vertical deflection is proportional to the brightness seen on the TV monitor. A conventional oscilloscope can be used in place of a video waveform monitor, although this makes it somewhat more difficult to carry out the appropriate tests.

The evaluation of the video waveform will allow you to determine if the components of the waveform are at the correct voltages and to determine the amount of inherent contrast in the image intensifier–video system. Also, you can check to determine if the grid and x-ray tube are appropriately aligned.

In our institution, we use the waveform monitor for a more extensive evaluation of the video system than we describe here. However, most of these tests are still in the developmental stages, and we are still collecting baseline data concerning the expected performance levels of video systems in diagnostic imaging. We do anticipate extensive use of the video waveform monitors in quality control and in the servicing of video systems in the future.

PROCEDURES

9.1. FLUOROSCOPIC IMAGE SIZE AND BEAM LIMITATION

Purpose

1. To assure that a fluoroscopic imaging system is displaying the entire area it was designed to display. [*Note:* The image area can be lost by improper image tube sizing, underscanning of the output phosphor of the image tube by the TV camera, or an improperly sized blanking ring.]
2. To prevent unnecessary patient exposure resulting from irradiation of an area larger than the image receptor.
3. To meet BRH beam limitation requirements.

Equipment Needed

1. Collimator alignment template with markings in either centimeters (preferred) or inches
2. A nonscreen film holder and film, or a ready-pack nonscreen film. If your system has a 6-inch (15-cm) image intensifier tube, an 8 × 10-inch (20 × 25-cm) film will be large enough, but a 9-inch (23-cm) intensifier will require a 10 × 12-inch (25 × 30-cm) film.
3. Masking or any other nongumming tape [*Note:* Avoid white hospital tape because of the residue left behind when the tape is removed.]

Procedure—To Determine Image Size and Collect Data for Beam Limitation

1. Place the fluoroscopic tower at its maximum height, with the collimators completely open.
2. Fluoroscopically center and tape the template to the input of the image intensifier, or spot film device if one is present, and prevent contact with the image tube. If your system has a 9-inch (23-cm) intensifier, place the long axis of the template across the length of the table to permit access for the 10 × 12-inch (25 × 30-cm) film.
3. Place the nonscreen film between the template and the intensifier or spot film device (Figure 9.1).
4. Measure and record the distance from the tabletop to the input of the image intensifier.
5. Fluoroscope and record the image size in both dimensions from the TV monitor or mirror if your system is a direct view system (Figure 9.2). [*Note:* Image intensifier sizing is the only factor that will affect sizing in direct viewing systems.]
6. If your system has a photofluorospot camera or cinecamera, record the template at approximately 50 kVp and the lowest operating mA possible (Figure 9.2c). [*Note:* If overexposure occurs repeat the exposure with a uniform-density phantom in the beam.]
7. After all the image size data have been collected, or after approximately 2 minutes of fluoroscoping time, remove and process the nonscreen film.
8. If you have a multimode intensifier repeat this procedure in all modes.
9. If your system has a photofluorospot camera or cine camera with exact framing where the entire image is seen on the film, you will be able to determine the sizing of the image tube by measuring the area exposed on the spot film, using the markings of the template. In general, most image intensifiers do not display an area as large as is quoted by the manufacturer. Normally, a 6-inch (15-cm) intensifier will be 5.5 to 5.9 inches (14 to 15 cm) in diameter and a 9-inch (23-cm) intensifier will be 7.8 to 8.7 inches (20 to 22 cm). To prevent an unnecessary service call, check with the manufacturer for the exact image intensifier tube size. By comparing the photofluorospot data with the fluoroscopic data, you can determine if the TV tube and blanking ring are properly sized. Direct viewing systems should, of course, display the entire image tube. If your system does not have a camera, you should display an area no smaller than 1 cm less than that specified by the manufacturer.

Procedure—Fluoroscopic Beam Limitation

1. A film of the actual beam size at maximum tower height has already been exposed while collecting the image size data. A second optional film can be made and measured at the minimum tower height, following the same procedure.

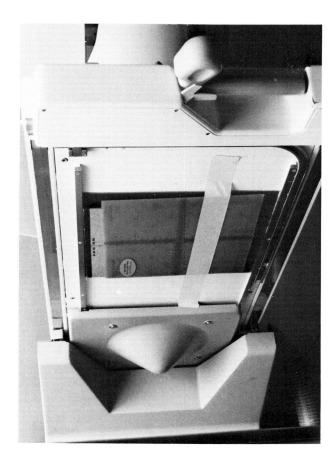

Figure 9.1. Fluoroscopic image size and beam limitation test setup.

2. Because the BRH regulations are tied to the source-to-image distance (SID), the distance from the x-ray focal spot to the tabletop must be determined. In some types of equipment, the x-ray tube can be reached to make this measurement, but in most cases you must find this information in the equipment manuals.
3. Compare the area exposed on the film with the area seen on the fluoroscopic image at both the minimum and maximum tower heights, and in all modes if your system is a multimode system, to determine if the beam limitation system is meeting acceptance limits (Figure 9.3).

Problems and Pitfalls

1. Conventional spot film devices, which prevent direct contact with the image tube, will somewhat reduce the appearance of the image size, but at maximum tower height the effect will be minimal if the system is sized properly.
2. Some types of image intensifiers have very little range in their sizing adjustment so you may not be able to change the sizing as much as you might wish.
3. Any change in image intensifier sizing will affect the focus of the intensifier. In some cases you may have to sacrifice sizing to be able to focus the system properly.
4. Image intensifiers that are grossly undersized lose gain because there is less minification; resizing may allow a reduction in the standard exposure rate.
5. Increasing the TV scan or blanking ring may uncover some alignment problems, which must be corrected.

Acceptance Limits

1. Image intensifiers should be sized to the maximum area that still allows proper focus.
2. TV tube scanning and blanking rings should be adjusted to cover the entire output phosphor of the image tube. [**Note:** This procedure may display a white ring around the outside of the image.]
3. Try to keep the total area loss to 1 cm or less than the actual size of the image intensifier.

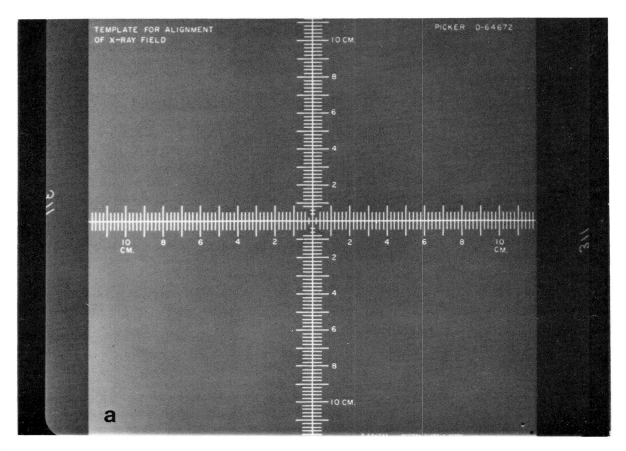

Figure 9.2a. Radiograph of the fluoroscopic image size and beam limitation test template.

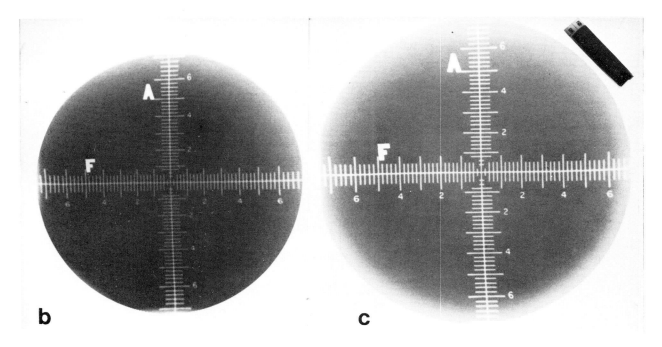

Figure 9.2b and c. Fluoroscopic image size and beam limitation test results. (b) Fluoroscopic image of test template. (c) Spot film image of template.

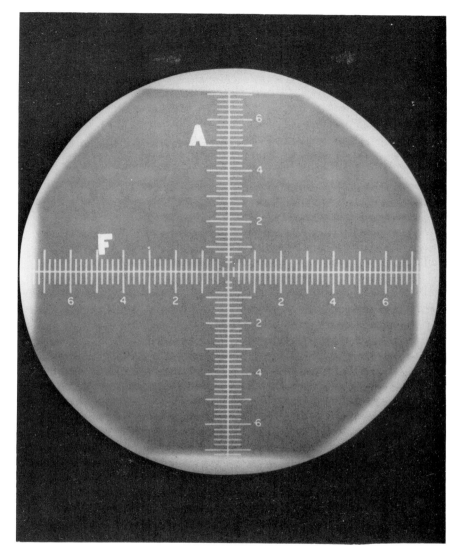

Figure 9.3. Nonscreen x-ray film showing template and collimator leaves location.

4. The total width or length of the x-ray field size should be no greater than 3% of the SID. In multimode systems, the collimation should automatically change to meet the size of the mode selected. In most modern systems, the x-ray field size can easily be kept within 1 cm of the image receptor size.

Corrective Action

1. Have a qualified service engineer correct any problems in sizing or beam limitation.
2. Before the service engineer leaves your facility recheck the sizing and beam limitation to be sure it meets the above acceptance limits.
3. One method to eliminate the necessity of the beam limitation test procedure is to have the shutters adjusted so they are just visible on the edge of the image at all times; then a simple visual check is all that is needed.

9.2. MAXIMUM FLUOROSCOPIC EXPOSURE RATE

Purpose

1. To assure an exposure rate adequate to perform quality fluoroscopic examinations on patients of all sizes.

2. To prevent excessive exposure to patients subjected to fluoroscopic examinations.
3. To assure that you meet Bureau of Radiological Health (BRH) maximum exposure rates.

Equipment Needed

1. Direct readout dosimeter (preferable)
2. Low-energy pen dosimeter with a range in excess of 1 R and a stopwatch (if direct readout dosimeter is not available)
3. Two 1/8-inch (3-mm) sheets of lead
4. Supports to hold lead above ionization chamber

Procedure—Fluoroscopic Systems with Undertable X-ray Tube, Performed with a Direct Readout Dosimeter

1. Set the fluoroscopic machine controls on automatic exposure (automatic brightness control) mode.
2. Turn mA and kVp controls to maximum, if controls are available.
3. Place dosimeter chamber on tabletop. [**Note:** Remove any padding if the system is used with and without padding.]
4. Precisely position the dosimeter chamber in the center of the radiation field with fluoroscopy. [**Note:** If *all* of the active volume of the chamber is not included in the field, the chamber cannot be used for this procedure.]
5. Adjust the fluoroscopic shutters so they are just visible on the edges of the image but do not cover any of the active volume of the chamber (Figure 9.4).
6. Turn the dosimeter to the exposure rate mode.
7. Place the two lead sheets on the supports to prevent damage, above the ionization chamber (Figure 9.5).
8. Fluoroscope long enough for the automatic exposure controls to stabilize, making sure the beam is completely attenuated. You should not be able to see any light areas on the fluoroscopic monitor.
9. Read and record the exposure rate in the QC room log. [**Note:** It may be worthwhile to record the indicated mA and kVp for future reference.]
10. Place the fluoroscopic machine in the manual mode with the mA and kVp controls at the maximum settings.
11. Read and record the exposure rate in the QC room log.

Procedure—Undertable Fluoroscopic Tube and Pen Dosimeter

Follow previous procedure except for:

1. Position the pen dosimeter in the center of the field (fluoroscopically).
2. Mark the position of the chamber with a piece of wire or a bent paper clip (Figure 9.6).
3. Place the lead sheets on the support and fluoroscope long enough for the automatic brightness controls to stabilize.
4. Charge and zero the dosimeter.
5. Position the dosimeter within the perimeter of the chamber position marker (paper clip).
6. Fluoroscope the pen dosimeter using a stopwatch to time the exposure:
   a. For a dosimeter with a maximum reading in the 1 to 1.5 R range, fluoroscope for 6 seconds.
   b. For a 5-R dosimeter, fluoroscope for 20 seconds.
7. Read the pen dosimeter using the reading light on the charger assembly.
8. Repeat Steps 4 through 7 three times and average the readings.
9. Multiply the reading by 10 for a 6-sec exposure or by 3 for a 20-sec exposure to get the exposure rate per minute.
10. Record the results in the QC room log.

Procedure—Overtable Fluoroscopic Systems

Follow previous procedures except position the chamber 30 cm above the tabletop (Figure 9.7).

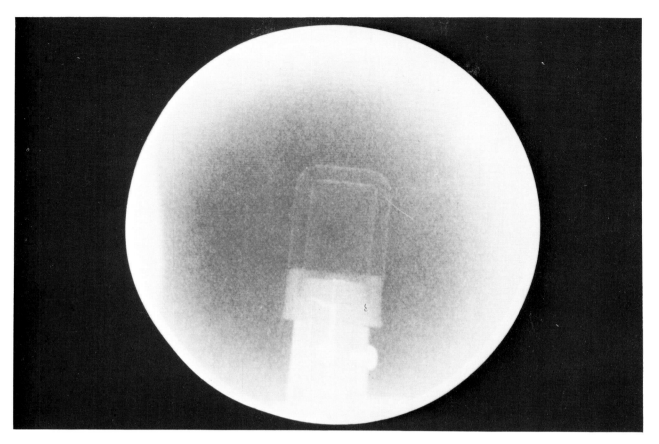

Figure 9.4.   Maximum fluoroscopic exposure rate test setup. Fluoroscopic image showing location of ionization chamber in the middle of the x-ray field with collimator leaves visible on all sides.

Procedure—C-arm Systems

Follow previous procedures except position the chamber 30 cm above the input to the image amplifier (Figure 9.8).

Problems and Pitfalls

1. Be careful to establish and outline, in writing, your procedure for controlling collimation, chamber position, and all other factors so that you or anyone in your department can *exactly* duplicate the procedure. The description of your procedure should be included in the QC room log.
2. Be extremely careful of the chamber position in systems that have x-ray tubes with anode angles of less than 12°. The heel effect can vary the exposure rate readings by 30% or more.
3. Reading with a pen dosimeter and a stopwatch may have a high degree of error. If the exposure rate is close to the acceptance limits, have your system rechecked with a direct readout dosimeter.
4. Reset the maximum exposure rate *only* with a direct readout dosimeter.

Acceptance Limits

BRH regulations for equipment certification (acceptance testing) state that the maximum fluoroscopic exposure rate shall not exceed 5 R/min in the manual mode and shall not exceed 10 R/min in the automatic exposure mode.

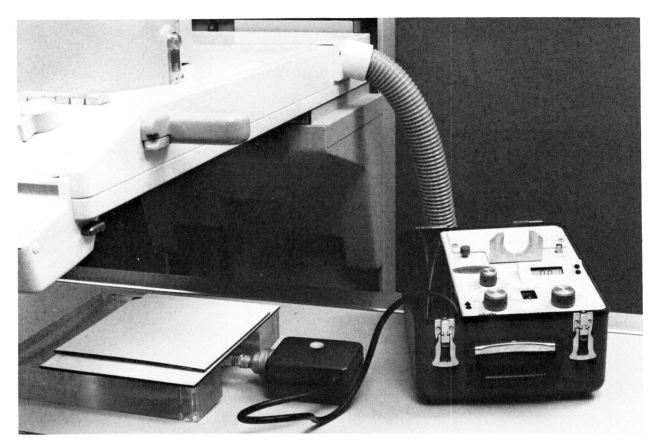

Figure 9.5.   Maximum fluoroscopic exposure rate test setup for undertable tubes.

Corrective Action

If the maximum exposure rates exceed BRH regulations, have a qualified service engineer reset them. Be sure to recheck the maximum exposure rate before the service engineer leaves.

9.3.   STANDARD FLUOROSCOPIC EXPOSURE LEVELS

Purpose

1.   To assure long-term consistency of the exposure rate.
2.   To establish and maintain the lowest reasonable exposure rate.

Equipment Needed

1.   Direct readout dosimeter (preferable)
2.   Low-energy pen dosimeter with a range in excess of 1 R and a stopwatch (if a direct readout dosimeter is not available)
3.   A phantom:
     a.   A standard patient equivalent phantom (PEP)
     b.   A smooth-bottomed water bath, at least 10 inch (25 cm) in diameter and with a water depth approximately 0.75 times the patient size you wish to simulate (i.e., 21 cm × 0.75 = 15.8 cm of water depth)
     c.   Two 7 × 7 × ¾-inch (18 × 18 × 2-cm) thick pieces of aluminum [**Note:**   This phantom is approximately equivalent to a 21-cm thick patient in absorption, but the scatter characteristics may be different since it is much smaller.]
4.   A support system to allow room under the phantom for the dosimeter chamber

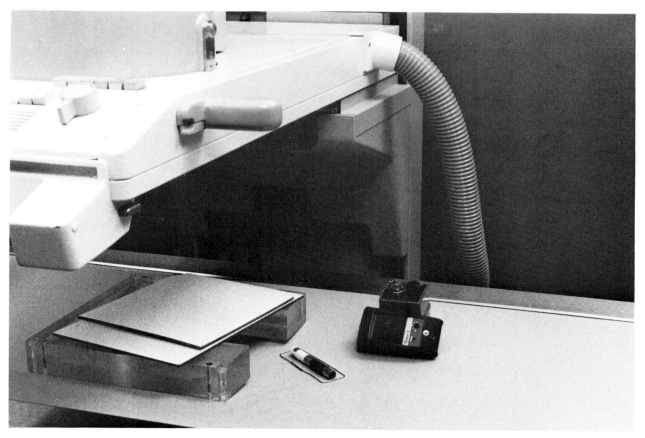

Figure 9.6. Maximum fluoroscopic exposure rate test setup for undertable tubes with a pen dosimeter. Although pen dosimeters are not recommended, it is possible to use them. It is necessary to locate the center of the field and mark this with paper clips so the dosimeter can be replaced in the exact center without fluoroscopic exposure.

Procedure

1. Carefully establish and outline, in writing, a repeatable procedure controlling collimation, tower height, operating mA and/or kVp if controls are available, dosimeter, and phantom position, e.g., collimators just visible on the edge of the field, tower 6 inches (15 cm) above the phantom, and the active volume of the chamber in the center of the x-ray field.
2. Place the phantom and the support system on the table with the dosimeter under the phantom and assure that the collimation, tower height, etc. are properly adjusted (Figure 9.9).
3. For the pen dosimeter and stopwatch follow the procedure describing measurement of maximum exposure rate on page 134.
4. Place the dosimeter in the exposure rate mode.
5. With the phantom and dosimeter chamber properly positioned, fluoroscope long enough for the reading to stabilize.
6. Read and record the exposure rate in the QC room log. [**Note:** It may be helpful to record the indicated mA and kVp. These data could be helpful in evaluating the cause of shifts in the standard operating exposure rate in the future.]
7. Make and record readings with and without the grid, and in the 6- and 9-inch (15- and 23-cm) modes for dual mode image amplifiers.
8. For overtable or C-arm systems, be extremely careful to fix and record the source-to-chamber distance.
9. Record the results in the QC room log.

Problems and Pitfalls

1. A poorly designed or improperly followed procedure will only provide erroneous and confusing data!

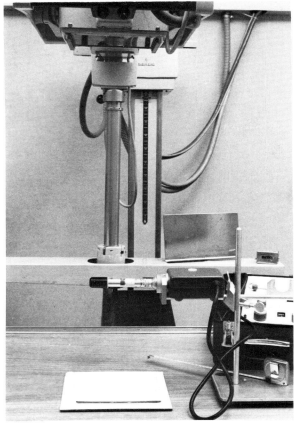

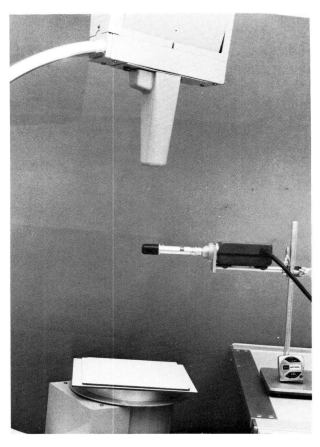

Figure 9.7. Maximum fluoroscopic exposure rate test setup for overtable tubes.

Figure 9.8. Maximum fluoroscopic exposure rate setup for C-arms.

2. Be very careful of the chamber position in systems that have x-ray tubes with an anode angle of less than 12°.

Acceptance Limits

The exposure rate needed for each individual machine is affected by many factors such as age, design, kVp range, and filtration, so the values given are only an approximation. A modern fluoroscopic machine operating without a grid through a 20–22-cm patient equivalent phantom with a tower height of approximately 14 inches (35 cm) above the table should have an exposure rate of 2–3 R/min in the 6-inch (15-cm) mode and from 1.5–2.5 R/min in the 9-inch (23-cm) mode. A system operating with a grid will have an exposure rate 1.5 to 2 times higher, depending on grid ratio and interspace material, than the exposures quoted for nongrid.

Corrective Action

With the help of a service engineer, adjust the exposure rate to the minimum needed to produce a quality image. [**Note:** See pages 190–192 on ways to reduce fluoroscopic exposure rates.]

9.4. AUTOMATIC BRIGHTNESS CONTROL (ABC), AUTOMATIC DOSE CONTROL (ADC), AND AUTOMATIC GAIN CONTROL (AGC)

Purpose

To assure that the automatic exposure and video gain controls are functioning properly. [**Note:** Not all fluoroscopic systems have the same combinations of exposure and gain control.]

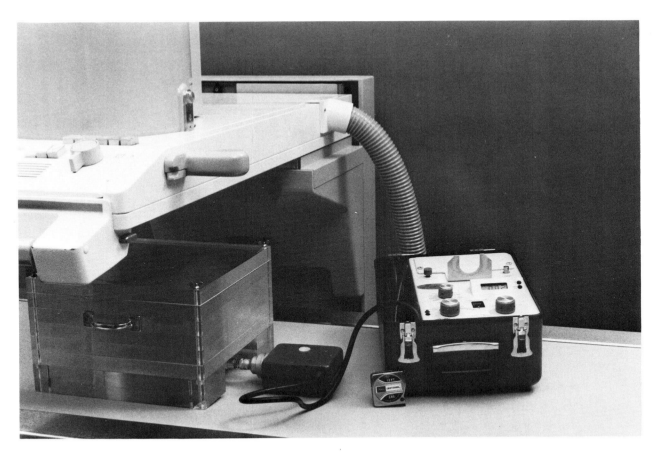

Figure 9.9a.   Standard fluoroscopic exposure level test setup with direct readout dosimeter (preferred).

Equipment Needed

1. Patient equivalent phantom (PEP)
2. Direct readout dosimeter (preferable)
3. Low-energy pen dosimeter with a range in excess of 1 R and a stopwatch (if direct readout dosimeter is not available)
4. Support system to hold phantom above dosimeter
5. Aluminum sheets used to measure the half-value layer

Procedure—ABC and ADC Controls

1. Set up the phantom and dosimeter following the same procedure you established to measure the standard fluoroscopic exposure rate, carefully controlling the field size, tower height, and chamber position. Be sure the controls are set in the automatic mode.
2. Fluoroscope long enough for the automatic exposure system to stabilize, then read and record the exposure rate for the full phantom (for the pen dosimeter follow the procedure described on page 134 in the description of measuring maximum fluoroscopic exposure rate).
3. Remove half the phantom [three 1-inch (2.5-cm) Lucite blocks or one ¾-inch (2-cm) aluminum block].
4. Read and record the exposure rate for the half phantom in the QC room log.

Problems and Pitfalls

1. Only well-designed and easily reproduced procedures will provide useful information.

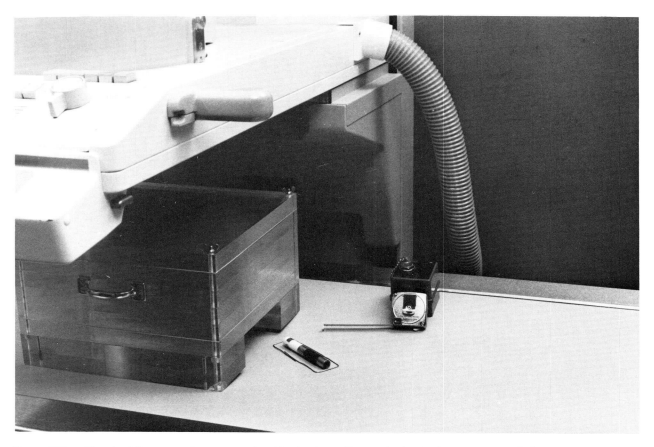

Figure 9.9b.   Standard fluoroscopic exposure level test setup with pen dosimeter (not recommended).

2.   There are several different styles of automatic exposure control systems. Some vary only the kVp, some vary only the mA, and some change the mA and kVp. Take the time to learn the function of the automatic exposure control system before making any judgment about the condition of your equipment.

3.   Do not attempt to compare the results of different models of automatic exposure control systems.

Acceptance Limits

1.   Because of the many different types of automatic exposure control systems, and exponential absorption of the x-ray beam, no specific values can be given, but the exposure rate for the half phantom should be approximately ½ the values for the full phantom.

2.   The ideal situation would be to perform this test just after the equipment was installed or after a service engineer has verified the condition of the automatic exposure control system. Follow-up checks should then produce similar results.

Corrective Action

If the automatic exposure control system fails, or if you question the function, consult a qualified service engineer.

Procedure—Automatic Gain Control (AGC) Functional Verification

An AGC system is incorporated in some, but not all, fluoroscopic equipment to provide a consistent brightness on the TV monitor. The AGC control varies the amplification of the video signal coming from the TV camera, and usually varies the video amplification along with but indepenently of automatic exposure control for changes in body part thickness. An additional benefit of an AGC system is that it broadens the useful range of a fluoroscopic unit beyond the limits of the automatic exposure control.

1.   Place the phantom, phantom support, and dosimeter on the table following the same procedure established to measure the standard fluoroscopic exposure rate.

2. Remove three of the six blocks if the Lucite phantom is used; if the aluminum phantom is used leave both ¾-inch (2-cm) thick blocks in place.
3. *Manually* match the mA, kVp, and exposure rate with the factors used by the automatic exposure control system.
4. Observe the image and mentally note the brightness and quality using the appearance of the dosimeter chamber as part of the impression.
5. Add one 1-inch (2.5-cm) thick Plexiglas block, or 2 mm of aluminum if the aluminum phantom is being used.
6. Observe the image brightness and quality. [*Note:* The image noise will increase because you are increasing the quantum mottle and electronic noise by increasing the video amplification.]
7. If the brightness did not change, add an additional 1 inch (2.5 cm) of Lucite or 2 mm of aluminum and observe image brightness and quality. Continue this procedure until the brightness of the TV image dims. If you have used all six of the Lucite blocks or 6 to 8 mm of aluminum and the image brightness has not changed, stop the procedure and assume the AGC system functions very well.
8. Record the mA, kVp, and dose rate used for the procedure, plus the amount of Lucite or aluminum needed to change the image brightness in the QC room log.

Problems and Pitfalls

1. Be very careful when setting the manual controls. If the mA, kVp, and exposure rate are not correctly set, you may have the AGC at minimum or maximum limits before you start the procedure, which will give you a false impression of the condition of the AGC system.
2. Before you make any judgment about the function of the AGC system, you must thoroughly understand how your system was designed to perform. Consult a service engineer who is familiar with your type of equipment for information about the function of the AGC system in your equipment.
3. This procedure is not a quantitative test, but rather a means of assuring that your AGC system is functioning.

Acceptance Limits

1. Expect the AGC system to function similarly on periodic checks.
2. Expect AGC systems from the same manufacturer and of the same design to perform similarly.

Corrective Action

If you feel the AGC is not functioning properly, consult a service engineer.

9.5. TV MONITORS AND VIDEOTAPE AND VIDEODISC RECORDERS

Purpose

To assure that the image display and recording systems are functioning properly.

Equipment Needed

1. Copper mesh resolution test target, or lead resolution target
2. Step wedge
3. Coarse mesh such as a screen contact test mesh
4. Video signal generator (ideal, but not commonly available)

Procedure—TV Monitors

Video signal generators with gray scale, resolution, and distortion patterns are the best method of checking TV monitors, but they are expensive and complex. Some simple checks include:

1. Observe the TV scan lines for sharpness from the center to the edge of the monitor.
2. Check the positions of the brightness and contrast knobs. If the settings are at one extreme or the other to produce the correct brightness and contrast, this could be an indication of weak components or an incorrect video signal entering the monitor. For most systems, a composite video signal including video and sync pulses should be between 0.9 and 1.2 volts.
3. To check for distortion, place a piece of coarse mesh flat on the table. Fluoroscope and observe the mesh pattern from center to edge. The mesh pattern will appear stretched at the edges of the image, but it should be distorted equally on all edges of the image (Figure 9.10).

Figure 9.10. TV monitors and videotape and videodisc recorder test results. Fluoroscopic image of coarse mesh (from screen-film contact test) showing the amount of distortion that may be anticipated in conventional fluoroscopic imaging systems.

4. Record the results in the QC room log.

Problems and Pitfalls

Monitors are an important link in a fluoroscopic system, yet it is very difficult to separate out the monitor from the other components of the system. The checks described may only provide an indication of problems. If you are suspicious of a problem, have a service engineer thoroughly check your monitor and the video signal entering the monitor.

Acceptance Limits

A judgment must be made by a qualified service engineer.

Procedure—Video Recording Systems

1. Fluoroscope the copper mesh or the lead resolution target and record the finest mesh or bar pattern visualized on the monitor. [**Note:** The copper mesh should be oriented at 45° to the TV scan lines and the lead test target should be at 90° to the scan lines.]
2. Replay the recorded image and record the finest mesh or bar pattern resolved (Figure 9.11).
3. Repeat the procedure with a step wedge and note any changes in contrast.
4. Record the results in the QC room log.

Acceptance Limits

1. For a high-quality videodisc recorder with a maximum response in the 4 MHz range, expect to lose 0.5 to 0.7 cycle/mm if a lead resolution target is used, or 1 mesh size if a copper mesh test tool is used.
2. For a videotape unit with approximately a 3 MHz response, expect to lose 0.8 to 1 cycle/mm on a lead resolution target and 2 mesh sizes for a copper mesh resolution test tool.

Figure 9.11a.   Videotape recorder test results (real-time fluoroscopic image). A lead resolution pattern was imaged fluoroscopically and then tape-recorded so the effects of tape recorder degradation could be noted.

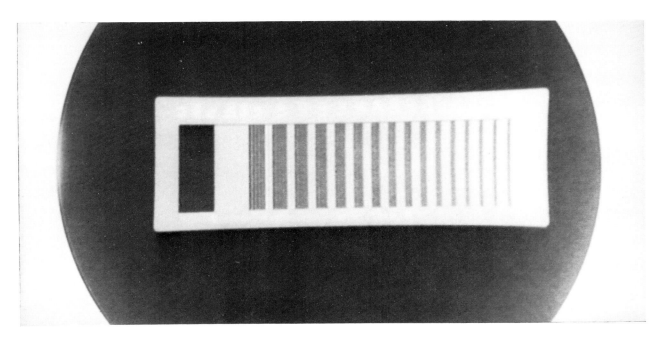

Figure 9.11b.   Image replayed from videotape recorder. Note the significant loss in resolution and sharpness.

3.   Little or no change in contrast should be seen between the live and the stored image.

Corrective Action

1.   Follow maintenance schedule for head cleaning.
2.   If excessive resolution is lost or the contrast changes greatly, consult a service engineer.
3.   If noise is excessive, try cleaning the recording and playback heads. If this does not help, consult a service engineer.

9.6. FLUOROSCOPIC IMAGE NOISE

Purpose

This test is only intended to help isolate the cause of troublesome image noise in televised fluoroscopy that results from either quantum mottle or electronic noise.

Equipment Needed

Patient equivalent phantom (PEP)

Procedure

1. Observe the monitor with no fluoroscopic image. Any noise will be electronic in nature. [**Note:** Many modern systems blank the TV monitor when no signal is present, which voids this part of the procedure.]
2. With the uniform density phantom in the beam and the system in the automatic exposure mode, fluoroscope and observe the amount of noise on the image (Figure 9.12).
3. With the system in the manual mode, match the fluoroscopic mA and kVp with the factors from the automatic mode.
4. While observing the fluoroscopic image noise, gradually increase the mA until the image is saturated. If the amount of noise decreases with the increased exposure rate (increased mA), the noise is probably quantum mottle. If the amount of noise does not change, it is probably electronic noise.

Problems and Pitfalls

There are many factors that can influence the amount of noise on an image. This test may well be influenced by any of these factors and confuse the test results.

Acceptance Limits

If the noise is so severe that it is affecting the ability of your radiologists to make a diagnosis, corrective action must be taken.

Corrective Action

1. Have a qualified service engineer evaluate your system.
2. If the problem is electronic in nature, the aperture in front of the TV tube should be opened, and the gain of the video amplifier reduced.
3. If the problem is quantum mottle, the exposure rate should be increased until the noise reaches an acceptable level.

9.7. IMAGE LAG

Purpose

To evaluate the lag, smearing, comet tailing, or persistence of video systems used for televised fluoroscopy. This phenomenon appears as a blur of objects in motion in the fluoroscopic image.

Equipment Needed

1. Patient equivalent phantom (PEP)
2. A fender washer, which is usually 2 inches (5 cm) in diameter with a ¼-inch (6-mm) hole in the center [**Note:** A similar-sized device made of lead will provide the same results.]

Procedure

1. Place the uniform density phantom on the table with the fender washer in the center of the phantom (Figure 9.13).
2. Fluoroscope the phantom, while moving the tower or tabletop smoothly in a circular pattern around the center of phantom.

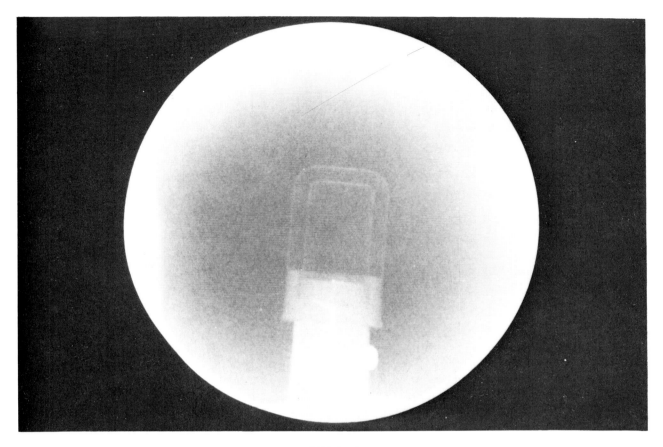

Figure 9.12a. Real-time fluoroscopic image noise at an 8-R/min dose rate.

3. While the tower or tabletop is in motion, note the comet-like tail originating from the hole in the washer and streaking onto the opaque portion of the washer (Figure 9.14).
4. Record your impression of the image in the QC room log.

Problems and Pitfalls

1. This test only results in a subjective impression on the part of the observer, with absolutely no hard data that can be documented.
2. The only way an observer can develop a feel for this problem is by observing several good and bad systems.
3. The use of an object that is too large, which will cause an increase in exposure by the automatic brightness system, may influence the results of the test.
4. Most vidicon camera tubes, by design, have more lag than plumbicon tubes. Before making any judgment about the condition of your system, find out which type of camera tube you are using.

Acceptance Limits

A system that exhibits excessive lag and consequently blurs a moving object is in need of repair or readjustment.

Corrective Action

1. Have your system evaluated by a qualified service engineer.
2. Some lag problems can be resolved by increasing the amount of light reaching the camera tube. This can be accomplished either by opening the aperture in front of the camera tube or by increasing the exposure rate.
3. Replace the camera tube.

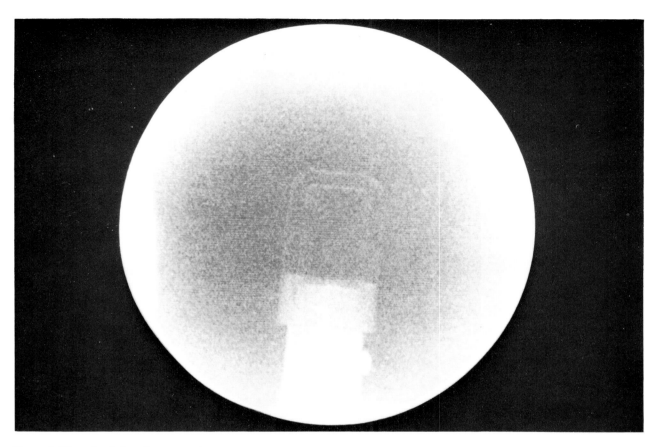

Figure 9.12b.   Real-time fluoroscopic image noise at a 3-R/min dose rate.

9.8.   SETTING AND MAINTAINING CINE AND PHOTOFLUOROSPOT (PFS) FILM CAMERA EXPOSURES

Purpose

To establish and then assure the correct exposure rate for camera systems that record images from image intensifier tubes.

Equipment Needed

1.   Direct readout dosimeter
2.   Patient equivalent phantom (PEP)
3.   Test stand or other device to hold the dosimeter in contact with the image intensifier

Procedure—Photofluorospot (PFS) Film Cameras

1.   Set the system to the automatic exposure control mode, and in most cases, to 80 kVp. [*Note:*   Check the manufacturer's recommendation in the equipment manuals.]
2.   Remove the grid from in front of the image intensifier. [*Note:*   On some types of systems the grid is not easily removed. In the case of some equipment a correction factor and instructions to correct for grid attenuation are found in the equipment manuals.]
3.   Raise the fluoroscopic tower to its maximum height.
4.   Place the PEP on the tabletop.
5.   With the dosimeter chamber supported by the test stand, and centered over the PEP, position the chamber as close as possible to the input of the image intensifier (Figure 9.15). [*Note:*   Systems with conventional

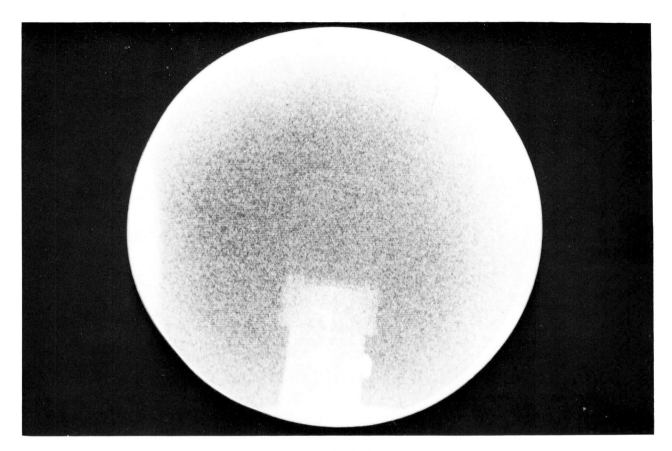

Figure 9.12c.   Real-time fluoroscopic image noise at a 0.75-R/min dose rate.

spot film devices will prevent contact with the image tube, but, in most cases, the distance difference will only amount to a slightly lower exposure reaching the image tube.]

6. Fluoroscopically center the chamber to the center of the image intensifier.
7. With the dosimeter in the exposure mode, make, record, and average the exposure for three separate exposures.
8. The typical exposure range, dependent on the image intensifier size and film quality requirements, is from 50 μR/frame (0.05 mR) to 200 μR/frame (0.2 mR). Systems that are used for angiography may need exposures in excess of the quoted figures to produce lower-noise films. [**Note:**   Check the manufacturer's recommended exposures for your equipment.]
9. With the assistance of a qualified service engineer, adjust the exposure to the desired level, then adjust the aperture in front of the spot film camera to produce the proper film density (typically 0.80–1.20).
10. Confirm the image intensifier entrance exposure and enter it, along with a careful outline of your setup and procedure, in the QC room log.
11. Check and record the entrance exposure to the phantom.
12. On follow-up visits check the entrance exposure to the image tube and the phantom.

Procedure—Cine Systems

1. Follow Steps 1 and 3–6 from the procedure for photofluorospot cameras.
2. Removal of the grid on most dedicated cine systems will expose the glass input of the image tube. Because there is some danger if this glass is broken, this procedure should be performed with the assistance of a qualified service engineer.
3. Set your dosimeter to the exposure rate mode.
4. Once the setup is complete, operate your system *without film* at your normal frame rate.

Figure 9.13.   Image lag test setup.

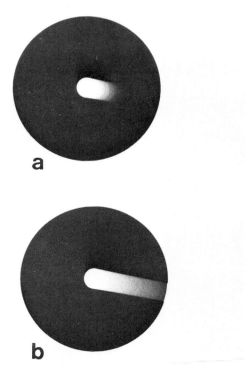

Figure 9.14.   Image lag test results. Sketch of fluoroscopic image of fender washer: (a) minimum lag; (b) objectionable lag. [*Note:*   The appearance of the image depends on many parameters in addition to the fluoroscopic system lag, such as dose rate and speed of moving the tower. Consequently, this is *not* a quantitative test, but a test requiring a visual impression.]

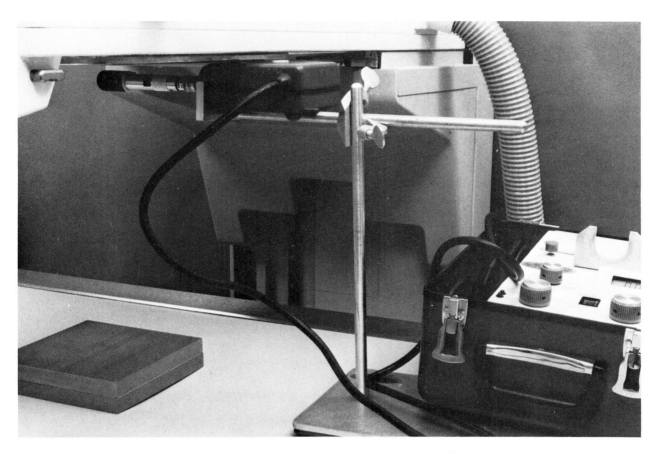

Figure 9.15. Setup for determining the entrance exposure rate at the image intensifier.

5. Run your system long enough for the automatic exposure controls to stabilize, then record the exposure rate (mR/min).

6. To calculate the exposure per frame, divide the exposure per minute by 60 to establish the exposure per second, then divide the exposure per second by the frame rate to determine the exposure per frame. For example, for an exposure rate of 72 mR/min with a frame rate of 60 frames per second (fps):

$$72 \text{ mR/min} \div 60 = 1.2 \text{ mR/sec}$$
$$1.2 \text{ mR/sec} \div 60 \text{ fps} = 0.02 \text{ mR } (20 \text{ } \mu R) \text{ per frame}$$

7. As with most measurements there is some backscatter reaching the dosimeter chamber from the glass and input phosphor of the image tube. Because this procedure is fairly critical, this backscatter must be taken into consideration. In most of the measurements of this type the backscatter amounts to approximately 10–15% of the exposure rate. You can simply subtract 10% of the exposure rate to correct for the backscatter, or attempt to move the image tube away from the chamber to minimize the amount of scatter reaching the chamber. If your automatic exposure system can be locked, run the system unlocked until it has stabilized, then lock it. Once locked in, raise the image intensifier from the chamber and make your measurements. A percentage calculation can be made at this point for future reference by using the measurements with and without backscatter.

8. If you find the entrance exposure rate doesn't meet your needs, adjust the exposure rate, with the assistance of a qualified service engineer, and enter the data in the QC room log.

9. Without moving the dosimeter chamber replace the grid, bring the image intensifier and grid back into contact with the chamber, and then make a measurement of the entrance exposure to the grid. With this data, you can establish a correction factor for the grid that will allow you to check the exposure rate in the future without removing the grid. The correction factor is determined by dividing the entrance rate without the grid by the entrance rate with the grid (e.g., 72 mR/min ÷ 90 mR/min = 0.80). Future measurements can be

made with the grid in place and, multiplying by the correction factor, you can obtain the entrance rate into the image tube. This value should be checked periodically because drifts in kVp will change the correction factor.
10. If the exposure rate is changed, an adjustment of the aperture of the cine camera may be needed to bring the film density to the desired level (typically 0.80 to 1.20).
11. Measure and record the entrance exposure to the phantom.
12. Carefully outline your setup procedure and calculations, and record these data in the QC room log so this procedure can be duplicated on future visits.

Problems and Pitfalls

If you do not place enough attenuator in the beam, or cannot lower the mA sufficiently, problems may occur with the minimum response time of the phototiming system. For most modern photofluorospot systems, slightly more than 10 msec will be sufficient. In cine systems try to use a pulse width of 2 msec or more to prevent problems.

Acceptance Limits

1. Photofluorospot film cameras: 50 to 200 μR/frame, or higher for special procedure applications.
2. Cine systems: 9-inch (23-cm) mode, 10–25 μR/frame; 6-inch (15-cm) mode, 20–50 μR/frame.
3. Check the manufacturer's recommendations for both cine and photofluorospot systems.

Corrective Action

1. If you find the exposure or exposure rate outside of the recommended range, adjust the exposure to the appropriate level with the assistance of a qualified service engineer.
2. Whenever possible, try to lower the exposure levels to the minimum that meet the imaging requirements of your system.

9.9. FLUOROSCOPIC, PHOTOFLUOROSPOT (PFS) FILM, AND CINE RESOLUTION

Purpose

To check the resolution capability of the imaging system

1. As seen on the television monitor
2. As recorded on photofluorospot film
3. As recorded on cine film

Equipment Needed

1. Copper mesh test target composed of eight pie-shaped segments of 16, 20, 24, 30, 35, 40, 50, and 60 mesh per inch
2. Patient equivalent phantom (PEP)

Procedure—Fluoroscopic Systems with Mirror Optics or Television Viewing

1. Center and tape the test target to the face plate of the image intensifier (Figure 9.16).
2. Collimate the beam and adjust the fluoroscopic factors.
   a. For manual brightness systems collimate the beam to the test target (Figure 9.17a) and adjust the fluoroscopic factors to best visualize the test target, e.g., about 50 kVp and 1 mA.
   b. For automatic brightness systems collimate to the test target. The system should automatically adjust to visualize the test target, but systems with minimum or fixed kVp should be set to approximately 50 kVp. Half of the PEP may be used to attenuate the beam if whiteout occurs because of the system's inability to adjust to extremely low radiation levels.
3. On television systems adjust the contrast and brightness controls on the TV monitor to best visualize the test target. The test target should be placed at 45° to the TV scan lines (Figure 9.17b).

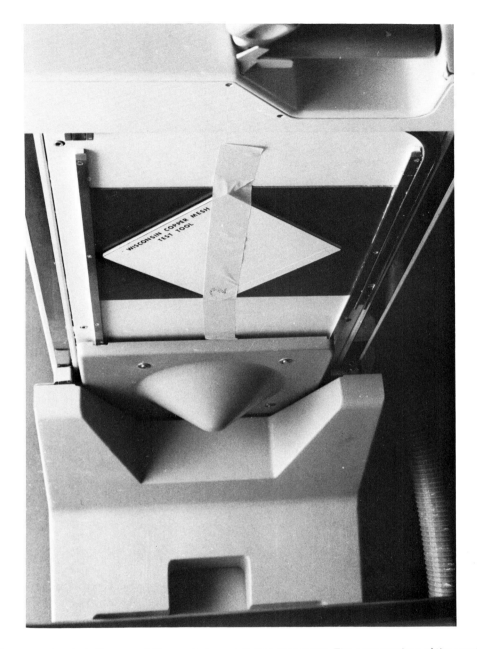

Figure 9.16. Fluoroscopic, photofluorospot film, and cine resolution test setup. The copper wires of the mesh pattern must be oriented at 45° to the television scan lines.

4. Note the finest wire mesh visible in the test target seen in the center and at the edges of the image. Also judge whether the lead numbers appear sharp and whether the entire test target is seen with minimal distortion.

5. Record the results in the QC room log.

Procedure—Photofluorospot Films and Cine Film

1. Set the kVp at the lowest level attainable on the system for making photofluorospots. Make three radiographs of the test target.

2. If the imaging system includes a cine system, set the kVp as low as possible and make a cine run of sufficient length to allow the automatic brightness system to stabilize (at least 5 seconds).

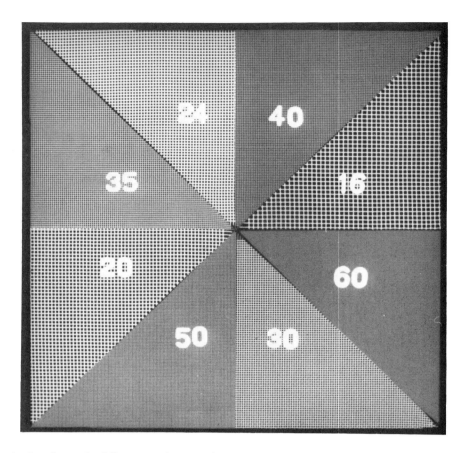

Figure 9.17a. Contact radiograph of fluoroscopic, photofluorospot film, and cine resolution mesh test pattern. The lead numbers indicate the mesh number, or number of wires per inch.

3. Process and view the photofluorospots and the cine film, noting the finest detail visible in the test target seen in the center and at the edges of the image in the films (Figure 9.17c).
4. Record the results in your QC room log.

Problems and Pitfalls

This test gives a measure of the information of the total imaging system. The information is subjective and can be influenced by the monitor settings and room lighting as well as the orientation of the test object. Problems noted in the images cannot be readily identified without further testing. However, the results of the PFS films or cinefilm tests may help narrow the search for the cause of the problem, e.g., if the TV resolution is poor, but the photofluorospot resolution is what you would expect, then the TV camera needs refocusing.

Acceptance Limits

| | Minimum mesh resolutions (mesh/inch) | | | |
| | 9-inch (23-cm) intensifier | | 6-inch (15-cm) intensifier | |
	Center	Edge	Center	Edge
Optical viewing	40	30	40 +	35 +
Standard TV	20–24	20	30–35	24–30
16-mm cine	35 +	30	40	35 +
35-mm cine and spot films	40	30	40 +	35 +

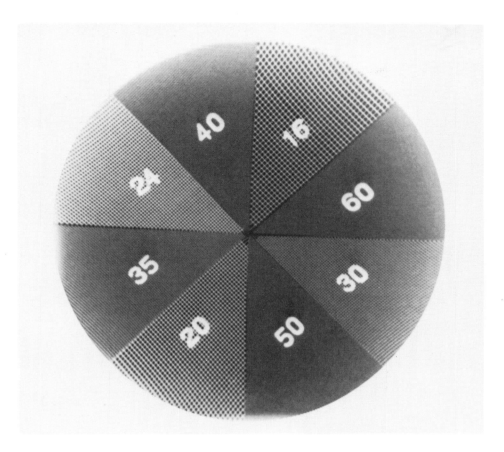

Figure 9.17b. Fluoroscopic image of the mesh test pattern.

Corrective Action

Evaluation and repair of the system by a qualified service engineer is indicated if the resolution is less than the minimum indicated.

9.10. LOW-CONTRAST FLUOROSCOPIC TEST

Purpose

To visually check for the ability of the imaging system to display low-contrast information.

Equipment Needed

Penetrameter consisting of:

1. Two ¾-inch (2-cm) aluminum plates, 7 × 7 inches (18 × 18 cm)
2. One sheet of 1.0-mm aluminum, 7 × 7 inches (18 × 18 cm), with two sets of four holes of the following sizes: 1.0, 3.0, 5.0, and 7.0 mm (¹/₁₆, ¹/₈, ³/₁₆, and ¹/₄ inch).

Procedure—Televised Fluoroscopic Systems

1. Place two aluminum plates plus the hole-drilled aluminum sheet on top of the x-ray table. With mobile C-arm equipment, place the phantom directly on the image intensifier face plate (Figure 9.18).

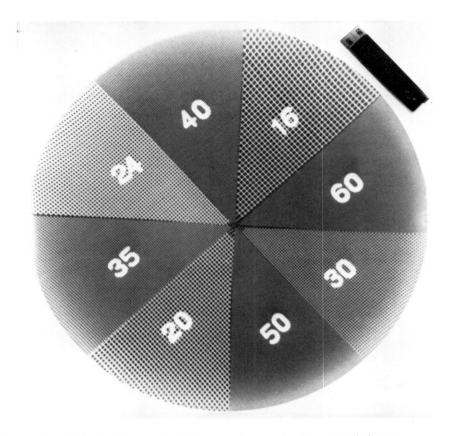

Figure 9.17c.   PFS image of mesh test pattern made at the same time as the fluoroscopic image.

2.   Set the image intensifier 10 inches (25 cm) above the x-ray tabletop with an undertable x-ray tube system.
3.   Allow the automatic brightness system to adjust the fluoroscopic factors and collimate the beam to the test object. The kilovoltage should be in the range of 85 to 90 kVp.
4.   View the image on the TV monitor and adjust the contrast and brightness controls to attain the best visualization of the penetrameter holes (Figure 9.19).
5.   There are two rows of equally sized and spaced holes. You should see both holes of the same size in order to count them as one hole set. Record the maximum number of hole sets seen.
6.   Record the results, including the operating mA and kVp, in the QC room log.

Procedure—Mirror-optic Fluoroscopic Systems

1.   Place the two aluminum plates plus the hole-drilled aluminum sheet on the x-ray tabletop.
2.   Set the image intensifier 10 inches (25 cm) above the x-ray tabletop with undertable x-ray tubes.
3.   Collimate the beam and adjust the fluoroscopic factors.
     a.   Collimate the beam to the test object and allow the automatic brightness system to adjust the fluoroscopic factors. The kilovoltage should be in the range of 85–90 kVp.
     b.   If fluoroscopic exposure factors are controlled manually, set the kVp between 85 and 90 and adjust the mA to attain the most pleasing image.
4.   There are two linear rows of equally sized and spaced holes. You should see both holes of the same size in order to count them as a hole set. Record the maximum number of hole sets seen.
5.   Record the results, including the operating mA and kVp, in the QC room log.

Problems and Pitfalls

1.   The ability to "see" the penetrameter holes is greatly influenced by the TV monitor settings, as is the ability to "see" detail in routine fluoroscopy.

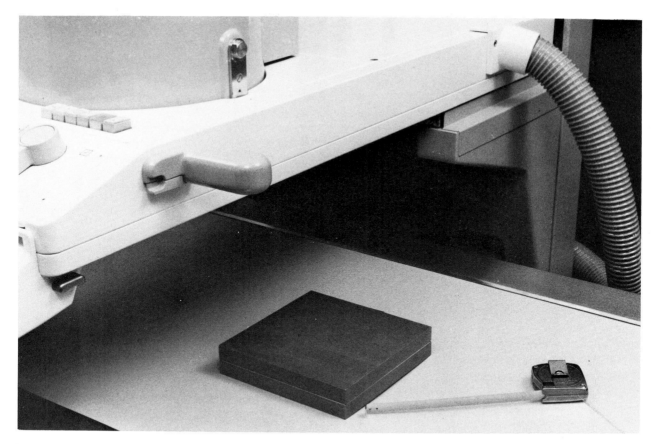

Figure 9.18a. Low-contrast fluoroscopic test setup for undertable x-ray tube.

2. Depending on the usage of your system, the inability to resolve the test holes may be of little consequence. Systems that are not used for chest fluoroscopy or other low-contrast procedures may be unaffected by the lack of low-contrast resolution.

Acceptance Limits

1. A properly adjusted video system should permit clear visualization of $^1/_4$- and $^3/_{16}$-inch (7- and 5-mm) holes clearly. The $^1/_8$-inch (3-mm) holes should be just barely visible. With better systems, you may be able to see the $^1/_{16}$-inch (1-mm) holes clearly.
2. For mirror-optic fluoroscopic systems you should be able to see the $^1/_4$-inch (7-mm) holes, but you will not be able to visualize the smaller holes except on systems of very high quality.

Corrective Action

Adjustment of the imaging system, kVp, and/or mA by a service engineer is required if the system does not perform properly.

9.11. VIDEO WAVEFORM MONITORING

Purpose

To assure that the video signal from the fluoroscopic system meets the appropriate standards in terms of voltages and wave shape, and to assure that the system is producing optimum contrast. This will ensure that the TV monitor or tape recorder is receiving an adequate signal and will be able to produce a quality image over the dynamic range of the system.

Figure 9.18b. Low-contrast fluoroscopic test setup for C-arm fluoroscopic system.

Equipment Needed

1. Oscilloscope or video waveform monitor (WFM) [**Note:** A WFM is an instrument similar to an oscilloscope, but it is designed for use in video signal analysis. Although this instrument is used in the broadcast industry, it is not commonly available to radiology service personnel. There are many features of this instrument that make it ideal for testing video systems. However, the major advantage is that you can select and display a single TV line, or any number of TV lines, for analysis. This allows for more precise measurement and a more complete evaluation of video signals.]
2. Oscilloscope camera
3. Patient equivalent phantom (PEP)
4. BNC T connector
5. A 75-ohm termination
6. A 1/8-inch (3 cm) thick lead strip as long as the input phosphor of the image intensifier and 0.1 times its width [e.g., for a 6-inch (15-cm) intensifier, the strip should be 6 inches (15 cm) long and 0.6 inches (1.5 cm) wide]

Procedure—Video Waveform Voltage and Shape

1. Center the phantom to the image intensifier with the system in the automatic exposure control mode.
2. Disconnect the video cable from the back of the TV monitor and connect this cable to the input of the oscilloscope using the T connector with the 75-ohm termination on one end of the T and the video line on the other end (Figure 9.20). Most systems use the BNC-type connectors; however, there are other types of connectors in use that will require an adapter to connect these with the oscilloscope. An alternate method is to loop through the monitor by connecting a video-quality shielded cable (Teleprompter RG 59 or RG 11, or Belden 8281) from the video output on the back of the monitor to the oscilloscope. This will allow simultaneous viewing of both the monitor and the oscilloscope display. If this approach is used, the termination of the

Figure 9.19a.   Low-contrast fluoroscopic test results. Contact radiograph of penetrameter showing four low-contrast holes.

monitor must be changed from 75 ohms to high impedance, or 3000 ohms. Failure to change the termination will result in incorrect voltage measurements. Normally, the termination is changed by use of a switch on the back of the TV monitor. However, some systems require removal of the back of the monitor to make the change. If an internal change is required, the loop-through method should not be used.

3.   Set the oscilloscope to display 0.2 V per division and 10 μsec per division. Adjust the trigger level to obtain a stable image waveform (Figure 9.21).
4.   Measure the sync voltage (Figure 9.22a).
5.   Measure the black level voltage. (The black level is often referred to as the pedestal or setup voltage.)
6.   Determine the time of the black level in the waveform to evaluate the blanking ring size in systems using video blanking. [***Note:***   Some systems use an external ring or mask on the face of the monitor.]
7.   Observe the shape of the video portion of the waveform, both with and without the fluoroscopic grid in place (Figure 9.22b).
8.   Make a picture of the video waveform with the oscilloscope camera. This will serve as a baseline waveform for future comparisons.
9.   Measure the peak-to-peak video voltage.

Procedure—Contrast or Flare Measurements

1.   Follow the setup procedure in Steps 1 through 3 above but without the use of the PEP.
2.   Adjust the system to operate in the 50–60 kVp range.
3.   Tape the lead strip to the center of the input of the image intensifier or the bottom of the spot film device so that the strip is perpendicular to the TV scan lines.
4.   Measure the peak white voltage (i.e., the maximum voltage), and the voltage of the image behind the lead strip (Figure 9.22c).

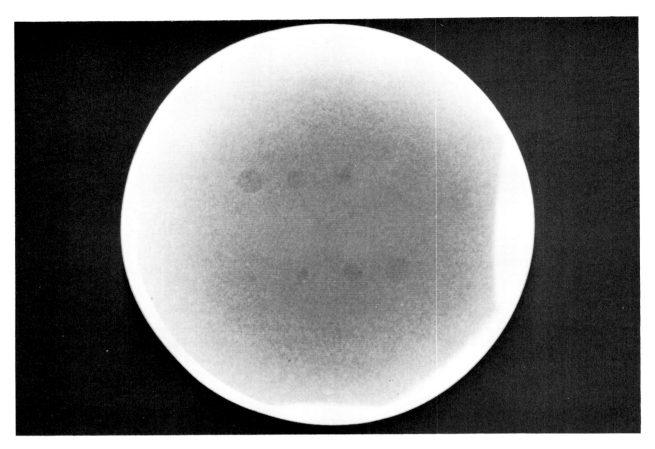

Figure 9.19b. Low-contrast fluoroscopic test results. Fluoroscopic image of the penetrameter.

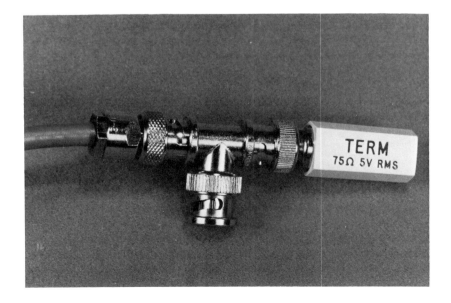

Figure 9.20. Video termination with a "T" connector.

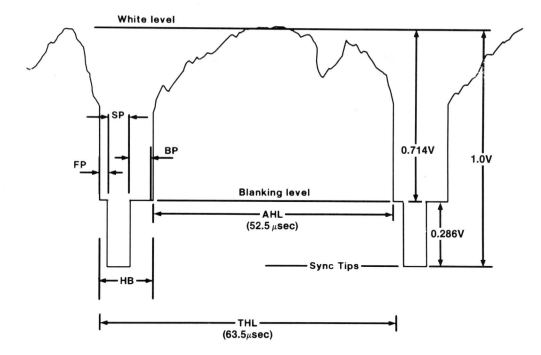

Figure 9.21.   Video waveform. This waveform is based on a 525–line, 30–frame per second (60–field per second) video image. [This is a display of video voltage (vertical) as a function of time (horizontal).] The components are as follows: SP—sync pulse, FP—front porch, BP—back porch, HB—horizontal blanking interval, AHL—active horizontal line (that portion of the scan line carrying image information), and THL—total horizontal line.

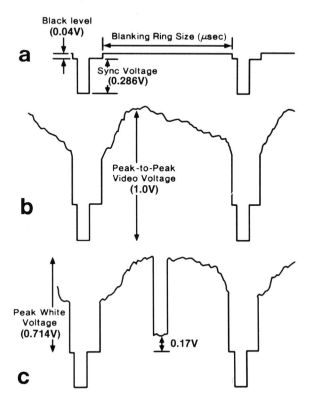

Figure 9.22.   Video waveform monitoring test results. (a) Measurement of the sync pulse and black level can be done without a fluoroscopic image, i.e., with no radiation being produced by the x-ray tube. The blanking ring size will always be less than 52.4 μsec (the active horizontal line length) and will probably be between 35 and 40 μsec at its longest point in the center of the TV field or frame. (b) The peak-to-peak video voltage is important, but you must also assure that the sync pulse voltage is correct. This is also an example of a nonuniform waveform, since the dome is not symmetrical about the center of the active horizontal line. This is probably due to grid misalignment. (c) In order to make the flare measurement it is necessary to determine the voltage difference between the peak white and the black level, and the voltage difference between the area behind the lead strip and the black level.

5. Calculate the percentage contrast using the formula

$$\left[1 - \left(\frac{\text{Voltage Behind Lead Strip}}{\text{Peak White Voltage}}\right)\right] \times 100\% = \% \text{ Contrast}$$

For example (from Figure 9.22)

$$\left[1 - \left(\frac{0.17}{0.714}\right)\right] \times 100\% = 76\%$$

Problems and Pitfalls

1. Improper termination of any monitor and/or tape recorder connected to the video system will result in incorrect waveform voltage. If all the voltages (sync, black level, and video waveform) appear to be higher or lower than expected, check the termination of each component. Under normal operating conditions, the last component and only the last component of the system must be terminated with a 75-ohm termination. All other components should be terminated with the high-impedance or 3000-ohm termination.
2. In some systems, the video signal is blanked once the signal drops to a predetermined level. In these systems, the black level voltage will not appear and cannot be measured without the assistance of an engineer.

Acceptance Limits

1. Specification for video signal voltages vary from manufacturer to manufacturer, so it is necessary to consult the service manuals or a service engineer for specifications for your equipment. In general, the sync pulse should be about 0.3 to 0.4 V. [In actuality, all video signals should comply with the EIA Standard RS-170 (Electronics Industries Association, 1957.)]
2. The black level voltage directly affects the contrast of the system and should be not more than 50 mV (0.05 V).
3. Composite video signal (sync plus video) should be between 0.9 and 1.4 V.
4. The blanking rings should measure, dependent on manufacturer, from 35 to 40 μsec. Similar pieces of equipment from the same manufacturer should be within $\pm$ 1 μsec.
5. The video waveform may vary in shape from unit to unit because of many factors. Some manufacturers use a shading or edge correction circuit that raises the video voltage along the periphery of the image to make up for differences in light output of an image tube over the surface. If an edge correction circuit is used, the waveform will appear flat to dome-shaped across the top of the waveform, or it may even appear depressed in the center if the circuit is overcorrecting. Systems without edge correction circuits will appear dome-shaped and this dome should appear symmetric with a variation from the center to edge of not more than 0.1 V. A change in the shape of the waveform with and without the fluoroscopic grid indicates grid cutoff due to misalignment of the x-ray tube grid combination.
6. Systems with 70% or greater contrast should produce excellent results. Systems with 55–70% contrast should produce acceptable results for general purpose work, but systems with less than 55% contrast are in need of repair or replacement.

Corrective Action

Discuss your findings with a service engineer. Semi-annual cleaning of the lenses of the TV chain, image intensifier–spot film–camera combination is recommended to prevent loss of contrast.

10 SPECIAL DIAGNOSTIC IMAGING SYSTEMS

Although the tests in this section are for equipment that may at first seem to have little in common (portable radiographic units, conventional tomographic equipment, and special procedures suites), they are indeed special applications of standard radiographic and fluoroscopic equipment. Each type of equipment presents special problems in everyday use and also presents special problems for quality control tests.

PORTABLE RADIOGRAPHIC AND CAPACITOR DISCHARGE UNITS

Portable radiographic equipment is not just conventional radiographic equipment on wheels. Although they are somewhat scaled down from permanent equipment, portable systems usually lack sophistication in timing circuits and do not have the extensive circuits available that are normally used for calibration purposes. In addition, battery-operated portables, especially those that use the same battery for both radiographic exposures and the power drive system, present special problems in that every use (exposure or movement of the portable unit) reduces the power available. Consequently, subsequent exposures may become lighter unless the unit is recharged frequently.

In capacitor discharge units, the peak kilovoltage drops continuously during the exposure. This means that the peak kilovoltage at the start may be 100 kVp but will drop to 80 kVp at the end of a 20-mAs exposure. [The peak kilovoltage will drop 1 kV for each mAs of exposure in a unit with a 1-microfarad capacitor (Weaver et al., 1978).] Consequently, special attention must be given to building a technique chart using higher kilovoltage and lower mAs than would

normally be used with a conventional generator. If the desired technique is 90 kVp at 20 mAs, then a technique of 100 kVp would be preferred since the average kilovoltage during the exposure would be about 92 kVp.

Portable equipment should meet all acceptance limits described for general radiographic equipment. This is also true for capacitor discharge units except that these units will not be able to meet the kVp requirements. After appropriate calibration by a qualified service engineer, the kVp should be measured by the QC technologist. On future checks, the kVp values obtained for the capacitor discharge units at this initial test should remain constant, or service is required.

CONVENTIONAL TOMOGRAPHY

Conventional tomography, as opposed to computerized tomography (CT), uses the standard techniques of x-ray source and image receptor motion to produce a thin-section image. In addition to all tests carried out on standard radiographic equipment, it is important to evaluate all aspects of the tomographic motion, thickness of cut, and level of cut on a regular basis. It has been our experience that "add-on" tomographic systems require considerably more attention and service at shorter intervals than even the sophisticated, complex motion tomographic units, assuming that the same number of cases is done per day on each.

Tomographic phantoms are relatively expensive but should be purchased if it is necessary to evaluate complex motion tomographic equipment. The simple tomographic test tool (described on pages 62–65) may be quite adequate for add-on linear motion systems, but the pinhole trace technique described in this chapter should also be used since this provides valuable information concerning the sweep motion of the equipment.

ANGIOGRAPHIC EQUIPMENT

Angiographic or special procedure suites deserve special attention for several reasons. First of all, angiographic equipment is the most sophisticated equipment in most radiology departments (excluding CT). It is necessary to have several interacting components all functioning optimally at the same time, especially in biplane systems. The patients being examined are the most critically ill so equipment failure will have significant consequences, not to mention the normal risk associated with large doses of arterially injected contrast media. The equipment in special procedure rooms is the most expensive in the department, and the cost of personnel to support these rooms is quite high, not to mention the loss of patient revenue if the rooms are out of service for long periods of time. Finally, the exposures received by patients and staff are the highest in special procedure rooms, especially those with cine systems, because of the limited amount of shielding that can be used and the high dose procedures and long fluoroscopic exposure times encountered.

If a hospital has one special procedures suite, then the cost of a complete set of quality control equipment can easily be justified, based on the cost of the special procedures equipment and operating personnel. Most of these rooms should be completely checked at least monthly, and, ideally, test phantoms should be imaged at the beginning of each case. In addition, the technologist responsible for the rooms should make a complete check of the equipment at the beginning of each day, *before* any patient is placed on the table, to assure that all equipment is functional. This should include not only mechanical checks, but checks of the fluoroscopic system using a phantom and checks of film changers to assure that they are functioning properly and loaded with sufficient film to do a complete study.

PROCEDURES

10.1. PORTABLE RADIOGRAPHIC AND CAPACITOR DISCHARGE UNITS

Purpose

To provide consistent, high-quality portable radiographs.

Equipment Needed

Full complement of QC test tools to check collimator and light field alignment, focal spot size, HVL, kVp, exposure time, and mR/mAs linearity and repeatability as described in the Procedures sections of Chapters 6, 7, and 8

Procedure—Conventional Portable Generators

1. Perform the full series of tests that you would perform on a fixed radiographic system.
2. Pay special attention to short exposure times such as those used in chest radiography.
3. On single mA station equipment do repeatability studies at a short (1/60–1/30 sec), medium (½ sec), and long (1 sec or over) exposure time.
4. Although not a true linearity, compare the mR/mAs for 3 or 4 time stations.
5. Record the results in the QC room log.

Procedure—Battery Powered Portables

1. Perform the full series of tests for conventional generator portables.
2. In addition, perform a battery depletion study:
   a. Completely charge the storage batteries.
   b. Select an average technique for the day-to-day work load.
   c. Measure with a dosimeter and record the exposure in mR for three exposures at the preselected technique.
   d. If your machine has power-assisted motion, drive the machine the typical distance one would travel between patient rooms.
   e. Repeat the three exposures and movement sequence until the mR output has fallen to 80% of the original output.
   f. Plot the mR versus the number of exposures on a piece of graph paper (Figure 10.1). If the typical number of exposures per portable run falls short of the number required to reduce the output to the 80% level, you should have little trouble producing consistent-density radiographs if all other radiographic factors are properly controlled.
   g. If your typical case load goes beyond the 80% mark, recharge the batteries for 5 minutes, and make a measurement of the exposure output. Typically, this brief recharge will bring the generator close to the original output. [*Note:* This brief recharge procedure should be implemented during heavy case load portable outings.]
3. Record the results in the QC room log.

Procedure—Capacitor Discharge Portable and Permanent Equipment

Perform the series of tests described above for conventional portable generators.

The kVp measurement on capacitor discharge equipment will need special acceptance limits. A typical capacitor discharge unit (1-microfarad capacitor) will lose 1 kVp for each 1 mAs of exposure. In other words, a typical kVp test cassette exposure for 80 kVp would require 20 mAs, and would yield a final minimum of 60 kVp with an average kVp of about 70. To further complicate the issue, the filtration used in the test cassette preferentially attenuates the lower-energy photons, which will yield a kVp reading higher than the average kVp.

Problems and Pitfalls

1. Portable radiographs of poor quality are often accepted because they are "just portables." The same performance characteristics can and should be expected from mobile equipment and fixed equipment.

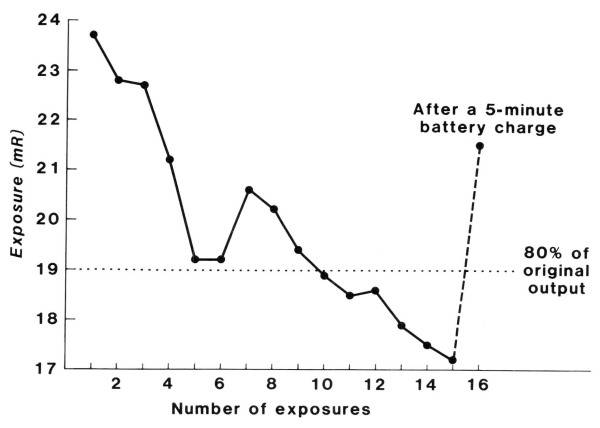

Figure 10.1. Output exposure as a function of the number of exposures for a battery-operated x-ray unit.

2. Special efforts should be made to provide the technologist with every possible aid to assure the correct source-to-image distance, angulation, beam alignment, and exposure factors.
3. Battery-powered portables should be recharged after *every* use to assure maximum consistency in output, i.e., they should be plugged in and charging at all times when not in use.
4. Capacitor discharge units require special consideration when building technique charts. It is advisable from the patient exposure standpoint to chart higher kVp and lower mAs than you would use for conventional generators.

Acceptance Limits

1. Conventional and battery-powered mobile equipment should meet the acceptance limits outlined for fixed equipment.
2. Capacitor discharge equipment should meet all acceptance limits outlined except for the measured kVp. Because there are no calibration curves provided with the kVp test cassette for capacitor discharge equipment, no specific limits can be given, but for an 80-kVp, 20-mAs exposure, expect a 72–74 kVp reading.

Corrective Action

If the acceptance limits are not met, have a service engineer correct the problems.

10.2. TOMOGRAPHY

Purpose

To assure maximum resolution in planes of interest and optimum blur of overlying structures, and that the patient entrance exposures are the same from room to room.

Equipment Needed

1. Tomographic phantom [commercially available, typically consists of varying-size mesh resolution patterns and lead numbers to indicate slice level and thickness (Figure 10.2)]
2. A 4 × 4 × ⅛-inch (10 × 10 × 0.3-cm) sheet of lead with a ¹/₁₆-inch (1.5-mm) countersunk pinhole in the center
3. Direct readout dosimeter

Procedure

1. Place the phantom and the lead pinhole on the table (Figure 10.3). [**Note:** For linear tomographic equipment turn the phantom so the lines of the mesh pattern are at 45° to the direction of the tube travel.]
2. Adjust the fulcrum to the appropriate level for the phantom being used. The pinhole should *not* be at the same level as the cut level. It should be about 2 cm above that level.
3. Set the arc to the maximum routinely used. Make sure the exposure time is long enough to cover the complete arc.
4. Cover the phantom, but not the pinhole, with a sheet of lead.
5. With the x-ray tube centered and perpendicular to the film, make a nontomographic exposure at the same kVp and about 10% of the mAs needed to properly expose the phantom. This exposure will mark the center of the pinhole trace.
6. Remove the lead, zero the dosimeter, and make a tomographic exposure of the phantom and the pinhole; read the exposure from the dosimeter. [**Note:** Depending on the phantom thickness, the pinhole trace may be too dark to interpret. An ideal density would be 0.6 to 1.2, and can be achieved by placing several millimeters of the aluminum used to measure the HVL over the pinhole.]
7. Repeat the procedure in the opposite direction for linear tomographic equipment that exposes in both directions.
8. The maximum arc should show any problems, if they exist, but if you wish to evaluate the slice thickness for lesser tomographic arcs repeat the procedure at the desired arc.
9. Interpretation
   a. Slice level—For the typical commercial type, read the lead number that is in best focus (Figure 10.4).
   b. Slice thickness—Observe the total number of lead numbers in focus.
   c. Resolution
      i. Observe the finest mesh size resolved (typically #30 to #50 mesh is present in most phantoms).
      ii. Compare films with films from a similar tomographic unit or with ones taken previously on the same equipment.

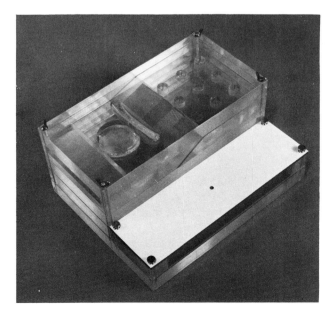

Figure 10.2a. A tomographic phantom developed for our quality control program that allows all sections to be imaged at one time, and allows for a pinhole trace to be made at the same time as the tomographic image.

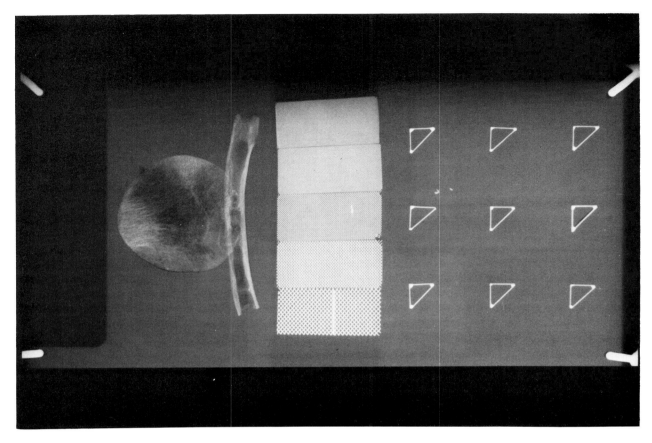

Figure 10.2b.   Radiograph of tomographic phantom shown in **a.** A portion of the femur lies in the plane of the tomographic cut with the rib lying above the plane. The mesh patterns lie at an angle through the plane of cut. A cutout for identification information (dark area on the left) lies in the plane of cut. The small triangles also lie in, above, and below the plane of cut, but are separated by 1 mm.

    d. Pinhole trace
       i. For linear tomography the pinhole trace should be equally divided on either side of the center mark.
      ii. Check any excessive change in density over the length of the trace. Areas of increased and decreased density will indicate hesitation or changes in the speed of the tomographic sweep.
    e. Blur
       i. Observe the edges of the resolution mesh or the lead numbers out of the plane of focus for smoothness of blur.
      ii. It may be helpful to place a paper clip bent into the shape of a triangle on top of the phantom, with one edge of the triangle parallel to the direction of the tomographic sweep. This arrangement will give an indication of the blur for objects parallel, 45° to, and 90° to the direction of travel.

10.   Record the results and the dosimeter reading in the QC room log.

Problems and Pitfalls

1.   Some linear units may produce better results in one direction of travel than the other. Make sure to test in both directions of travel. If efforts to correct the problem fail, establish a procedure to have all tomographic exams done in the direction that produces the best results.
2.   Pay special attention to the blur capability of the tomographic unit. A phantom film may give the appearance of a properly functioning machine, but if the blur is poor, the results will be less than adequate.
3.   When comparing resolution between different machines (using the same screen-film combination) keep in mind that different-size focal spots will have an effect on resolution.

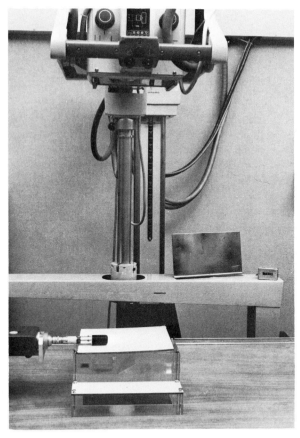

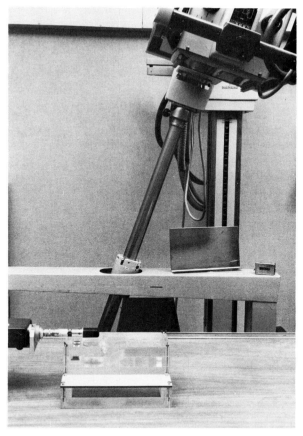

Figure 10.3a. Tomographic test setup. A light exposure is first made (with lead over the imaging portion of the phantom) with the tube in the center position so that a pinhole image is produced marking the center of the sweep.

Figure 10.3b. Tomographic test setup. A conventional tomographic exposure is then made so that both pinhole images and a tomographic image of the thick section are made at the same time.

4. The dosimeter must be located in the same position relative to the anode-cathode axis (parallel and perpendicular) for consistent results. Also, the dosimeter should be placed such that it will be exposed to radiation during the entire tomographic sweep.

Acceptance Limits

1. The slice level should be within 5 mm of the indicated level.
2. The slice thickness varies with arc, but a linear sweep with a 30° arc should have a slice thickness of 2 to 2.5 mm. A complex motion tomographic unit operating in excess of 30° of arc should have a slice thickness of about 1 mm.
3. The resolution will be dependent on the focal spot size, the magnification (phantom thickness), and the smoothness of the tomographic motion. A good-quality unit will resolve the finest mesh (#50 mesh). A typical linear tomographic unit should resolve the #40 mesh. A unit that can resolve only the coarsest mesh size (#20 or #30) is in need of repairs.
4. The pinhole trace for a linear unit should be equally divided on either side of the center mark. If it is not, check to see that the correct exposure time was used. Complex motion units should not leave large gaps or greatly overlap on the trace pattern. The density of the trace should be relatively smooth and follow a smooth, uniform course (Figure 10.5).
5. The blur of objects out of the plane of focus should be smooth and not a series of repeating images of the object.

Figure 10.4. Commercially available tomographic phantom. This phantom requires several exposures to obtain the necessary information.

6. For similar tomographic systems using similar generators, tubes, collimators, tabletops, and screen-film combinations the entrance exposures to the phantom should be within ± 10% of each other. If there is a greater variation, then you should investigate the cause, paying particular attention to the HVL, the output of the x-ray tube, and any other factors that may affect the exposure to the patient. If rooms do not use similar equipment, then exposure variations will be greater than noted above. However, you should investigate the reason for these variations and consider differences in the tabletops, HVLs, collimator design, x-ray tubes, and any other factors that may affect the output of the x-ray generator and the patient exposure. Measurements of the PEP for Bucky uniformity and motion and of the exposure consistency (pages 89–90) should also be made. With these measurements, you can compare entrance exposures in the room under two different conditions.

Corrective Action

1. Observe the motion of the x-ray tube and film tray for hesitation or adverse motion. If adverse motion is seen or indicated on the pinhole trace, try to locate and correct the cause of the problem.
2. Clean any dirt from the tube and Bucky tracks or support rails.
3. Tighten any loose screws, bolts, or connecting pins.
4. Look for loose or worn bearings.
5. Make sure the tube and film tray locks are releasing during the tomographic motion.
6. Correct the exposure time and check position-sensing microswitches if the pinhole trace is not equal on either side of the center.
7. Consult a qualified service engineer if your efforts fail to correct the problem.

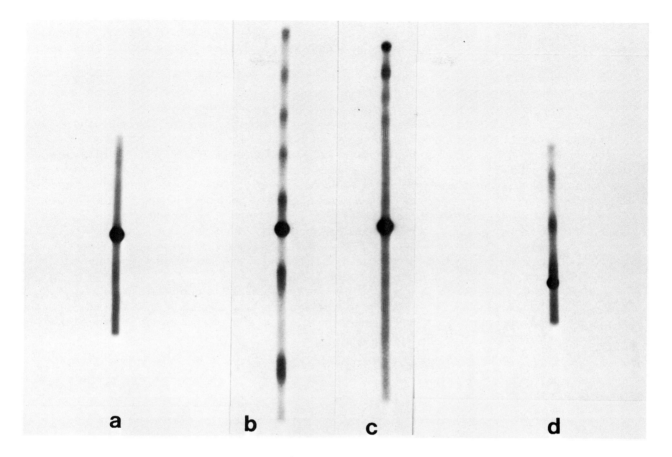

Figure 10.5.   Pinhole traces. **(a)** Good pinhole trace with image located symmetrically on either side of center mark. **(b)** Unacceptable motion, probably due to dirt or lack of lubrication on the rails of the tube and cassette system. **(c)** Note the heavy exposure at the top end of the trace. This could be due to either the tube not starting to move before the x-ray exposure is initiated or the tube motion terminating before the exposure terminates. **(d)** In addition to poor motion this exposure was not symmetric about the center mark. This may be due to the x-ray exposure time terminating the exposure before the entire tomographic swing has been completed.

10.3.   ANGIOGRAPHIC EQUIPMENT

Purpose

To assure optimum-quality angiographic examinations.

Equipment Needed

1.   A full complement of test tools to check collimator alignment, focal spot size, HVL, kVp, exposure time, mR/mAs linearity, and repeatability
2.   Star focal spot test target (for focal spots of 0.3 mm or less)
3.   Copper mesh resolution test tool, and a low-contrast resolution test tool to check fluoroscopic and cine resolution
4.   Lead resolution target
5.   Screen contact test mesh
6.   A homogeneous patient equivalent phantom (PEP)
7.   Direct readout dosimeter

Procedure—Roll or Cut-Film Angiographic Equipment

1. Perform the full series of tests on the generator(s) and x-ray tube(s) as described in the Procedures section of Chapter 8.
2. Test the high- and low-contrast resolution parameters (pages 150–155) and the maximum and standard operating exposure levels (pages 133–138) of the image intensifier.
3. Check the screen contact of the film changer at the maximum frame rate used in your aniographic suite, then compare the rapid film contact test with a static (single-exposure) film from the film changer.
4. Check and compare the resolution (with a phantom) of the film changer with static and serial films at the maximum filming rate used. If magnification work is performed check the resolution both in contact and at the normal magnification ratio used. The phantom can consist of a variety of test objects placed on top of the uniform density phantom used to measure the fluoroscopic exposure rate. A lead resolution target with a bar pattern that goes to 5 cycles/mm or beyond would be ideal, but a copper mesh pattern can be used [***Note:*** Turn the mesh pattern 45° to the grid lines, and the lead target 90° to the grid lines.] A magnification phantom can be constructed of loosely bound steel wool, small catheters, fine wire, and small pieces of bone placed on the uniform density phantom (Figure 10.6). These objects could also be used with the lead resolution target or copper mesh to check the resolution in contact (non-magnification) situations. Save the static film and one of the serial films for comparison on return checks.
5. Measure focal spots used for magnification with a star focal spot test target at a 3:1 or 4:1 magnification ratio as described on pages 79–80. In addition to measuring the focal spot at the NEMA-specified mA and kVp (one-half the maximum mA and kVp), measure the focal spot at the maximum mA used to check for excessive focal spot blooming.

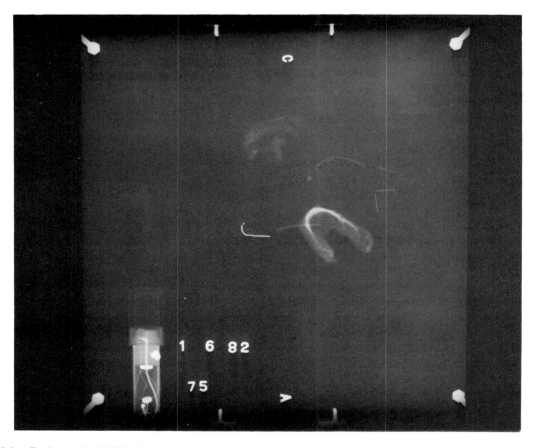

Figure 10.6. Radiograph of PEP with objects added that are common in the angiographic environment.

Problems and Pitfalls

1. An angiographic suite consists of many key components that can greatly affect the quality of the final product. Each component must be thoroughly tested on a regular basis.
2. Some film changers are not capable of producing good-quality angiograms at a high frame rate, because of either poor design or excessive wear. Check them at all frame rates normally used, and use the frame rate that produces the best results whenever possible.
3. Focal spots that have excessive bloom and produce less than adequate images are not covered under any manufacturer's warranty. Situations like this must be handled on a one-to-one basis with the vendor.

Acceptance Limits

1. Generators, x-ray tubes, and fluoroscopic systems should meet acceptance limits outlined in the respective Procedures sections of Chapters 7, 8, and 9.
2. Film changer screen contact may deteriorate somewhat on the outside edges of the image during serial runs because of the lack of adjustment points at the very edge of the pressure plates, but the center contact must be uniform throughout. If the contact problems cannot be corrected because of poor design or excessive wear, try to limit the use to the slowest possible frame rate.
3. Resolution loss due to serial motion should be minimal—up to 6 frames/sec on a good quality film changer. You may lose one group of bars (approximately 0.2 to 0.3 cycle/mm) on a lead resolution target, and you should not lose a full mesh size if a copper mesh pattern is used.

Corrective Action

1. If you experience excessive resolution loss, check for vibration, film movement during exposure, or changer motion that could cause blurring of the image. If none can be found consult a service engineer.
2. For generators or x-ray tube problems consult a service engineer.

Procedure—Cine Systems

1. Check the fluoroscopic maximum and standard exposure rate as outlined on pages 133–138.
2. In addition, regularly check the standard cine exposure rate following the same procedure outlined on pages 146–150. Clearly outline all the parameters, such as tower height, collimation, frame rate, and selected kVp, so this procedure can be easily duplicated on return checks. The ideal time to start this program would be just after a service engineer has calibrated the system. The typical method of setting the exposure rate is to remove the grid from the face of the image intensifier and then set the entrance exposure rate through an attenuator to the input phosphor to approximately 18 to 20 μR/frame or 70 mR/min.
3. Regularly check the high- and low-contrast resolution of the cine system as described on pages 150–155.
4. Check and record the film density produced by the cine system by reading the density from a low-contrast test target or from a cardiovascular phantom if one is available.
5. A simple phantom and patient identification marker can be constructed from inexpensive materials that can provide a continuous check of a cine system performance (Figure 10.7). This phantom can be used to identify the patient before each case and will continuously give an indication of any changes in resolution and contrast. The attenuator can be copper (best) or aluminum. A small step wedge (3 or 4 steps) can be made out of lead foil, such as the lead backing in a cassette or the lead in a dental film back. Steps with 1, 2, 4, and 8 thickness of lead foil from a dental pack can be used. Copper screen can be used for a simple resolution pattern. [*Note:* Check with a local hardware dealer for copper screen mesh.] The date and the patient's identification number can be placed on the phantom with lead numbers.
6. With the assistance of a service engineer set up a program to clean the lenses of the image amplifier and cine camera every 6 months. Excessive dust and dirt can greatly reduce the contrast of a system.
7. Set up a program to clean the viewing screen and lenses of your cine projector monthly.

Problems and Pitfalls

Cine systems are complex systems that have more stringent requirements than most radiographic equipment. Work closely with the manufacturer of your equipment to learn these requirements, and establish a quality control program that meets the needs of your equipment.

Acceptance Limits

1. The standard cine exposure rate is dependent on many factors, such as the frame rate, kVp, filtration, and exposure requirements of your image amplifier. A change of 1 μR/frame at the entrance to the image inten-

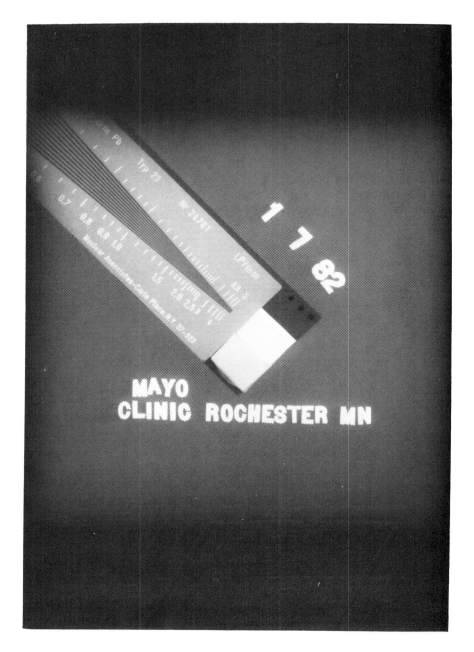

Figure 10.7a. Contact radiograph of the cine patient identification and test phantom. Patient ID information is added to this phantom and it is imaged before each patient is placed on the table for an examination.

sifier can mean a difference of several R/min at the entrance to a 21-cm patient equivalent phantom. You will have to establish acceptance limits that meet the needs of your equipment. To give you some idea of the magnitude of the entrance exposure rate, our equipment at 60 frames per second in the 6-inch (15-cm) mode operates at about 70–75 R/min through a 21-cm patient equivalent phantom (at 70 kVp).

2. A good-quality cine system will be able to easily resolve #60 mesh in the center of the image. If a lead resolution target is used expect to resolve 2 cycles/mm or better. The low-contrast resolution test should resolve the smallest hole size [1/16 inch (1.5 mm)].

3. The typical film density range selected is from 0.80 to 1.2 (these are not control limits).

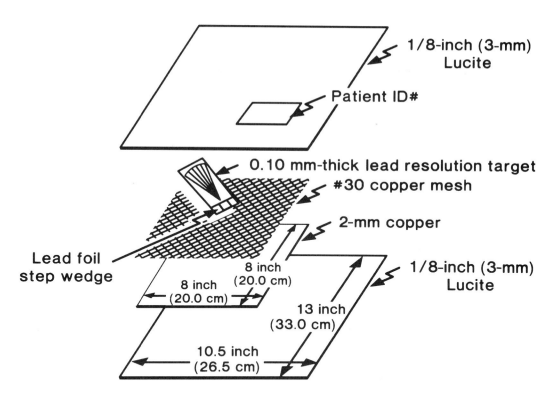

Figure 10.7b. Sketch of the cine patient identification and test phantom.

Corrective Action

1. Carefully follow the manufacturer's maintenance schedule and particularly the cine camera film loading and maintenance instructions.
2. For exposure rate or resolution problems consult a qualified service engineer.

11 _____ MISCELLANEOUS TESTS AND TECHNIQUES

In almost any book, certain topics defy classification in a logical manner. Consequently, we have grouped a series of unrelated tests in this chapter. This is not to imply that these tests are unimportant or that they have been added as an afterthought. In fact, some of the topics in this chapter may be more important than those that have already been covered.

VIDEO HARD-COPY CAMERAS

Any diagnostic imaging system is only as good as the weakest link in the imaging chain. This is equally true with video hard-copy cameras used to make permanent images from CT scanners, ultrasound equipment, fluoroscopic video images, and digital radiographic systems as well as from many imaging systems in nuclear medicine. These cameras, also known as multiformat cameras, take a video signal and display it on a cathode ray tube (CRT) and then optically transfer it to film.

Many of the older cameras used phototiming circuits with a photocell monitoring the output phosphor of the CRT. These systems usually work for CT applications, but they create many problems in ultrasound, where the amount of image information may vary from scan to scan, especially with B-mode scans. Since there is less information on the monitor (i.e., less light) in some images, the photocell attempts to compensate for this by increasing the exposure time. We strongly recommend that, if you have this type of camera, the phototiming circuit should be disabled and you should work with a fixed exposure time on the order of 1 second. (This feature is not to be confused with the microprocessor-controlled circuits

on newer cameras that monitor the video signal levels.)

On many cameras, the video monitors are not black-level clamped. This means that as you change the contrast, the brightness will shift to a different level. This creates considerable difficulty in that changes in contrast also change the overall density of the film, making adjustments difficult and time consuming.

Whenever adjustments are being made to these cameras, or to any video device, changes should be made in only the contrast or brightness. Never change both contrast and brightness at the same time. Adjust the brightness to obtain the desired density on the film (usually in the background or low-density area) and then adjust the contrast to give a pleasing image. In addition, when adjusting the brightness and contrast, view the monitor and assure that you can see a dim, low-contrast image. If the brightness and contrast are driven to a high level on the monitor, the scanning spot tends to increase in size, decreasing the sharpness and resolution of the images.

The more recent developments in hard-copy cameras have included the addition of microprocessor circuits that monitor the video level of the signal entering the camera and set the exposure appropriately. Most of these devices work quite well as long as the video signal meets the EIA standard RS–170 (Electronics Industries Association, 1957). Many pieces of imaging equipment do not meet this standard. For example, one ultrasound camera produced a 1.5-V signal for the alphanumerics and white mask overlaying the image (a maximum of 1.0 V is specified in

RS–170) while the image information was contained in the signal between 0.0 and 0.6 V. Since the camera monitored the peak video signal, it did an excellent job of assuring that the 1.5-V signal was reproduced correctly on the film, but the diagnostic information was produced at an exceedingly low contrast and was quite dark. It is essential that the signal output from any video equipment meets the RS–170 standard if an optimal image is to be displayed and recorded.

Some of the newer cameras offer a raster blending feature. Contrary to popular belief, this is not achieved by making the scanning spot larger, but rather by moving either the scanning spot or the entire raster up and down slightly (less than one line width) to fill in the space between the scanning lines. This does not affect the vertical resolution since the blending only fills in the open spaces, nor does it affect the horizontal resolution since the scanning spot is as small as it would be if the feature was not used (Figure 11.1). However, to realize the best possible results from raster blending, it is necessary to record at least eight video frames. If you record one frame, no blending will be present; with two frames some im-

provement will be noticed; and so on. It is recommended that you record at least 16 frames for the best results or (ideally) 30 frames, which results in a 1-sec exposure and also allows the use of the camera with minimum brightness settings on the CRT.

Some of the new cameras offer "frame-grabbing" or "on-the-fly" modes. This is particularly useful when real-time recording is desired, such as in real-time ultrasound or in the recording of fluoroscopic images where motion is a problem. However, in recording a single frame, the image quality will be poorer (contain more noise) than if you record (average) more frames in a single image. This is the inevitable trade-off between low-noise images with long exposures and the need to make images with a short exposure time to reduce motion.

IMAGE QUALITY TESTS FOR PRODUCT COMPARISONS

It is frequently necessary to evaluate new products to assess their effects on image quality and patient exposure. This may be done to assure that the depart-

Figure 11.1a.   Video image demonstrating the effects of raster blending. Video image of entire display of an electronically generated gray scale.

Figure 11.1b. Close-up of gray scale without raster blending.

ment is using the best available and/or most economical products, such as screens and films, in its patient examinations. Since the QC technologist is the person in the department who has the test equipment and the expertise in its use, product comparisons are a logical part of his or her duties.

A vendor should make samples of new products available at no cost to your department. Also, the evaluation should be carried out in your department in the way the product will be used. One firm showed comparison chest films of two patients made using two products. The old product was used to make a chest radiograph of a 250-pound (115-kg), 5-foot 5-inch (165-cm) male; the new product was used to make a "comparison" chest radiograph of a 120-pound (55-kg), 5-foot 8-inch (170-cm) female (best described as having "centerfold anatomy"). Needless to say, everyone can predict in advance which chest radiograph will look "best."

In blind product comparisons, and in many other evaluations, the individuals doing the comparison will spend most of their time trying to determine which of the two films, for example, is the new one. In order to avoid this problem, all markings on the films should be eliminated except for numerical markings

used for identification purposes, which should have no relationship to the speed or types of products being evaluated. This includes trimming off *all* edge markings on the films and from the screens.

Slight differences in the way the films are made can influence the impressions of the individuals making comparisons. Through experience, we have found that the density on phantom films, be they PEP films or anatomical phantom films, must be matched to ±0.05 in density at a density of about 1.0. If they are not matched to this level, differences will be noted by the radiologists, who will attribute this to differences in the products.

Before a final decision is made to purchase a new product or change to another brand, clinical films must be made for comparison purposes since phantom films are sometimes misleading. Even anatomical phantom films do not really provide images identical to patient films since phantoms are made with dry bones, material *simulating* tissue, and materials that do not really mimic the patient and various anatomical information. However, patient studies must be carried out with extreme care.

Any time a second film is made on the same patient that is not needed for diagnosis, this must be

Figure 11.1c.   Close-up of gray scale with raster blending. Note that the edge sharpness is maintained with raster blending.

considered as human research or human studies. Such films should not be made without the informed consent of the patient. In addition, most institutions require that such studies be approved by the radiation control committee and the human studies committee. In all cases, before any new product is introduced into the clinical environment, the technologist should discuss this completely with the chairman of the department and be sure of all the implications of the tests and the test procedure.

Ideally, you should expose two films on the same patient in comparing screens or films. For example, if chest radiography is of interest, then two films should be made on the same patient, in the same position, exposed within a short period of time, and in such a manner that the densities match as closely as possible. (In this case, ±0.10 is usually acceptable in terms of density variation between films.) However, this involves informed consent and approval by various committees, and, in fact, in many institutions studies requiring two exposures of the same patient, where the second provides no additional diagnostic information, may not be approved.

There are alternative methods that can be used. For example, the various images in a series for ex-

cretory urograms may be made on different films. Where both left and right extremities are to be radiographed, one film or screen to be compared can be used on the left and the other on the right. For mammography comparisons, the left breast can be imaged with one image receptor and the right with the other. Although this is not the best way to evaluate new products, it does avoid the problem of committee approval and informed consent. If this method is used, then the left should not consistently be radiographed on the old product and the right on the new; rather, the products being compared should be used randomly. Also, the total number of patients involved in such a study should be kept to the absolute minimum, both to minimize the dose and risk to the patient and to avoid as much confusion as possible with multiple imaging systems in the radiology department.

ATTENUATION MEASUREMENTS

Attenuation is the proportion of radiation that is absorbed by the item being measured, whereas transmission is the proportion of radiation that is transmitted through the item. In other words, the transmission is equal to 100% minus the percentage of attenuation. We discuss the measurement of the attenuation in this section since the transmission can be derived from that.

In evaluating various products, it is often necessary to determine the attenuation or transmission of the product. In addition, you should determine the attenuation of the tabletop and grid combination to assist in balancing technique charts and to assist in reducing patient exposure differences from room to room.

In the determination of attenuation, it is essential to make all measurements using the same beam quality you would encounter where the product is being used. For example, if you were to measure the attenuation of a cassette front at 70 kVp with no phantom in the beam, you would find that the attenuation is much higher than if the measurements were made at 70 kVp through the PEP. In the first case, all of the soft radiation in the beam reaches the cassette front and is preferentially absorbed. In the second case, with the phantom, the soft radiation is absorbed by the phantom so that primarily harder radiation is reaching the cassette front, showing a relatively lower attenuation. This is particularly important in comparing materials that have different spectral absorptions, such as aluminum and carbon fiber. One manufacturer claimed that a carbon fiber product had 50% less attenuation than an aluminum counterpart. Making the measurements as described in this section, we noted only 7% less attenuation, a difference that was substantiated in clinical tests.

COPY FILM

Next to the excuse for the poor quality of portable radiographs being "well, they are just portables," comes the often-heard excuse that "the films are not good because they are just copies." Neither of these are really excuses and should never be accepted in a radiology department that is concerned with quality.

Copy films are specifically designed by the manufacturer to reproduce *faithfully* the exact densities of the original film up to a density of 2.3 to 2.5. Since copy film is a single-emulsion film, the entire density range of a radiograph (in excess of 3.0) will never be duplicated with presently available films. However, for 95% of the uses, a duplicate with today's films will look identical to the original radiograph (except for the shiny surface on some copy films).

One of the major failures in copying films comes from attempting to lighten a radiograph that is too dark or darken one that is too light. This will *never* produce a quality duplicate, let alone produce a duplicate of the radiograph as it should have been made in the first place. The copy procedure should be set up as described in this chapter to duplicate exactly the density and contrast of the original, and changes should only be made when deviations from these ideal settings are required because of changes in the copy film or light source.

You should be able to display a properly made duplicate on a viewbox next to the original radiograph without a radiologist being able to consistently tell which is the duplicate and which is the original.

METHODS OF LOWERING THE FLUOROSCOPIC EXPOSURE RATE

In many cases, a piece of fluoroscopic equipment is set up to produce the best image quality with little attention to the exposure rate. One method of producing a high-quality, noise-free image is to operate the generator at a high exposure rate. These high-dose images are very pleasing to the eye but may not, and in most cases do not, increase the ability to make the diagnosis over a slightly noisier, less pleasing image, especially in high-contrast procedures such as GI studies. With current awareness and concern about the effect of exposure to ionizing radiation, many radiology departments have found that they can lower the fluoroscopic exposure rate considerably and not hamper the ability to make the diagnosis. This can be done by eliminating the use of grids (Gray and Swee, 1982) and by the techniques described in this section.

Before considering changing the exposure rates, a thorough evaluation of the use of your equipment and the needs of your department must be made by everyone involved. In addition, some judgment must be made on what quality of image is needed to make the diagnosis.

The most noticeable change in a low-dose image will be an increase in image noise (quantum mottle) and a loss of low-contrast resolution. There should be little or no change in the medium- to high-contrast resolution and very little change in the overall contrast.

The age and condition of your equipment is an important factor. An older piece of equipment may not allow the degree of exposure reduction that a new piece of equipment can tolerate. Some types of fluoroscopic equipment have an optional high-exposure mode. This option gives you the opportunity to lower the dose rate in the standard mode, but still have a higher exposure mode for exams that require a lower-noise image, such as chest fluoroscopy. Fluoroscopic systems that have vidicon camera tubes can tolerate lower exposure rates better than systems with plumbicon tubes since the lag in the vidicon system smooths the appearance of the quantum mottle or noise.

Particular areas that should be considered for reduced-dose fluoroscopy include portable image intensifiers used in surgical procedures, fluoroscopic localization used for tomography or GI filming, catheter placement during special procedures, and GI studies.

WHAT TO DO BEFORE
THE SERVICE ENGINEER LEAVES

One word that should be emphasized in this section is *"before."* Before the engineer leaves and even *before* the covers are put back on the equipment, the QC technologist should verify the integrity of the equipment and the quality of the images being produced. This also assumes that the QC technologist will verify that the original problem has been corrected and that the equipment is producing images of a quality similar to or better than before service was requested.

The main reason for testing the equipment before the service engineer leaves is to assure that the problem has been corrected, and that more problems have not been introduced so that the service engineer will not have to return later. Remember that every service call is billed at the rate of about $60 per hour including travel time! Also, this helps to avoid developing an adversary relationship between the QC technologist and the service engineer. If the QC technologist can work with the service engineer in sorting out problems, a better relationship will result than would be the case with the technologist calling the engineer after he has left and telling him that he did not do the job properly, to say nothing of the cost involved in this latter approach.

FILM VIEWBOXES

Although no specific procedure has been included for the quality control of film viewboxes, standard policies and procedures should be developed to assure consistency throughout the department. Improper or inconsistent illumination can affect the diagnostic potential of even the finest radiograph. A difference in illumination or ambient lighting conditions between the film stacking and film interpretations areas can create misunderstanding and confusion within a diagnostic imaging department.

One way to approach the problem is to establish a policy of cleaning the viewboxes and changing *all* of the bulbs in the viewboxes periodically. Only one type of bulb should be used in all viewboxes throughout the department, and that type should be made by one manufacturer only. If one bulb needs to be replaced in a viewbox, then all bulbs in that bank of viewboxes should be replaced at the same time. This may seem like a costly policy, but it assures that all viewboxes will be of the same brightness and color. In addition, the investment in equipment and manpower required to produce quality radiographs must be kept in mind; in looking at the total cost of producing radiographs, the cost of replacing all viewbox light bulbs is minimal.

How often should bulbs be replaced and viewboxes cleaned? Bulbs should be replaced annually if they are used for even a few hours each day. The boxes should be cleaned at least twice a year—this means cleaning the inside and outside surfaces of all viewboxes, including the area behind the light bulbs. The outside surfaces should also be cleaned at any time dirt or marks are apparent.

Alternate methods of assuring consistency through measuring viewbox light levels with a photometer or a photographic light meter are described by Hendee and Rossi (1979).

PROCEDURES

11.1. VIDEO HARD-COPY CAMERAS

Purpose

To assure that the film images of video displays, e.g., from CT, ultrasound (US), and digital radiographic systems, reproduce the full range of information displayed on the cathode ray tube (CRT).

Equipment Needed

1. Densitometer
2. Processor control chart

Procedure—Setting up Video Hard-Copy Cameras

1. It is our feeling that older-style phototiming in CT and US applications creates more problems than it solves. We recommend that you have the phototiming circuits in your camera disconnected by a service engineer.
2. If the phototimer has been disconnected, or if your camera doesn't have phototiming, set the exposure time to approximately 1 sec for recording static images. (This will assure a complete fill-in of the CRT image.)
3. Set the lens aperture at f/5.6 to f/8 if an aperture setting is present.
4. View the displayed image and adjust the CRT to produce a dim, low-contrast image with no flare.
5. Make a series of films varying *only* the *brightness* control.
6. Select the image that produces a density approximately 0.05 above base-plus-fog (B + F) for US (or a density of 0.20 above B + F in the background for a black-on-white display) and 0.10 above B + F for CT on the lightest step of the step wedge.
7. Make a series of images varying *only* the contrast control, using the brightness setting selected in Step 6.
8. Select the contrast setting that produces the most pleasing image.
9. Recheck the density of the lightest step to assure that it has not changed. If the density has shifted make another series of films varying *only* the *brightness.*
10. Repeat this procedure until the proper density and a pleasing image is produced (Figure 11.2).
11. White-on-black US images require a slightly different approach. Follow Steps 1 through 9 but read the densities from an average US image, not the step wedges. Adjust the CRT brightness to produce a density of 0.05 to 0.10 above B + F for the strongest echoes (skin reflection at the scan surface). Then adjust the contrast to produce a density as close as possible to 1.6 above B + F from the weakest echoes.

Procedure—QC Monitoring

1. After the correct density and contrast have been established, select the step from the step wedge that has a density closest to 1.0 above the B + F to be monitored as the mid-density level. Use a step near 0.20 above B + F (low) and a step that has a density closest to 1.8 above B + F (high) to calculate the density difference (the high minus the low density).
2. Monitor these steps on a daily basis initially, then on a weekly basis if it is apparent that the density levels are not shifting on a day-to-day basis.
3. Record the mid-density and the density difference on a processor control chart.
4. If you do not wish to disconnect your phototiming system and still wish to monitor the film density, a perfectly reproduced phantom scan must be used to produce the film and gray scale needed for monitoring the film density.
5. If you use Polaroid film, follow the setup procedure (Steps 1 through 11 above), then visually check the step wedge on the edge of the image regularly. You should be able to see the difference in density between the two lightest steps and between the two darkest steps.

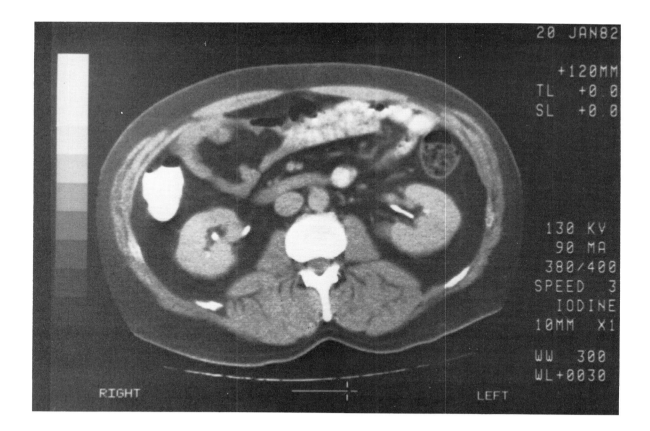

Figure 11.2a.   CT image produced with a video hard-copy camera.

6.   Be sure to record all the exposure factors, including f-stops, exposure time, brightness, and contrast settings, on the control charts.

Problems and Pitfalls

1.   Phototimed systems make it almost impossible to carry out quality control since the exposure depends on the image.
2.   Some older and poorly designed multiformat cameras are designed so that the brightness and contrast controls are not independent, making it impossible to adjust the contrast without changing the brightness.

Acceptance Limits

If your processor is in control, set your limits for the mid-density and density difference at ± 0.10.

Corrective Action

1.   Adjust the brightness and contrast controls to bring the density and contrast back within the control limits.
2.   Clean the face of the CRT and camera lens monthly with a soft brush, then use lens tissue and lens cleaning solution.

11.2.   IMAGE QUALITY TESTS FOR PRODUCT COMPARISONS

Purpose

To compare under clinical conditions the differences in image quality from different products, such as intensifying screens, films, or grids.

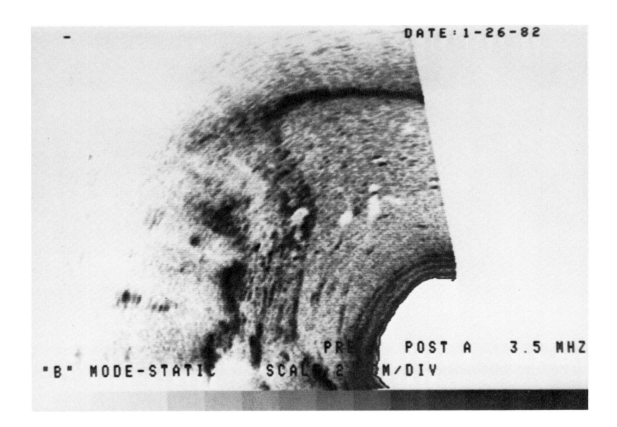

Figure 11.2b. Ultrasound image produced with a video hard-copy camera.

Equipment Needed

1. Anatomical phantom
2. Flat metal washer with 3/8-inch hole
3. Densitometer
4. Lead markers
5. Dosimeter

Procedure

1. Tape the flat metal washer to the top surface of the anatomical phantom in a location such that its image will appear in an exposed portion of the radiograph (an area where the density will be about 1.0). For example, if an abdomen phantom is used, locate the washer over the kidney region. This is done to assure that densitometer readings used to obtain a close density match are made at the same point on the comparison radiographs.
2. Set up the generator, phantom, and x-ray tube for routine radiography. Position the dosimeter chamber on the phantom to record entrance exposure to the skin in the area of interest. The setup will vary depending upon the product being evaluated.
3. Place lead markers on the cassette to identify the products being evaluated, but do not use the product names—use only numerical identification.
4. Make a radiograph using technical factors appropriate for the anatomic phantom for the product currently used in the department and record the dosimeter reading.
5. Process this radiograph and check for proper positioning of the phantom, metal washer, and dosimeter chamber (Figure 11.3).
6. Repeat Step 4 if needed to obtain a typical radiograph and satisfactory location of the metal washer.

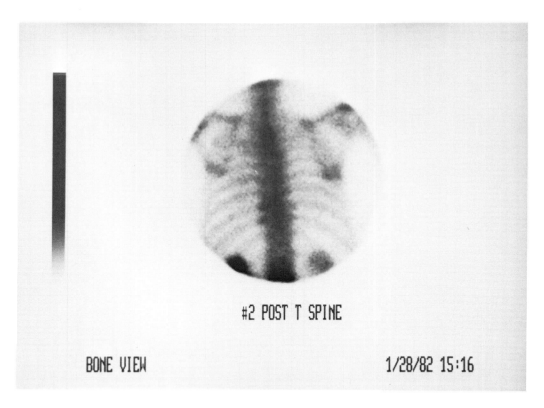

#2 POST T SPINE

BONE VIEW   1/28/82 15:16

Figure 11.2c. Nuclear medicine digital image produced with a video hard-copy camera.

7.   Do not alter the radiographic setup once a satisfactory radiograph has been obtained until the testing series has been completed.
8.   Expose a radiograph with technical factors appropriate for the product being tested and record the dosimeter reading.
9.   Process the comparison radiograph in the same processor.
10. Make densitometer readings in the open area of the washer and record the readings. Repeat radiographs if necessary to attain a density match within ± 0.05 (ideally), or within ± 0.10 if necessary.

Problems and Pitfalls

1.   It is essential that the test be conducted in a manner such that the only difference that will be noted in the comparison radiographs will be due to differences in the products tested—in this case, between the currently used and new product. For this reason, problems will be avoided if you:
     a.   Make the comparison radiographs at the same kVp setting.
     b.   Make exposure adjustments with exposure time. Avoid changing mA initially, if possible. Calibration of the x-ray generator may be inaccurate between mA stations and changing to a different mA station may also result in a change of the focal spot size.
     c.   Use the same cassette when comparing films or grids.
     d.   Process the radiographs in as short of a time period as possible in the same processor.
2.   A mismatch in light level or color on adjacent illuminator panels used to view comparative radiographs can significantly affect results.
3.   Unbiased evaluations require that other observers not be able to identify the product from the identification markers, or manufacturer's edge markings, on film and screens.
4.   It is essential that densities of the comparison films are matched as closely as possible. A slight difference in density can significantly alter the appearance of the radiographic contrast and sharpness.

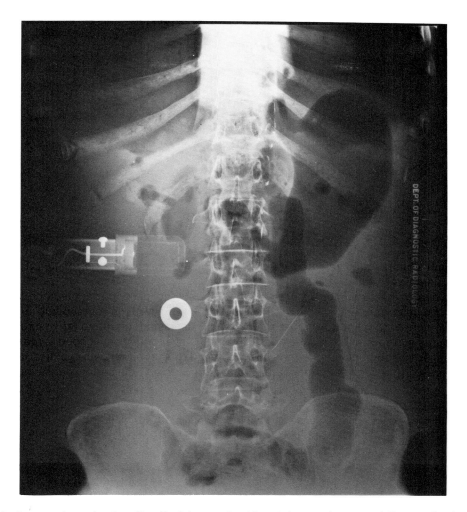

Figure 11.3.   Product comparison phantom film. Each image should contain a washer to mark the spot for density matching, lead letter identification information that is not related to the product name, and an ionization chamber for monitoring the phantom entrance exposures. All edge markings are then trimmed from the film so that neither the film nor the screen can be identified by the viewer.

Acceptance Limits

Densitometer readings on the comparison radiographs should be in the general range of 0.80–1.0 and should ideally match within ± 0.05, but you may have to accept ± 0.10. Make additional radiographs if needed to attain matched densities within these limits.

Image Analysis

1. View comparison radiographs on adjacent panels of well-matched viewboxes under normal viewing conditions for interpretation. Form and record subjective impressions regarding differences, i.e., information equally well visualized, better visualized, or less well visualized.
2. Review the results with a radiologist to determine further action. If the new product at this point offers sufficient advantages to warrant clinical use (i.e., provides the same information at a lesser dose or more information at the same dose), further testing that may involve comparison patient radiographs will be required before a final decision is made.

    If comparison patient radiographs are made, good radiation safety practices dictate that these be:
    a. Kept to a minimum
    b. Made only on patients who require a particular examination
    c. Made only on patients beyond the usual childbearing age

d. Limited to not more than one comparison radiograph on any given patient
e. Made only after approval by the chairman of the radiology department and in many institutions after approval by the human studies and radiation control committees.

11.3. ATTENUATION MEASUREMENTS

Purpose

To accurately determine the attenuation or transmission of materials under clinical conditions.

Equipment Needed

1. Patient equivalent phantom (PEP) with base
2. Direct readout dosimeter with an ionization chamber that fits in the Bucky tray plus a large conventional chamber
3. A 14 × 17-inch (35 × 43-cm) sheet of ½-inch (1.3-cm) plywood backed with lead. An opening should be cut into the plywood to hold the ionization chamber and assure that it is centered in the Bucky (Figure 11.4).

Procedures—Measuring Attenuation of Cassette Fronts, Grids, Tabletop Pads, Lead Aprons, etc.

1. Place the PEP and base on the table, set the x-ray tube at the normal working distance, and center it to the PEP.
2. Place the large chamber in the base opening under the PEP and assure that it is centered under the phantom.
3. Set the generator to about 50 mAs and to a kVp that would be typical for the use of the product you are working with.
4. Make three exposures, determine the average of the three, and record the data in a log book.
5. Place the item that you are measuring between the phantom and the base (Figure 11.5). Care should be taken not to damage the product being tested.
6. Repeat Step 4 above.
7. Determine the attenuation using the following formula:

$$\left[1 - \left(\frac{\text{Exposure with sample}}{\text{Exposure without sample}} \right) \right] \times 100\% = \%\ \text{Attenuation}$$

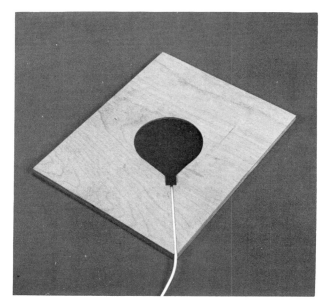

Figure 11.4. Bucky tray ionization chamber holder. This holder is designed to center the ionization chamber in the Bucky tray as well as to provide protection from variations in backscatter (by utilizing lead backing under the plywood sheet).

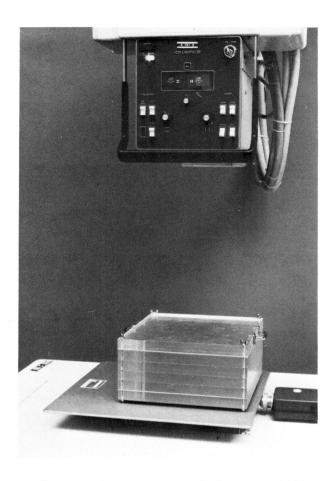

Figure 11.5. Attenuation measurement test setup for product evaluation. Care must be taken not to damage the product being evaluated when the PEP is placed on top of it.

For example, assume your dosimeter read 100 mR without the sample and 10 mR after the sample was inserted in the beam; then

$$\left[1 - \left(\frac{10 \text{ mR}}{100 \text{ mR}} \right) \right] \times 100 = 90\% \text{ attenuation}$$

The transmission is equal to 100% − percentage of attenuation; i.e., (100% − 90%) = 10% transmission.

8. If the attenuation of another product is to be determined at this time, place the product between the phantom and the base. Note that it is not necessary to make the initial three measurements without the product (Step 4) again, since the exposure will be the same.

Procedure—To Measure Tabletop and Grid Attenuation

1. Place the PEP and base on the table, set the x-ray tube to the normal working distance, and center the tube to the phantom.
2. Place the 14 × 17-inch (35 × 43-cm) sheet of plywood in the Bucky tray and center the Bucky tray to the x-ray tube.
3. Collimate to the phantom.
4. Place the Bucky ionization chamber under the phantom, on top of the table, assuring that it is centered under the phantom and x-ray beam.
5. Set the generator to about 50 mAs and the typical kVp used in the room.
6. Make three exposures, take the average of the three, and record the data in a log book.
7. Place the Bucky ionization chamber in the cutout of the plywood sheet in the Bucky tray (Figure 11.6).
8. Make three exposures, take the average of the three, and record the data in a log book.
9. Use the formula in Step 7 of the procedure above to determine the attenuation.

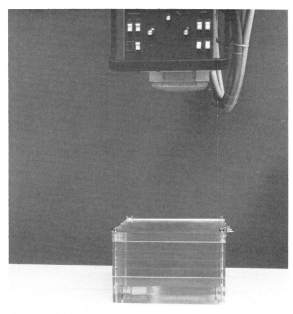

Figure 11.6. Attenuation measurement test setup for tabletop and grid attenuation. Care must be taken not to damage or crimp the cable coming from the Bucky ionization chamber. Since the signal is not digitized at this point, the cable is carrying extremely low currents and is sensitive to induced currents as a result of flexing the cable.

Problems and Pitfalls

1. If the product being evaluated is to be used over a wide range of kVp values, then the attenuation must be determined over the same range (usually 20-kVp increments is sufficient).
2. It is essential to evaluate the product under the conditions that are typical of its use. For example, measurements made of cassette fronts must be made through a phantom and, ideally, through a grid also. Grids, whether of primary or secondary interest in making attenuation measurements, must be used at the proper distance to assure accurate data.
3. **Do not change the generator** between the various measurements, since it is difficult to reset the generator to the identical technique.

Acceptance Limits

There are no acceptance limits for this test. However, table pads should have a minimum amount of attenuation, as should cassette fronts and tabletops. Under the conditions described, grids will appear to have large attenuation factors since they are removing scattered radiation. You may also want to measure the attenuation of grids without the phantom. This attenuation value (for primary radiation) should be minimized. In general, a difference in attenuation of 10% or less between two products will not result in a visible difference in the radiographs produced.

11.4. COPY FILM

Purpose

To provide copy films of quality similar to the original.

Equipment Needed

1. Aluminum step wedge (2 mm–thick steps)
2. Copper mesh resolution target or lead resolution target
3. Aluminum used to measure HVL
4. Fine-screen mesh

Procedure

1. Make a radiograph of the step wedge and resolution target. Make sure that a full range of useful densities (0.25 to 2.5) is exposed on the wedge. For an average step wedge you will need to place about 8 mm of aluminum over the resolution target to prevent overexposure of the target. (You should obtain a density of about 1.0 *beside* the test target.) Also, make a radiograph of the fine-screen mesh (Figure 11.7).
2. Expose a copy film with the original test film made in Step 1. Also expose a copy film of the fine-screen mesh radiograph.
3. Read and compare the densities of the original and the copy with a densitometer.
4. Match the density of the original and copy film to within 0.10 at the density on the step wedge closest to 1.0. This is accomplished by adjusting the timer or the light intensity setting on the copy machine.
5. Compare the resolution of the original and the copy film.
6. Check the copy of the mesh radiograph for contact over the entire image.
7. Repeat this procedure on a monthly basis.
8. Save the original and the current copy film in your QC room log.

Problems and Pitfalls

1. Typically, the high and low density may be less dense than the original.

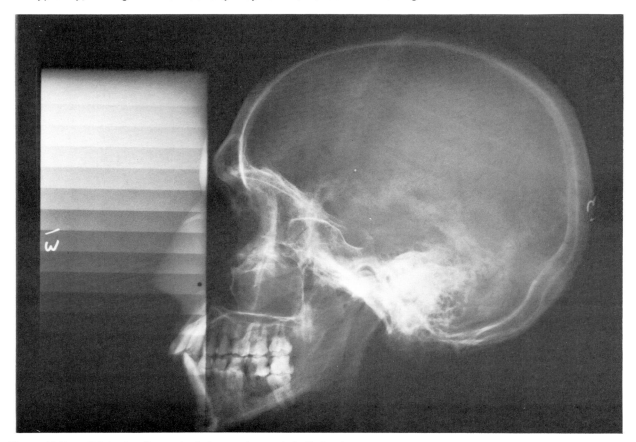

Figure 11.7a. Original radiograph of step wedge and skull phantom.

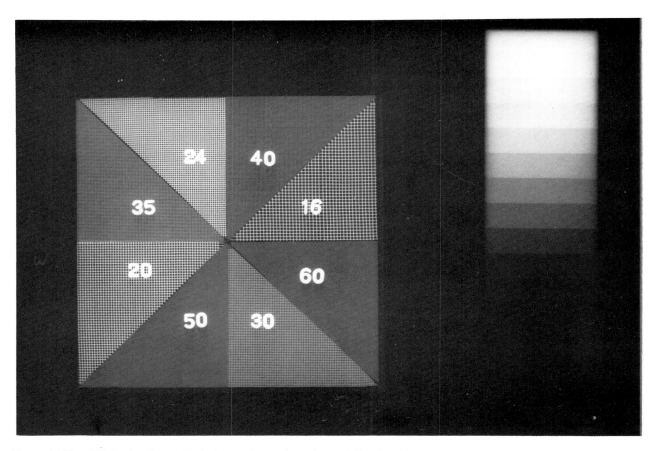

Figure 11.7b.   Original radiograph of step wedge and mesh resolution target.

2.   If the duplicating bulb must be replaced, make sure to use the bulb recommended by the manufacturer.

Acceptance Limits

1.   The copy film density should be within 0.10 of the original at a density around 1.0. Visually, there should be very little difference between any original and copy.
2.   There should be little or no loss of resolution between the original and the copy film.

Corrective Action

1.   Adjust the timer or light intensity to produce the correct density.
2.   If the densities cannot be matched, or if resolution is lost, consult a service representative from the copy film or machine manufacturer.

11.5.   METHODS OF LOWERING THE FLUOROSCOPIC EXPOSURE RATE

Purpose

To minimize the fluoroscopic procedure dose to the patients and staff while maintaining image quality sufficient for diagnostic purposes.

Equipment Needed

1.   Patient equivalent phantom (PEP)
2.   Copper mesh resolution test tool or lead resolution target
3.   Low-contrast resolution test tool

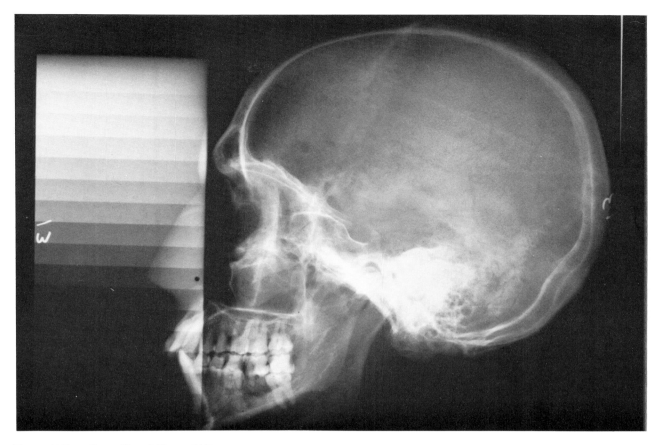

Figure 11.7c. Copy film of Figure 11.7a.

4. Dosimeter (and stopwatch if pen dosimeter is used)

Procedures—Fluoroscopy

1. Measure and record the standard fluoroscopic exposure rate as described on pages 136–137 before changing the exposure rate.
2. Place the copper mesh or lead resolution target on the PEP and note the maximum resolution before the exposure rate is changed.
3. Place the low-contrast test tool on the table and note the smallest hole size resolved before the exposure rate is changed (see Figure 9.18).
4. Observe the noise level during all tests before the exposure rate is changed.
5. With the assistance of a service engineer, gradually lower the fluoroscopic exposure rate. [**Note:** Changes in the aperture of the TV camera lens will have to be made to meet the light requirements of some TV cameras. In fiberoptically coupled systems it will be necessary to vary the video gain.]
6. Check and compare the image quality (resolution, contrast, and noise) and exposure rate with each step until the desired image quality and/or exposure rate is obtained.
7. Record the final exposure rate, kVp, mA, and image quality data in the QC room log.

Procedure—Grid Versus Nongrid Fluoroscopy and Photofluorospot (PFS) Films

1. Compare the image quality and exposure levels as described above through the PEP with and without the fluoroscopic grid.
2. Make PFS films of all the test objects through the PEP with and without the grid. [**Note:** The kVp used for the PFS films without the grid may have to be lowered if the exposure time is in minimum response range of the phototiming circuit, typically 10 msec.]

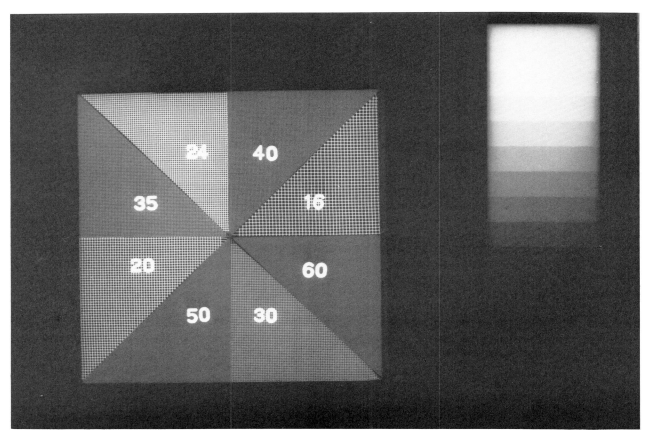

Figure 11.7d.   Copy film of Figure 11.7b.

3. Consult your radiologists with the data and exposure measurements. [See Gray and Swee (1982) for further information and data.]
4. Initiate a patient trial if the data are favorable.
5. If it is apparent that the fluoroscopic exams and PFS films can be performed without the grid, discontinue its use; this will reduce both patient and staff exposure.
6. Record the exposure levels for the standard phantom and the image quality data in the QC room log.

11.6.   WHAT TO DO BEFORE THE SERVICE ENGINEER LEAVES

Purpose

To assure that the x-ray equipment that you as a technologist are responsible for is mechanically and electrically safe and that the equipment is producing high-quality, consistent radiographs at a minimum dose to the patient.

Equipment Needed

1. The entire quality control test kit that you have developed
2. The QC room log
3. Patient equivalent phantom (PEP)
4. An understanding of the x-ray equipment, how it functions, and the problems the service engineer is trying to correct
5. Good rapport between the quality control technologist and the service engineer

Procedure

1. Verification of the integrity of x-ray equipment after it has been serviced is an important part of the quality control program that is often overlooked. This is the responsibility of the QC technologist and is best taken care of *before* the service engineer leaves. In fact, it is even better if it can be taken care of before the service engineer replaces all of the covers on the equipment.

2. Work closely with the service engineer, if possible, so that he understands the problem that you called him to repair and to assist him in any way possible. In some cases your test tools may provide results that differ from the engineer's measurements, so you will have to work together to resolve this problem.

3. Provide the service engineer with whatever test equipment he needs that you may have, which can make his job easier. For example, provide him with your phantom and dosimeter so he can set the fluoroscopic exposure rates to the levels you specify and under the conditions you normally use in evaluating the equipment.

4. Before the service engineer leaves test all aspects of the equipment function that he may have affected through his service. Most service engineers will be pleased to have you do this while they are there so that they can see what you are doing and to avoid the necessity of a second trip to your institution to correct a problem they thought was already corrected. In addition, avoiding this second trip can be financially advantageous to your institution since most vendors now charge between $50 and $60 per hour for service work, door-to-door. In other words, you are paying for the time the service engineer takes to get to your institution from his office, do his work, and return to his office from your institution, plus mileage.

5. Finally, make several radiographs of the PEP to assure that patient films will be acceptable.

Problems and Pitfalls

Often the QC technologist is not available when the service engineer is ready to leave or an adversary relationship develops between the QC technologist and the service engineer. Remember, your institution is paying for the engineer's services so you should make every effort to assist him and make his job as easy as possible. There is no sense in developing an adversary relationship (e.g., "I'm checking up on you since we don't trust the work you do"), because this will benefit no one. Good rapport and a close working relationship are essential—e.g., "I would like to work closely with you and assist you in any way that I can to better explain the problem we are having and to minimize the number of return trips you have to make to eliminate this problem."

12 EQUIPMENT SPECIFICATION, PURCHASE, AND ACCEPTANCE TESTING

The purchase of new x-ray equipment is complex, the equipment is expensive, and attempting to understand the differences in the equipment from various vendors can be overwhelming. We do not go into detail concerning how to go about specification and acceptance testing, but we do provide some general guidelines and suggestions on how to make this task easier and how to make sure you get what you want.

The first thing to consider is that the more complex the equipment and the more flexible the usage of the room, the more expensive the equipment will be to purchase and the more difficult it will be to maintain. However, inexpensive equipment may not be reliable and may require more service than slightly more expensive equipment. If the service for a particular manufacturer's equipment is difficult to obtain, if it takes a long time for the service man to respond to calls, and if parts are difficult to locate, then, for the most part, that manufacturer should be excluded from consideration unless you have an adequate in-house service organization.

The best way to start the specification process is to consider what you really need from the equipment you are about to purchase. Many single-phase units now provide excellent timing capabilities and with the faster screen-film systems now in use it may not be necessary to consider three-phase equipment. Be sure to determine not only what maximum mA is required (e.g., 600 mA is satisfactory for most radiographic and fluoroscopic rooms) but also what kVp is required. Many generators are capable of producing 150 kVp, but most radiographic examinations are carried out at 125 kVp or below so it is not necessary to pay for the additional kVp capability. Do not indicate to the vendor that you wish to purchase a 600-mA, 125-kVp generator without indicating a kW rating. A firm could quote, for example, a 600-mA, 125-kVp generator that is rated at only 50 kW, which means that the 600 mA station can only be used up to 80 kVp. To be able to use the entire capability of 600 mA and 125 kVp you need a generator that is rated at 75 kW.

Most practical radiographic and fluoroscopic imaging systems today should be equipped with 0.6-mm and 1.2-mm focal spot x-ray tubes for the best detail and the most flexibility. However, it will not be possible to use the small focal spot for more than about 200 mA unless you specify a high-speed rotor for the x-ray tube. Consequently, many vendors will quote a 1.0-mm and 2.0-mm focal spot combination and not mention the possibility of the smaller focal spots with a high-speed rotor, which would cost $3,000 to $4,000 more but allow you much more flexibility and use of the small focal spot at higher techniques.

Many other considerations must be reviewed before asking for quotations from the vendors. Remember that the vendors' job is to sell equipment and they may or may not have your best interests at heart. Talk to several vendors and ask what they would suggest. Talk to other x-ray departments that have equipment similar to that which you are considering and see what the service history has been. Visit other institutions and assure yourself that the equipment you are considering is easy to use. Especially, talk to the technologists who are using the equipment on a day-to-day basis and see what they have to say about it.

What about quotes and specifications? We will assume that you have decided what type of equipment you wish to purchase. You can ask several vendors to provide you quotes and specifications on the equipment. However, this results in a deluge of brochures with the pertinent information scattered throughout and makes the job of comparing the various vendors' quotes almost impossible. In addition, most vendors prefer to quote a package price, so you have no idea what you are paying for separate options. For example, a 4-way power tabletop may cost as much as $15,000 to $20,000 more than a comparable 2-way power top, but this won't be obvious from a package price quote. Since most vendors are reticent to provide prices for each item in a room of x-ray equipment, the easiest way to determine the cost differences is to ask them to "option" certain items. For example, a high-speed rotor for an x-ray tube may be optioned at $4,000, a 100-mm camera may be optioned at $30,000, and a 2-way power top may be optioned at "less $16,000" (compared to the price of the 4-way power top). Most vendors will give you a package price and then list the options, either as add-ons or subtractions from the package price at the end of the quote. Never tell one vendor that you favor his equipment over another during the specification and quoting process.

Equipment specifications are difficult to obtain from most vendors in a manner in which they can easily be compared. There are two approaches you could take to help solve this problem. One is to write up your own *detailed* specifications and ask the vendors to bid on the basis of these. However, this means that you must specify such things as what the kVp calibration accuracy must be, what the resolution in the center and edges of the image intensifier must be (and how it will be tested), and how the television system will perform. In addition, the vendors may not be able to meet some of your specifications and decide not to bid. This also tends to promote an adversary relationship between your department and the vendors, since you are telling them how to build the equipment.

We have found that it is much easier to ask the vendors to fill out a standard specification form (Appendix B) and provide the information necessary to determine how the tests were carried out. Most importantly, the vendor must be advised verbally, and in writing as part of the final purchase order, that the equipment must meet these specifications after delivery and installation at your facility. (Some vendors will want to specify that the equipment meets their specifications when it is preassembled at their factory!) If you cannot carry out all of the tests necessary for acceptance testing, then it would be worthwhile to hire a consulting service engineer and physicist to assure that the equipment meets the appropriate specifications.

The standard specification form saves you many hours in comparing equipment specifications from various vendors since you can lay out each page from the different vendors side by side and see how the equipment compares. This in itself may be educational in that some vendors may note that their equipment cannot do this or that, so you should immediately question whether their competitors' equipment is of the same type. As an example, one vendor noted that his equipment did not meet the EIA RS-170 video standards set by the broadcast industry and two others left this question blank. After inquiring it was discovered that none of the three vendors' equipment met the standard. (This standard is especially important if you want to tape-record your video images on conventional recording equipment.)

The acceptance testing process is the responsibility of the QC technologist. You may have considerable assistance if you have in-house service engineers who can be with the vendor's installation crew during the entire installation, assuring that the equipment is being installed to your standards and being properly calibrated. (When the in-house engineer works with the vendor's crew during installation, two other benefits result: 1) the engineer is receiving training on the new equipment and will become quite familiar with the entire installation, including the setup and calibration procedures; and 2) the engineer is providing an extra pair of hands to assist in the installation, so the vendor should be willing to compensate your facility in some way for this by either reducing the equipment price slightly or by providing, at no cost, service schooling at the manufacturer's facility on the new equipment.)

If you have similar equipment in your facility the standards that should be expected from the equipment are already known and will make acceptance testing easier. For the most part, acceptance testing means working through the entire room QC checks you would normally carry out on similar equipment and assuring that each item meets the standards of similar equipment and the specifications set forth by the vendor in his specification sheet and price quote. (This is why it is important that the vendor be advised, and that the purchase order note, that the specifications must be met prior to final payment for the equipment.)

Most vendors are willing to work closely with your department to assure that the equipment is meeting their specifications. They will normally replace x-ray tubes if the focal spots are too large, replace image intensifiers if the resolution does not meet specifications, and so forth. However, some difficulties may be encountered in that the measurement techniques they use may be considerably different from yours. In this case you can request that they provide their test equipment and demonstrate to you that the system meets the specifications that they have provided you.

Only after *all* problems have been corrected and *all* specifications have been met should the final payment be made for the equipment.

REFERENCES

American College of Radiology. 1981. Quality Assurance in Diagnostic Radiology and Nuclear Medicine—The Obvious Decision. HHS Publication No. (FDA)81-8141. U.S. Department of Health and Human Services, Washington, D.C.

American National Standards Institute. 1980. American National Standard Method for the Sensitometry of Medical X-Ray Screen-Film-Processing Systems, PH 2.43, Draft No. 7. American National Standards Institute, New York.

Blackham, W. C. 1977. Cost reduction through quality assurance. In: Proceedings of the Second Image Receptor Conference: Radiographic Processing. HEW Publication No. (FDA)77-8036. U.S. Department of Health, Education and Welfare, Washington, D.C.

Bureau of Radiological Health. 1980. Regulations for the Administration and Enforcement of the Radiation Control for Health and Safety Act of 1968. HHS Publication No. (FDA)80-8035. Bureau of Radiological Health, U.S. Department of Health and Human Services, Washington, D.C.

Burkhart, R. S. 1977. Diagnostic Radiology Quality Assurance Catalog. HEW Publication No. (FDA)77-0828. Bureau of Radiological Health, U.S. Department of Health, Education and Welfare, Washington, D.C.

Burkhart, R. S. 1978. Diagnostic Radiology Quality Assurance Catalog. Supplement. HEW Publication No. (FDA)78-8028. Bureau of Radiological Health, U.S. Department of Health, Education and Welfare, Washington, D.C.

Crow, E. L., Davis, S. A., and Maxfield, M. W. 1960. Statistics Manual. Dover Publications, New York.

Electronics Industries Association. 1957. Electrical Performance Standard—Monochrome Television Studio Facilities. EIA Standard RS-170. Electronics Industries Association, Washington, D.C.

Fields, T., Griffith, C. R., and Hubbard, L. B. 1980. What price quality? A quality assurance program for diagnostic radiology. Appl. Radiol. 57-65.

Frank, E. D., Gray, J. E., and Wilken, D. A. 1980. Flood replenishment: A new method of processor control. Radiol. Technol. 52:271-275.

Goldman, L., Vucich, J. J., Beech, S., and Murphy, W. L. 1977. Automatic processing quality assurance program: Impact on a radiology department. Radiology 125:591-595.

Goldman, L. W. 1979. Analysis of Retakes: Understanding, Managing, and Using an Analysis of Retakes Program for Quality Assurance. HEW Publication (FDA)79-8097. U.S. Department of Health, Education and Welfare, Washington, D.C.

Gray, J. E. 1975. Light fog on radiographic films. How to measure it properly. Radiology 115:225-227.

Gray, J. E. 1976. Photographic Quality Assurance in Diagnostic Radiology, Nuclear Medicine, and Radiation Therapy. Volume 1. The Basic Principles of Daily Photographic Quality Assurance. HEW Publication No. (FDA)76-8043. Bureau of Radiological Health, U.S. Department of Health, Education and Welfare, Washington, D.C.

Gray, J. E. 1977. Photographic Quality Assurance in Diagnostic Radiology, Nuclear Medicine, and Radiation Therapy. Volume 2. Photographic Processing, Quality Assurance and the Evaluation of Photographic Materials. HEW Publication No. (FDA)77-8018. Bureau of Radiological Health, U.S. Department of Health, Education and Welfare, Washington, D.C.

Gray, J. E., and Swee, R. G. 1982. The elimination of grids during intensified fluoroscopy and photofluorospot imaging. Radiology 144:426-429

Gray, J. E., and Trefler, M. 1980. Pin-hole cameras: Artifacts, modifications, and recording of pin-hole images on screen film systems. Radiol. Technol. 52:277-282.

Hall, C. L. 1977. Economic analysis from a quality control program. Proceedings of the Society of Photooptical Instrumentation Engineers 127:271-275.

Hendee, W. R., and Rossi, P. 1979. Quality Assurance for Radiographic X-Ray Units and Associated Equipment. HEW Publication No. (FDA)79-8094. U.S. Department of Health, Education and Welfare, Washington, D.C.

Inter-Society Commission for Heart Disease. 1976. Optimal resources for examination of the chest and cardiovascular system. Circulation 53: A-1-A-37.

Jacobson, A. F., Cameron, J. R., Siedband, M. P., and Wagner, J. 1976. Test cassette for measuring peak tube potential of diagnostic x-ray machines. Med. Phys. 3:19-25.

Joint Commission on the Accreditation of Hospitals. 1980. Accreditation Manual for Hospitals. Joint Commission on Accreditation of Hospitals, Chicago.

Linton, O. W., Properzio, W. S., and Steele, J. P. 1979. Quality assurance: An idea whose time has come. Editorial. AJR 133:989–992.

National Electrical Manufacturers Association. 1974. Measurement of Diagnostic X-Ray Tubes. NEMA Standard Publication Number XR5–1974. National Electrical Manufacturers Association, New York.

Nelson, R. E., Barnes, G. T., and Witten, D. M. 1977. Economic analysis of a comprehensive quality assurance program. Radiol. Technol. 49:129–134.

Noyes, R. S. 1980. The economics of quality assurance. Radiology/Nuclear Medicine Magazine, pages 7–9, 24, 28.

Poznanski, A. K., and Smith, L. A. 1968. Practical problems in processing control. Radiology 90:135–138.

Rao, G. U. F. 1966. Influence of Focus and Off-Focus Radiation on Radiographic Detail (Modulation Transfer Function) and Patient Exposure in Diagnostic Radiology. Report on Contract #FAPH 76496. U.S. Public Health Service, Washington, D.C.

Rausch, P. L. 1981. Performance characteristics of diagnostic x-ray generators. In: Acceptance Testing of Radiologic Imaging Equipment, Proceedings of a meeting at St. Charles, IL, October 1–2, 1981.

Rickmers, A. D., and Todd, H. N. 1967. Statistics, An Introduction. McGraw-Hill, New York.

Stears, J. G., Gray, J. E., and Winkler, N. T. 1979. Evaluation of pH monitoring as a method of processor control. Radiol. Technol. 50:657–663.

Suleiman, O. H., Showalter, C., and Koustenis, G. 1981. A sensitometric evaluation of film-chemistry processor systems in the State of New Jersey. (Submitted for publication)

Thomas, S. R., Freshcorn, J. E., Krugh, K. B., Henry, G. C., Kereiakes, J. G., and Kaufman, R. A. 1982. Characteristics of extrafocal radiation and its potential significance in pediatric radiology. Radiology (In press).

Thomas, W., Jr. 1973. SPSE Handbook of Photographic Science and Engineering. John Wiley & Sons, New York.

Thompson, T. T. 1978. A Practical Approach to Modern X-Ray Equipment. Little, Brown & Company, Boston.

Titus, D. E. 1979a. Flooded Replenishment Method for Cine Processing. Publication #MPA 7.236. Eastman Kodak Company, Rochester, New York.

Titus, D. E. 1979b. Flooded Replenishment Method for Low Volume Industrial X-Ray Processors. Publication #MPA 7.237. Eastman Kodak Company, Rochester, New York.

Titus, D. E. 1979c. Flooded Replenishment System for Dedicated or Low Volume Kodak RP X-Omat Processors. Publication #MPA 7.235. Eastman Kodak Company, Rochester, New York.

Weaver, K. E., Barone, G. J., and Fewell, T. R. 1978. Selection of technique factors for mobile capacitor energy storage x-ray equipment. Radiology 128: 223–228.

Weaver, K. E., Wagner, R. F., and Goodenough, E. J. 1975. Performance considerations of x-ray tube focal spots. Proceedings of the Society of Photo-optical Instrumentation Engineers 56:150–158.

Winkler, N. T. 1975. Quality control in diagnostic radiology. Proceedings of the Society of Photo-optical Instrumentation Engineers 70:125–131.

Appendix A
QUALITY CONTROL FORMS AND CHARTS

CONTENTS

Location _____

From _____ To _____

Reject/Repeat Analysis

Cause	Number of Films	Percentage of Rejects	Percentage of Repeats
1. Positioning			
2. Patient Motion			
3. Light Films			
4. Dark Films			
5. Clear Film			
6. Black Film			
7. Tomo Scouts			
8. Static			
9. Fog—Darkroom			
10. Fog—Cassettes			
11. Mechanical			
12. Q.C.			
13. Miscellaneous (?)			
14. Good Films			
Total Waste (1–14) _____ %			
Total Rejects (All except 5 and 12)			
Total Repeats (1–4, 6, 8–11, 14)			
Total Film Used _____			

Processor: _____ Month: _____

Month:

Date:

Density Difference (High-Low)

+0.20

+0.10

-0.10

-0.20

Medium Density

+0.20

+0.10

-0.10

-0.20

Base Plus Fog

+0.10

-0.10

REPLENISHMENT RATE		
Date	Developer	Fixer

TEMPERATURE		
Date	Developer	Wash

REMARKS			
Date	Action	Date	Action

Building _____ Section _____ Room # _____ MDH # _____

X-RAY GENERATOR:

Manufacturer _____

Model _____

Serial # _____

Date purchased _____

Fixed _____ Mobile _____

CD _____ Battery _____ 110 _____ 220 _____

Single phase _____ Three phase _____

Maximum kVp _____ Maximum mA _____

OVERHEAD:

Manufacturer _____

Date purchased _____

Model _____

COLLIMATOR:

Manufacturer _____

Model _____

Serial # _____

Date purchased _____

Source-to-image distance _____ cm

Source-to-tabletop distance _____ cm
                (fluoro)

GRID:

Manufacturer _____

Date purchased _____

Grid ratio _____

Lines per inch _____

Focus _____ to _____ cm

Interspace material _____

Stationary: yes _____ no _____

HEAD UNITS:

Manufacturer _____

Model _____

Date purchased _____

TOMOGRAPHIC UNITS:

Manufacturer _____

Model _____

Serial # _____

Date purchased _____

Linear _____ Circular _____

Oval _____ Tri-spiral _____

Hypocycloidal _____

FILM CHANGERS:

Manufacturer _____

Serial # _____

Date purchased _____

Model _____ Film size _____

Cut film _____ Roll film _____

USAGE:

Maximum kVp used _____

Maximum time used _____

Number of exams per week _____

Number of films per week _____

Maximum mA used _____

Maximum mAs used _____

MISCELLANEOUS/COMMENTS:

Building _____ Section _____ Room # _____

X-RAY TUBES:

Manufacturer _____   Fixed _____ Mobile _____

Model _____   Focal spot sizes _____

Serial # _____   Radiographic _____ Fluoro _____

Date installed _____   Grid pulse _____ High speed _____

Date removed _____   Bias focus _____

Horns: 0° _____ 90° _____ 135° _____

180° _____ 270° _____

OVERLOAD PROTECTION FACTORS:
Single (   ) or Three (   ) Phase

The following techniques should be allowed by the overload protection circuits:

The following techniques should *NOT* be allowed by the overload protection circuits:

mA	kVp	Time		kVp	or	Time
			Low speed			
_____	_____	_____		_____		_____
_____	_____	_____		_____		_____
_____	_____	_____		_____		_____
_____	_____	_____		_____		_____
			High speed			
_____	_____	_____		_____		_____
_____	_____	_____		_____		_____
_____	_____	_____		_____		_____
_____	_____	_____		_____		_____

Building _____ Section _____ Room# _____

- -

TV MONITOR:

    Manufacturer _____   Fixed _____ Mobile _____

    Model _____   Size _____

    Serial # _____

    Date purchased _____

- -

IMAGE INTENSIFIER:

    Manufacturer _____   Fixed _____ Mobile _____

    Model _____   ZnCds _____ CsI _____

    Serial # _____   Size - Input _____ (cm)

    Date purchased _____   Output _____ (cm)

- -

TV CAMERA:

    Manufacturer _____   Fixed _____ Mobile _____

    Model _____   Plumbicon _____ Vidicon _____

    Serial # _____   Other (Specify) _____

    Date purchased _____   525 _____ Other (Specify) _____

- -

MISCELLANEOUS/COMMENTS:

Building: _____ Section: _____ Room # _____ Tube: _____

		DATE														
OVERHEAD TUBE CRANE	TFD indicator or marks															
	Angulation indicator															
	Locks (all)															
	Perpendicularity															
	Field light															
	Bucky center light															
	High tension cable/other cables															
TABLE	Overhead crane movement															
	Bucky lock															
	Cassette lock															
	Float and power top switches															
	Measuring caliper															
	Step stool															
	Angulation indicator/stop															
	Foot board and shoulder braces															
CONTROL BOOTH	Hand switch placement															
	Window															
	Panel switches/lights/meters															
	Technique charts															
	Overload protection															
FLUOROSCOPIC SYSTEM	Locks (all)															
	Power assist															
	Motion smoothness															
	Switches/lights/meters															
	Compression device/spoon															
	Fluoroscopic monitor															
	Fluoroscopic grid															
	Fluoroscopic timer															
	Fluoroscopic drapes															
	Park position interrupt															
	Fluoro shutters visible-high															
	-low															
OTHER	Gonad shield/aprons/gloves															
	Bucky slot cover															

PASS = ✓
FAIL = F
DOES NOT APPLY = NA

mR/mAs

Building _____ Section _____ Room # _____ Tube _____ Focal spot _____

TECHNIQUE: Time _____ Source-detector distance _____ Bucky _____ Tabletop _____

Phantom _____

mA

60 kVp   80 kVp   100 kVp   120 kVp

Date →

Building _____ Section _____ Room # _____ Tube _____

TECHNIQUE:

kVp _____ Focal spot _____ SID _____

Tabletop _____ Bucky _____

mA _____ _____ _____ _____ _____

Time _____ _____ _____ _____ _____

mAs _____ _____ _____ _____ _____

Average mR/mAs   Variation (± %)

Date ➔   Date ➔

Building _____ Section _____ Room # _____ Tube _____

TECHNIQUE:

kVp _____ Focal spot _____ SID _____

Tabletop _____ Bucky _____

Variation (± %)

_____ mA

_____ mA

_____ mA

_____ mA

Date ➔

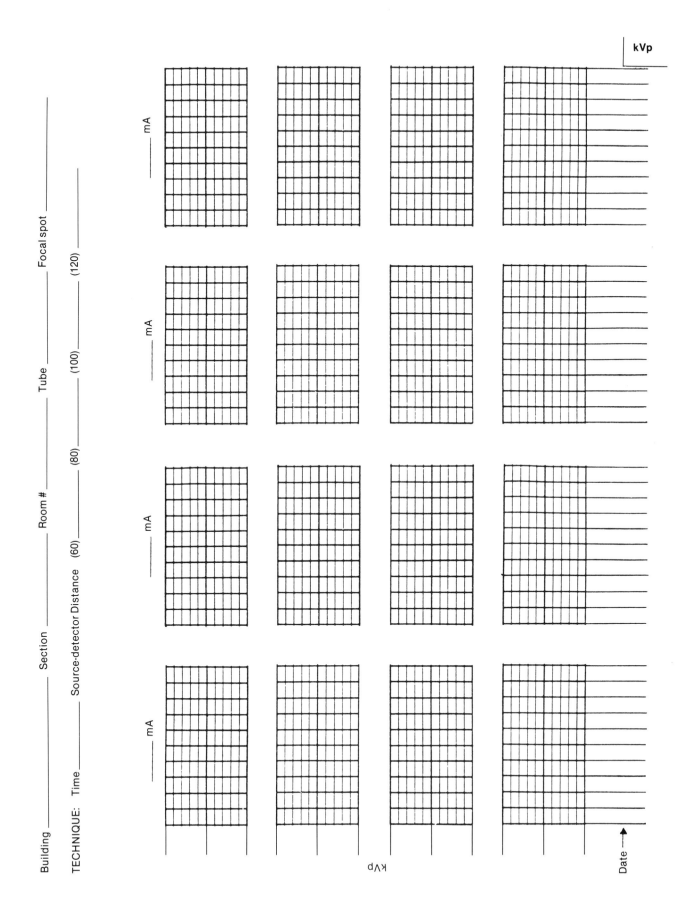

Building _____ Section _____ Room # _____ Tube _____ Focal spot _____

TECHNIQUE: Time _____ Source-detector Distance _____ (60) _____ (80) _____ (100) _____ (120) _____

mA _____

mA _____

mA _____

mA _____

kVp

kVp

Date

Timer Accuracy

Building ______________________ Section __________________ Room # ________________ Tube _________

TECHNIQUE: kVp ________________________ mA ___________________ Focal spot _____________

Time

Setting

Time

Setting

Setting

Date →

Setting

Date →

Half-Value Layer

Building _____ Section _____ Room # _____ Tube _____

TECHNIQUE:

kVp _____ mA _____ time _____

Added filtration _____ Focal spot _____

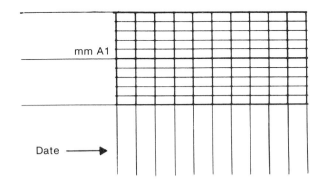

Focal Spot Size

Building ____________ Section ____________ Room # ____________ Tube ________

TECHNIQUE:

kVp ____________

Screen-film type ____________

SID ____________ SOD ____________

Test tool ____________

Small Focal Spot

Nominal size ____________ mm

mA ________ time ____________

mm

Date →

mm

Date →

Large Focal Spot

Nominal size ____________ mm

mA ________ time ____________

mm

Date →

mm

Date →

Building _____ Section _____ Room # _____ Tube _____

TECHNIQUE:

SID _____

kVp _____ mA _____ Time _____

Tabletop _____ Bucky _____

Date	Deviation (mm)				Align-ment	Automatic Field Size			
	Left	Right	Top	Bottom		8 × 10	10 × 12	11 × 14	14 × 17

Building _____ Section _____ Room # _____ Tube _____

Standard phantom (6″ Lucite, 3 mm Al) on support, image intensifier 6″ above phantom.

Measurement distance (if other than standard setup) _____

Entrance exposure rate (R/min)

6″ mode   9″ mode

Exit exposure rate (mR/min)

mA

kVp

Date ⟶   Date ⟶

Maximum Fluoroscopic
Exposure Rate

Building _____ Section _____ Room # _____ Tube _____

Tabletop _____ Measurement distance (if other than tabletop) _____

Automatic   Manual

Exposure rate (R/min)

mA

kVp

Date ⟶   Date ⟶

Building _____ Section _____ Room # _____ Tube _____

MAXIMUM EXPOSURE TIME:

kVp _____ mA _____ FFD _____

MINIMUM EXPOSURE TIME:

kVp _____ mA _____ FFD _____

Milliseconds

Milliseconds

PHANTOM RADIOGRAPHS:

mA _____ FFD _____ Detector: R _____ C _____ L _____

Film density

4-inch acrylic

kVp _____

8-inch acrylic

kVp _____

kVp _____

Date ⟶

Building _____ Section _____ Room # _____ Tube _____

TECHNIQUE: (21-cm lumbar spine technique from chart)

kVp _____ mA _____ time _____

Focal spot _____ FFD _____ phantom _____

ENTRANCE EXPOSURE (mR) (including backscatter)

FILM DENSITY (read at 1:00 open position on step wedge)

DENSITY UNIFORMITY (Pass/Fail)

Date ⟶

Building _____ Section _____ Room # _____

TECHNIQUE: Use charted tomographic factors for a 15-cm lateral skull or AP abdomen

kVp _____ mA _____ Time _____ Focal spot _____

Motion _____ Angle _____

Level _____ Thickness _____

Phantom _____

Date	Resolution	Level	Thickness	Pinhole OK?	Comments

ENTRANCE EXPOSURE (mR)

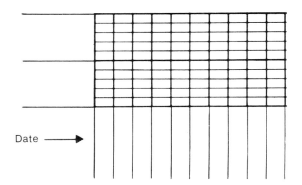

Date ⟶

Maintenance Log

Building _____ Section _____ Room # _____

Date	Action	Service Hours	QC Hours

X-Ray Service Request Form

(White copy)

(Gold copy)

(Pink copy)

TO BE COMPLETED BY ORIGINATOR — TO BE COMPLETED BY SERVICEMAN — PARTS REPLACED — REQUESTED BY — TIME — DATE — AM PM — DAY MO YR

TO BE COMPLETED BY ORIGINATOR

REQUESTED BY	TIME	DATE		
	AM PM	DAY	MO	YR

CALLED TO MAINTENANCE   YES☐   NO☐

PRIORITY   ☐IMM.   ROOM WILL BE AVAILABLE
☐SCHED.   ☐24 HR.   DATE _____ TIME _____

ROOM NO.   BLDG.   CMF ☐
MAYO ☐   RMH ☐   DAMON ☐
ST. M. ☐   PLUMMER ☐   MED SCI ☐

DESCRIPTION OR PROBLEM—PLEASE BE SPECIFIC

X-RAY SERVICE REQUEST NO. 12555

TO BE COMPLETED BY SERVICEMAN   (Yellow copy)

PARTS REPLACED

REPAIRS MADE OR WORK PERFORMED

DONE ☐   NOT DONE ☐   RESCHEDULE ☐   ORDER PARTS ☐
DATE _____ TIME _____

COPY   COPY TO
TO LOG☐   UNIT SUPR. ☐ | SERVICEMAN | TOTAL HOURS | SUPR. INIT.

EXAMINATION	TIME/SEC	mA	kVp SCALE	TFD	CASSETTE
SKULL					
SKULL, AP, Lateral 0–3yrs.					
4–7 yrs.					
Adult					
CERVICAL SPINE					
Cervical AP 10°↑				48″	8 x 10 in
Lateral (Cross Table)				48″	24 x 30 cm
¾ (Table Top)				48″	24 x 30 cm
Swimmer's (Grid or Bucky)				48″	24 x 30 cm
Odontoid				30″	8 x 10 in
Piller 30°↓				48″	24 x 30 cm
SHOULDER					
Shoulder AP				48″	24 x 30 cm
Neer View				48″	24 x 30 cm
Transthoracic Lateral				48″	35 x 43 cm
Axillary View (Grid)				48″	24 x 30 cm
Scapula AP & Lateral				48″	24 x 30 cm
Clavical PA				48″	24 x 30 cm
Humerus AP & Lateral				48″	35 x 43 cm
THORACIC					
Dorsal AP (Filter)				48″	35 x 43 cm
Lateral Dorsal (Filter)				48″	35 x 43 cm

EMACIATED	THIN	AVERAGE	PORTLY	OBESE
_____mA	_____mA	_____mA	_____mA	_____mA

EXAMINATION				TFD	CASSETTE
Dorso-Lumbar Junction 10 ↓				48″	24 x 30 cm
Dorsal Lower Lateral				48″	24 x 30 cm
Lumbar Upper Lateral				48″	24 x 30 cm
LUMBAR AND ABDOMINAL					
Lumbar AP 5°↑ and Abdomen					
≤18 cm				48″	35 x 43 cm
19–23 cm				48″	35 x 43 cm
≥24 cm				48″	35 x 43 cm
Lumbar ¾, 42° Oblique 5°↑					
≤18 cm				48″	24 x 30 cm
19–23 cm				48″	24 x 30 cm
≥24 cm				48″	24 x 30 cm
Lumbar Lateral Meas L-2				48″	30 x 35 cm
Lumbar Loc lateral meas L-5				48″	6 x 10 in
Lumbar Graft Lateral				48″	24 x 30 cm
Lumbar Flexion & Extension				48″	30 x 35 cm

EXAMINATION	TIME/SEC	mA	kVp SCALE	TFD	CASSETTE
LUMBAR AND ABDOMINAL (cont'd)					
Pancreatic Area (AP (Both 15° Obl) 24 × 30 cm Transverse					
≤ 18 cm				48″	24 x 30 cm
19–23 cm				48″	24 x 30 cm
≥ 24 cm				48″	24 x 30 cm
PELVIC REGION					
Pelvis & Hips AP				48″	35 x 43 cm
Hips Lateral & Oblique 5°↓				48″	24 x 30 cm
Sacrum AP 5°↑				48″	24 x 30 cm
Sacrum Lateral				48″	24 x 30 cm
Coccyx AP 10°↓				48″	24 x 30 cm
Coccyx Lateral				48″	24 x 30 cm
S-1 Joints (R & LPO 20°)				48″	24 x 30 cm
FEMUR, KNEE					
Femur AP				48″	35 x 43 cm
Lateral & Oblique for Vessels				48″	35 x 43 cm
Knee AP, Lateral				48″	24 x 30 cm
Intercondylar Notch				48″	Non-Bucky
Houston View 45°↑				48″	35 x 43 cm
CHEST					
AP Supine, All				48″	35 x 43 cm
Lateral Supine (Bucky)				48″	35 x 43 cm
Lateral Decubitus (Grid)				48″	35 x 43 cm
Lateral Sternum				48″	30 x 35 cm
RIBS					
Ribs Above Diaphragm				48″	24 x 30 cm

EMACIATED	THIN	AVERAGE	PORTLY	OBESE
_____mA	_____mA	_____mA	_____mA	_____mA

EXAMINATION	TIME/SEC	mA	kVp SCALE	TFD	CASSETTE
Ribs Below Diaphram					
≤ 18 cm				48″	24 x 30 cm
19–23 cm				48″	24 x 30 cm
≥ 24 cm				48″	24 x 30 cm
EXTREMITY					
Wrist, Hand, Forearm, Foot—Use Extremity Cassette, 48″					
Extremity— sec, mA—kV from Extremity Cassette Scale as measured					

Wrist & Hand	Small	Medium	Large
Finger & Toes	kVp	kVp	kVp

EXAMINATION	TIME/SEC	mA	kVp SCALE	TFD	CASSETTE
Ankle, Leg, Elbow, Patella, Intercondylar Notch—Use Regular Cassette					
Extremity—Regular Cassette				48″	Non-Bucky

EXAMINATION	TIME	kVp	DIAPHRAGM	ANGLES	REMARKS
SKULL ROUTINE					
Towne					
PA					
Stereo Lateral					
SINUS ROUTINE (Non-Bucky)					
Caldwell					
Waters					
Lateral					
ORBITS (Bucky Sinuses)					
Caldwell					
Waters					
Stereo Lateral					
METASTATIC BONE SURVEY					
Towne					
Lateral (Single)					
Cervical Lateral Bucky					
STEREO BASE					
MASTOIDS					
Towne					
Stenvers					
Laws					
Owens					
FACIAL BONES					
Stereo Caldwell					
Stereo Waters					
Lateral					
SLIT VIEWS					
Orbit (Straight-in-AP)					
Towne					
PLATYBASIA VIEWS					
PA					
Lateral					
OPTIC CANALS					
STYLOID FOR TMJ					
JAW UPRIGHT					
PA					
Lateral					
JUGULAR FORAMEN					
LOCALIZED SELLA					
NASAL BONES					
Orbits (Above)					
Soft Tissue Lateral (Non-Bucky)					
PAROTID AREA					
Towne					
Lateral					
EYE LOCALIZATION					
Orbits (Above)					
Special View (Sweets)					

SCALE 8	SCALE 4	SCALE 2	SCALE 1	CM	1/2 SCALE	1/4 SCALE	1/8 SCALE
				6	54	60	68
				7	55	62	71
				8	56	63	73
				9	57	65	75
				10	59	66	77
				11	60	68	80
				12	62	71	82
				13	63	73	85
				14	65	75	88
				15	66	77	91
			60	16	68	80	95
			62	17	71	82	100
			63	18	73	85	104
			65	19	75	88	109
			66	20	77	91	115
49	54	60	68	21	80	95	120
50	55	62	71	22	82	100	126
51	56	63	73	23	85	104	132
52	57	65	75	24	88	109	138
53	59	66	77	25	91	115	144
54	60	68	80	26	95	120	150
55	62	71	82	27	100	126	
56	63	73	85	28	104	132	
57	65	75	88	29	109	138	
59	66	77	91	30	115	144	
60	68	80	95	31	120	150	
62	71	82	100	32	126		
63	73	85	104	33	132		
65	75	88	109	34	138		
66	77	91	115	35	144		
68	80	95	120	36	150		
71	82	100	126	37			
73	85	104	132	38			
75	88	109	138	39			
77	91	115	144	40			
80	95	120	150	41			
82	100	126		42			
85	104	132		43			
88	109	138		44			
91	115	144		45			
100	126	150		46			
104	132			47			
109	138			48			
115	144			49			
120	150			50			
132				51			
138				52			
144				53			
150				54			

EXTREMITY CASSETTE

CM	kVp
1	47
2	51
3	54
4	57
5	60
6	63
7	66
8	69
9	72
10	75

Appendix B
EQUIPMENT SPECIFICATION FORMS

These equipment specification forms have been developed in order to simplify both the request for specifications and the comparison of different vendors' specifications. Copies of the General Information (see following page) and all pertinent forms are sent to each vendor under consideration when new equipment is to be purchased. Forms are included for the following equipment:

CONTENTS

Generators (3 pages)
X-ray Tubes
X-ray Tube Housings
Heat Integrators
Image Intensifiers (2 pages)
Video Systems
Disc or Tape Recorders
Cameras
Exposure Control Systems
Grids
Video Systems Performance
Camera Systems or Changer Performance

These forms may be copied for individual use without the permission of the authors or publisher (with appropriate credit given). They may not be copied for resale.

GENERAL INFORMATION

The attached forms are provided so that we may more fairly evaluate your specifications compared to those of your competitors. It is hoped that the majority of the specification data are readily available and that it will not be necessary to specially test the equipment that is under consideration. If for any reason you feel that you cannot supply certain data, please let us know, stating the reasons that such information is not available. If you feel that your product is not properly represented by the data requested in these forms, please let us know and provide us with what you believe is the appropriate data.

The following guidelines should assist you in preparing the necessary information for our evaluation:

1. All blanks on the attached forms must be filled in for the equipment upon which you are bidding.
2. All data must be provided in the units noted.
3. We have not specified the methods of evaluation; therefore it will be necessary for you to provide the appropriate conditions for the tests you have carried out (e.g., kVp, mA, exposure time, focal spot size, scattering material (if any), geometry, test target used, etc.).
4. The specification data provided on these forms will become part of the purchase order and, hence, the specifications for acceptance.
5. If alternate (optional) equipment is to be considered a complete evaluation form will be required for each alternate item. For example, if two generators are being considered, one bid and the other as an option, two sets of the generator specification forms must be provided, one for each generator.
6. After completion of the forms please number all pages (e.g., page *1 of 10*) to assure that none of your material is overlooked.
7. Please provide all other available data and specifications for equipment quoted (e.g., single exposure rating, anode thermal characteristic, housing cooling, angiographic rating, cine-radiographic rating, and fluoroscopic rating charts for x-ray tubes and housings).
8. On your quote, please provide list and net price for all units of equipment comprising a component of the system (e.g., spot film camera system).
9. Price quotes for components should include the cost of necessary additional fixtures. For example, the quote price for a spot film camera system should include the cost of all mounting, support, and interfacing components.
10. These forms along with your detailed quotation and other supporting information should be supplied to _____ _____. A total of three copies would be appreciated.

If you have any questions concerning the forms, the information requested, or any other matters, please contact _____ _____.

GENERATORS (page 1)

Manufacturer _____

    Model Number _____

Power Requirements

    Preferred Mains Voltage _____ V
    Single or Three Phase _____ Ø
    kVA _____ kVA

kVp

    Push-button or Dial _____
    Minimum kVp _____
    Maximum kVp _____
    Steps _____
    Specified Accuracy _____
    _____
    _____

mA

    Push-button or Dial _____
    Minimum mA _____ mA
    Maximum mA _____ mA
    mA Stations—Small Focus _____
                Large Focus _____
    Specified Accuracy _____
    _____
    _____

Timing

    Type (e.g., forced extinction) _____

    Manual—Minimum   _____ msec ± _____ msec   at _____ kVp _____ mA
           10 msec   10 msec ± _____ msec   at _____ kVp _____ mA
         100 msec   100 msec ± _____ msec   at _____ kVp _____ mA

    Automatic—Minimum   _____ msec ± _____ msec   at _____ kVp _____ mA
           10 msec   10 msec ± _____ msec   at _____ kVp _____ mA
         100 msec   100 msec ± _____ msec   at _____ kVp _____ mA

GENERATORS (page 2)

Timing (cont.)

Maximum Exposure Time   _____ sec
Is maximum exposure time adjustable?   _____ yes   _____ no
Exposure Time Settings   _____
                                             _____

Phase-In Interrogation Time   _____ msec   at _____ kVp   and _____ mA
Maximum Exposures per Second   _____ exposures/second
Exposure Time Display (Type)   _____
Falling Load   _____ yes   _____ no

kW Ratings

at 70 kVp   _____ kW
     80 kVp   _____ kW
     90 kVp   _____ kW
   100 kVp   _____ kW
   110 kVp   _____ kW
   125 kVp   _____ kW
   150 kVp   _____ kW

Premagnetization Time   _____ msec

Time Sharing Capability   _____ yes   _____ no

Fluoroscopy

kVp   Range   _____ kVp   to   _____ kVp
        Steps   _____

mA   Range   _____ mA   to   _____ mA
        Steps   _____

Timer   Range   _____ min   to   _____ min
        Steps   _____

Automatic Exposure Control   _____ kVp only _____ mA only _____ mA-kVp
                                                                      combined

GENERATORS (page 3)

Focal Spot Size Selection

    Available Independent of mA?   _____ yes   _____ no

Rotor Speeds

    Available   _____ rpm

        _____ rpm

Percentage Ripple

    (Measured as x-ray output)

        _____ % at 80 kVp, 100 mA

        _____ % at 80 kVp, 200 mA

        _____ % at 80 kVp, 400 mA

        _____ % at 80 kVp, 600 mA

        _____ % at 80 kVp, 800 mA

        _____ % at 80 kVp, 1000 mA

X-RAY TUBES

Manufacturer   _____

    Tube Model #   _____

Focal Spot Size

	Unbiased		Biased	
Small	_____	mm	_____	mm
Large	_____	mm	_____	mm
Will you accept star measurements for testing purposes?	_____	yes	_____	no

kW Rating

Small Focal Spot	_____	kW	_____	kW
Large Focal Spot	_____	kW	_____	kW

Maximum kVp   _____ kVp

Anode Characteristics

Angle—Small Focal Spot	_____	°
Large Focal Spot	_____	°
Heat Capacity	_____	HU
Cooling Rate	_____	HU/min (maximum)

Rotor Speed Requirements

Fluoroscopic—Small Focal Spot	_____	rpm
Large Focal Spot	_____	rpm
Radiographic—Small Focal Spot	_____	rpm
Large Focal Spot	_____	rpm

Bias Power Supply

Bias Voltage	_____	V
Number of Tubes per Supply	_____	

_____   _____

Vendor   Date

X-RAY TUBE HOUSINGS

Manufacturer

       Housing Model #   _____

Housing Characteristics

       Heat Capacity   _____ HU

       Cooling Rate—Without Fan   _____ HU/min (maximum)

                With Fan   _____ HU/min (maximum)

                With Liquid Circulation System   _____ HU/min (maximum)

_____   _____
Vendor   Date

HEAT INTEGRATORS

Manufacturer   _____

         Model #   _____

Number of Tubes   _____

Display and Warning

         Digital or Analog Display   _____

         All Tubes Simultaneously?   _____ yes   _____ no

         % of Maximum or % Remaining   _____

         Audible Overload Indicator   _____ yes   _____ no

         System Lock at Overload?   _____ yes   _____ no

               Manual Lock Override?   _____ yes   _____ no

IMAGE INTENSIFIERS (page 1)

Manufacturer
_____

    Model #
_____

Input Field Size

    Small
_____ in   ±   _____ in

    Medium
_____ in   ±   _____ in

    Large
_____ in   ±   _____ in

Output Phosphor Size
_____ in   ±   _____ in

Phosphor Types

    Input
_____

    Output
_____

X-ray Absorption at 60 keV
_____ %

Resolution*

    Small Field—Center
_____ cycles/mm

        50%
_____ cycles/mm

        Edge
_____ cycles/mm

    Medium Field—Center
_____ cycles/mm

        50%
_____ cycles/mm

        Edge
_____ cycles/mm

    Large Field—Center
_____ cycles/mm

        50%
_____ cycles/mm

        Edge
_____ cycles/mm

*Please state measurement technique (e.g., kVp, target type, scatter).

IMAGE INTENSIFIERS (page 2)

Brightness Falloff*

    Small Field   _____ %

    Medium Field   _____ %

    Large Field   _____ %

Contrast Sensitivity*

    Small Field   _____ %

    Medium Field   _____ %

    Large Field   _____ %

Contrast Ratio*

    Small Field   _____ %

    Medium Field   _____ %

    Large Field   _____ %

Conversion Factor* $\left(\dfrac{cd}{m^2\ mR/sec} \right)$

	Minimum	Maximum
Small Field	_____	_____
Medium Field	_____	_____
Large Field	_____	_____

Flare or Veiling Glare*

    Small Field   _____ %

    Medium Field   _____ %

    Large Field   _____ %

*Please state measurement technique.

_____ _____
Vendor   Date

VIDEO SYSTEMS

Video Tube (Please provide manufacturer's data sheet)

    Manufacturer _____

    Type (e.g., vidicon, lead-oxide vidicon, or plumbicon) _____

    Model # _____

    Target Voltage _____ V

Camera–Video Tube–Amplifier Chain

    Manufacturer _____

    Model # _____

    Bandwidth _____ MHz at −3 dB

    Signal-to-Noise Ratio _____ dB

    Scan Lines Per Frame _____

    Shading Correction? _____ yes _____ no

    Gamma Correction? _____ yes _____ no

    Other Signal Processing (e.g., white clip or crush)?
      Describe _____

    Composite Video Signal _____ mV

    Sync Pulse _____ mV

    RS/170 Standard Signal? _____ yes _____ no

    Does video signal contain serrations and equalizing
      pulses? _____ yes _____ no

    AGC or ATC? _____

    Aspect Ratio (4:3, 1:1, etc.) _____

Monitor

    Manufacturer _____

    Model # _____

    Size (diagonal) _____ in

    Bandwidth _____ MHz at −3 dB

    Signal-to-Noise Ratio _____ dB

    Black Level Clamping _____ yes _____ no

DISC OR TAPE RECORDERS

Manufacturer   _____

       Model #   _____

       Type (U-matic, hard disc, floppy disc, etc.)   _____

Bandwidth   _____ MHz at − 3 dB

Signal-to-Noise Ratio

       Inner track   _____ dB

       Outer track   _____ dB

Maximum Number of Images   _____ fields _____ frames

Real-Time Recording

       Frames/sec—Record   _____ fps

                 Playback   _____ fps

       Is (single frame) playback field or frame?   _____ yes _____ no

       Last Image Hold?   _____ yes _____ no

Composite Video Signal   _____ mV

Sync Pulse   _____ mV

RS-170 Standard Signal?   _____ yes _____ no

Does video signal contain serrations and equalizing pulses?   _____ yes _____ no

Automatic Video Level Control   _____ yes _____ no

_____   _____
             Vendor   Date

CAMERAS

Manufacturer   _____

        Model #   _____

Film Size   _____ mm

                                           _____ mm
Image Size

Film Holders

        Maximum Input Capacity   _____ sheets or feet

        Maximum Output Capacity   _____ sheets or feet

Frame Rates   _____ fps

Lens

        Focal Length   _____ mm

        Widest Aperture   _____ f/#

        f/# Stops Available   _____

            Continuous or Waterhouse   _____

Resolution* (Camera only—i.e., lens plus film during
        maximum speed run)   _____ cycles/mm

*Please state measurement technique.

_____   _____
Vendor   Date

EXPOSURE CONTROL SYSTEMS

Fluoroscopic

    Manufacturer   _____

    Model #   _____

    Type (ionization, PMT, peak video, average video)   _____

    % of Image Area View for Exposure Control   _____ %

    Technique (mA-kVp variable, mA variable,
       kVp variable, etc.)   _____

    Manual Overrides (Types and Techniques)   _____

Spot Film and/or Spot Film Cameras (Specify)

    Manufacturer   _____

    Model #   _____

    Type (ionization, screen-PMT, etc.)   _____
       If screen, what type?   _____

    Technique (Fixed mA and kVp with variable time,
       floating mA and/or kVp with fluoro, etc.)   _____

    Maximum Exposure Time   _____ msec

    Minimum Exposure Time   _____ msec

    Manual Technique (mA and/or kVp and/or Time)   _____

    Density Selector

      Type   _____

      Number of Steps   _____

      % Exposure (not density) Change per Step   _____ %

_____   _____
Vendor   Date

GRIDS

Application

         (Bucky, fluoro, image intensifier, film changer, etc.)   _____

Manufacturer   _____

         Model #   _____

Ratio   _____

Lines/cm   _____ lines/cm

Lead Content   _____ g/cm^2

Focus Range   _____ in to _____ in

Removable?   _____ yes _____ no

_____   _____
Vendor   Date

VIDEO SYSTEMS PERFORMANCE

Total Video Chain Including Image Intensifier
  but Excluding Image Storage Devices

Bandwidth	_____ MHz at -3 dB		
Signal-to-Noise Ratio	_____ dB		

	Small Field	Medium Field	Large Field
Brightness Fall-Off*	_____ %	_____ %	_____ %
Contrast Sensitivity*	_____	_____	_____
Contrast Ratios*	_____	_____	_____
Flare or Veiling Glare*	_____	_____	_____
Resolution*—Center	_____ cycles/mm	_____ cycles/mm	_____ cycles/mm
50%	_____ cycles/mm	_____ cycles/mm	_____ cycles/mm
Edge	_____ cycles/mm	_____ cycles/mm	_____ cycles/mm

Total Video Chain Including Image Intensifier
  and Image Storage Devices

Bandwidth	_____ MHz at -3 dB		
Signal-to-Noise Ratio	_____ dB		
Inner Track	_____ dB		
Outer Track	_____ dB		

	Small Field	Medium Field	Large Field
Resolution—Center	_____ cycles/mm	_____ cycles/mm	_____ cycles/mm
50%	_____ cycles/mm	_____ cycles/mm	_____ cycles/mm
Edge	_____ cycles/mm	_____ cycles/mm	_____ cycles/mm

*Please state measurement technique.

_____   _____
            Vendor   Date

CAMERA SYSTEMS OR CHANGER PERFORMANCE

Image Intensifier–Camera, Spot Film
  System, or Film Changer

Resolution*	Small Field	Medium Field	Large Field
Single Frame—Center	_____cycles/mm	_____ cycles/mm	_____cycles/mm
50%	_____ cycles/mm	_____ cycles/mm	_____cycles/mm
Edge	_____cycles/mm	_____ cycles/mm	_____ cycles/mm
Nominal Frame Rate (_____ fps)			
Center	_____cycles/mm	_____ cycles/mm	_____cycles/mm
50%	_____cycles/mm	_____ cycles/mm	_____cycles/mm
Edge	_____ cycles/mm	_____ cycles/mm	_____cycles/mm
Maximum Frame Rate (_____ fps)			
Center	_____cycles/mm	_____cycles/mm	_____cycles/mm
50%	_____cycles/mm	_____ cycles/mm	_____cycles/mm
Edge	_____ cycles/mm	_____ cycles/mm	_____ cycles/mm
Brightness Falloff*	_____%	_____%	_____%
Contrast Sensitivity*	_____	_____	_____
Contrast Ratio*	_____	_____	_____
Flare or Veiling Glare*	_____	_____	_____

*Please state measurement technique.

INDEX

dosimeter used with, 11, 14
position of, 16–17

Joint Commission on the Accreditation of Hospitals (JCAH), quality control and, 1

kVp
for mR/mAs measurement, 100–101
x-ray generator evaluated, 95, 102–103, 104–106
repeatability and, 101–102

Lag, in fluoroscopic imaging, 128, 144–145, 148
LCL, see Lower control limit
Lead aprons, attenuation measurement for, 186–187
Light field
x-ray field alignment with, 52, 58–60, 70, 84–90, 91
Lights, visual and manual quality control check for, 54
Linearity, see x-ray generator
Locks, visual and manual quality control check for, 53
Low contrast fluoroscopic test, 128–129, 153–155, 156, 157, 158
Lower control limit (LCL), 20, 21, 22

mA
exposure time and, 101
selection of for mR/mAs measurements, 100
x-ray generator evaluated, 97, 102, 103
Maintenance log, 22, 24
maintenance of photographic processor recorded in, 39
Mammography, 102, 124
ionization chamber used in, 11
Manual quality control checks, 51, 53–55
Manual spinning top, for exposure timing, 95, 107–108
Maximum fluoroscopic exposure rate, 126, 133–136, 137
Measuring caliper, visual and manual quality control check for, 53
Mechanized processors, 33
see also Photographic processing equipment
Mesh test pattern, 150, 151, 152, 153
Meters, visual and manual quality control check for, 54

Minimum exposure time test, 122–123
Mirror-optic fluoroscopic system, low-contrast fluoroscopic test for, 154–155
Motion smoothness of fluoroscopic tower, visual and manual quality control check for, 54
Motorized synchronous top
for exposure timing, 95, 108–109
for linearity of x-ray generator, 119
mR/mAs, x-ray generators and, 97–102, 115–119, 120, 121
Multiformat cameras, see Video hard-copy cameras

National Electrical Manufacturers Association (NEMA), focal spot size of x-ray tube and, 69, 70, 83
Nine-penny test, 52, 58–60
Noise, in fluoroscopic imaging, 128, 144, 145, 146, 147
Nongrid fluoroscopy, lowering exposure rate, 191–192

Off-focus radiation, mR/mAs measurement and, 100
"On-the-fly" modes, video hard-copy cameras and, 176
Operating level, 21–22
Oscilloscope
video waveform monitoring with, 156, 157
for x-ray output waveforms, 96, 112
Output waveform, from x-ray generator, 96–97, 111–115
Overhead crane movement, visual and manual quality control check for, 53
Overload protection
visual and manual quality control check for, 54
x-ray tube and, 69, 78–79
Overtable fluoroscopic system, maximum fluoroscopic exposure rate for, 134, 138
Overtable x-ray tube, half-value layer measurement of, 91–92

Panel switches, visual and manual quality control check for, 54
Park position interrupt, visual and manual quality control check for, 54
"Pass-fail" tests, visual and

manual quality control checks as, 51, 53–55
Patient equivalent phantom (PEP), 7–11, 12–13
for basic homogeneous phantom test, 52, 60–62
for fluoroscopic images, 144
mR/mAs value changes and, 97–98, 99
for phototimer, 120
for standard fluoroscopic exposure level, 136
PBL, see Positive beam limitation systems
Peak video voltage, 157, 159
Pelvis phantom, 8, 9
Pen-type dosimeters, see Dosimeter
PEP, see Patient equivalent phantom
Perpendicularity of x-ray beam, 85–89
visual and manual quality control check for, 53
pH and developer activity, 37
Phantoms
extremity, 8–10
pelvis, 8, 9
skull, 8, 9
tomographic, 161, 165, 166, 168
water, 60
see also Patient equivalent phantom
Photofluorospot (PFS) film units, phototiming system checked for, 121
Photofluorospot film cameras
lowering exposure rate of, 191–192
resolution, 128, 151–152
setting and maintaining exposure of, 128, 146–147
Photographic processing equipment
cleaning and maintenance, 37, 39, 41, 47–48
daily quality control program for, 35–38, 44–47
cross-over of control emulsions, 38
dip test, 38
for mechanized film processors, 38–39, 45–47
procedure, 44–47
flood replenishment, 40–41, 48–49
problem with, 33
purchasing, 33–34
standby kit for, 38
wash water temperature for, 38–39
Photographic processor
control chart for, 21
operating level for, 21–22

DATE DUE

Demco, Inc. 38-293